SCHOLARS
WHO
TEACH

Steven M. Cahn
Editor

SCHOLARS
WHO
TEACH

the art of college teaching

Nelson-Hall nh Chicago

Library of Congress Cataloging in Publication Data
Main entry under title:

Scholars who teach.

    1.   College teaching.   I.   Cahn, Steven M.
LB2331.S355   378.1'2   78–944
ISBN 0–88229–373–7 (cloth)
ISBN 0–88229–598–5 (paper)

Manufactured in the United States of America

10   9   8   7   6   5   4   3   2   1

To Ronald Bettauer
who helped as always

Contents

STEVEN M. CAHN

Introduction

It is a sad but indisputable fact that much of the teaching that goes on in our colleges and universities is of very poor quality. Indeed, virtually any college student can relate stories about the incredible tribulations he suffered at the hands of incompetent instructors. I myself have never forgotten my English composition teacher who mumbled incoherently in class, refused to speak to students outside class, and gave no grade higher than C+. Few college teachers, however, can be accused of intellectual incompetence. Why, then, the poor quality of college teaching?

Two popular explanations are the large size of college classes and the demand that professors publish as well as teach. But poor teaching is to be found as much in small classes as in large ones. And as to that familiar slogan "publish or perish," writing articles for scholarly journals sustains and facilitates good teaching rather than hindering it, for such scholarship develops a teacher's ability to think critically by leading him to submit his ideas to the judgment of his peers.

The crisis in college teaching is not due in any significant measure to these factors but results, rather, from a failure to recognize the crucial principle that intellectual competence and pedagogic competence are two very different qualities. One cannot be an outstanding teacher without thorough knowledge of subject matter, but to possess that knowledge does not guarantee the ability to communicate it to a student. And this ability is by no means easy to acquire. The number of great teachers is as small as the number of great artists or scientists. And just as an artist or scientist needs to master necessary skills, so a teacher must do the same.

That there are such skills is obvious to anyone who has ever stood in front of a class of twenty or thirty restless fifth-graders. Admittedly, teaching college students is easier than teaching elementary-school students. Youngsters quickly indicate their boredom or disapproval by yelling or throwing chalk. Older students faced with poor teaching simply fall asleep. This reaction is in one respect quite unfortunate, since an elementary-school teacher is made immediately aware of his pedagogic inadequacy, while a college teacher may go on for years without ever realizing his incompetence. Some time ago, for example, I asked a colleague of mine about the progress of several of his students. He turned out to be unaware that they were in his class, since, as he confessed, he did not know the names of any of his students. His ignorance did not seem to bother him, despite the fact that the term was half over and the class enrollment was but twelve.

Unfortunately, like most other college instructors, he had never spent even a moment of his academic career learning how to teach. He was learning on the job, while the students served as guinea pigs. Indeed, in applying for a position as a college teacher, an applicant need not present any evidence of teaching ability. A Ph.D. or its equivalent is usually required in order to show scholarly competence, but nothing whatever is required in order to demonstrate pedagogic competence, competence in the very skills one is expected to use on the job.

What can be done to alleviate this situation? The most practical solution rests in the hands of those who administer graduate-school programs. They have the responsibility to provide courses in methods of teaching for students intending to enter the profession. And these courses should be required of all to be recommended for teaching positions.

But what material should be read by prospective college teachers or by one who wishes to improve the quality of his teaching? Many books discuss the problems and techniques of elementary- and secondary-school teaching, but hardly any are devoted to the problems and techniques of college teaching. This book is designed for that purpose.

The seven contributors to this volume were chosen on the basis of their recognized excellence as college teachers, as attested to by both their colleagues and their students. Of course, no essay will convey the thrill of experiencing a class taught by a great teacher. Nevertheless the essays in this volume serve at least two purposes. First, they provide the opportunity to read what outstanding teachers have to say about their work. And although a reader may disagree with some of the ideas expressed, still much is to be learned, for the authors are undeniably masters of their art. Second, these essays will lead a teacher or future teacher to think through his own approach. And this activity is of vital importance, for the most serious failure of college teachers is the reluctance to think seriously about their teaching. Reading this book will not turn a poor teacher into a great one. But it will turn an unreflective teacher into a reflective one, and that is the crucial step on the path toward better teaching.

RUSSELL H. BOSTERT

Teaching History

RUSSELL H. BOSTERT (Ph.D., Yale University) is Stanfield Professor and chairman of the history department at Williams College. He also has taught at Tufts University and, in the John Hay Program, at Bennington College and the University of Oregon. During the academic year 1976–77 he was a Fulbright Lecturer in Taiwan, associated with Fu Jen University and Tamkang College. He is the author of *American Foreign Policy to 1880* and has contributed to various periodicals, including the *Journal of American History, Yale Review, Hispanic-American Historical Review,* and *Berkshire Review.*

During the decade of the 1970s the challenge for college teachers of history has been one of growing intensity. Students, educators, even historians, increasingly express doubts about the value of the subject. A few years ago many undergraduates demanded that their courses relate to social problems of the present; now they seem increasingly to perceive higher education as preparation for a career. Neither emphasis seems likely to revive the study of history in college classrooms.

Some educators believe that only branches of history remote in time and alien in content, like medieval studies, will feel the long-run effects. But in fact the current emphasis has led to skepticism about the value of any part of the past, including our own national history. What does our urban-industrial society, for example, have to learn from that long stretch of its history when the economy was chiefly agricultural and social patterns predominantly rural? What useful meaning is there for Americans now plagued by problems of over-concentrated population, polluted environments, and sick cities, in a previous social experience characterized by European immigrants moving into a virgin wilderness or helping to settle new and dynamic cities? Summing up a pessimistic response to those who demand relevance in their education, one well-known historian, Martin Duberman, wishes that "we [historians] could find a way of making the past yield information of vital concern to contemporary needs," but he has "little hope that we can."[1]

Such skepticism is hardly novel. In 1537 the Swiss physician-philosopher Paracelsus bluntly asked in his classic *Seven Arguments*: "What profits the rain that fell a thousand years ago? Benefit comes from rain that falls now. . . . Our concern should be for the present, not for the past."[2] But to many teachers of history the issue of whether a study of the past has value is being raised today in a disturbingly extreme manner, and they are ill-equipped to cope with it.

Nor are they prepared to meet the arguments of those who would turn over the study of human experience to the behavioral scientists in psychology, anthropology, sociology, economics, and political science. This case against the teaching of history maintains that the historical method (about which historians are often vague and ill-informed) has failed because it lacks a clear conceptual framework, is deficient in intellectual rigor, and produces conclusions that cannot withstand analytical criticism.

As a result, many professional educators are turning for guidance to such men as Jerome Bruner, professor of cognitive psychology at Harvard University. In one of his books, *Toward a Theory of Instruction,* Bruner predicts a "move towards instruction in the sciences of behavior and away from the study of history."[3] The past must be made to serve the present, Bruner thinks, not by following the historians' emphasis upon its details and its discreteness, but by purposeful use of historical examples. In recent years, particularly in many secondary schools, the teaching of history in effect has been replaced by the study of social science concepts, and the construction of theoretical models, using selected evidence from the past, often of a quantitative sort. Hypotheses about past human experience are tested, to discover by the "inquiry" method what are termed the "underlying principles" of history as subject matter.[4]

At the college level some teachers of history, admitting the inadequacies of their own approach, are trying hard and at times with modest success to retool themselves and make some use of the methodology practiced by at least one of the behavioral sciences. Other historians remain either indifferent or antagonistic. Many take refuge in writing narrow monographic studies, or concentrating in the classroom on what they consider to be "traditional" history. Whatever the result, the teaching of history has become visibly affected, its content and methods clearly put on the defensive.

Historians themselves currently are showing cannibalistic tendencies about their own subject. Pulitzer-Prize winning George Dangerfield of the University of California at Santa Barbara has declared: "History is, after all, a set of intellectually enchanting abstractions. It bears very little relation to your sordid reality; . . . it's like higher mathematics, where an argument can be beautiful even if it's wrong."[5] Dangerfield's conclusion that history is meaningless, and historians' work probably absurd, is certainly extreme. But one suspects that some teachers of history, caught in the uncertainties of the contemporary scene, sympathize with his view, at least to some extent, though they are understandably reluctant to express it.

Another line of criticism during the last decade has come from within the profession—from a group of historians, mostly young and some of a "New Left" persuasion, who challenged what they termed an "establishment" school of American historians.[6] This school, they contend, has exaggerated the continuities, the agreements, the felicitous part of America's past, and in so doing produced a false image to the effect that Americans throughout their history essentially have been in consensus. "For many," writes Barton Bernstein of Stanford, "the rediscovery of poverty and racism, the commitment to civil rights for Negroes, the criticism of intervention in Cuba and Vietnam, shattered many of the assumptions of the fifties and compelled intellectuals to re-examine the American past."[7] A New Past needs to be resurrected, Bernstein and others insist, one that will take account of the darker side of American life, recognize its many conflicts, its violence, its radicals, its imperialistic tendencies, and its often savage treatment of minority and ethnic groups—in short, a history that will seek "explicitly to make the past speak to the present, to ask questions that have a deep-rooted moral and political relevance." Some of those who call for a New Past are very much interested in shaping America's future. "Recourse to the past," writes Staughton Lynd, "can be a means of retrogression and escape; but it can also be the first step in a process of liberation. . . . With or without the help of historians . . . Americans concerned to change the society around them have made appropriate use of the past as a source for forgotten alternatives, for encouragement to endure."[8] Lynd and historians of similar persuasion clearly intend to help.

As if these internecine struggles among historians were not disturbing enough, the national trend in college history enrollments continues to slump. At a time when higher education is in deep financial trouble, and the teaching market in history is overwhelmed with qualified teachers who cannot find jobs, many liberal arts colleges, where undergraduate history teaching traditionally has been strong, find themselves especially hard hit.[9] No one can say whether this combination of regrettable trends will continue. But if it is combined with an increased emphasis in the schools on the teaching of social science rather than history, prospects for the future of college history offerings would appear to be distressingly poor.

Such considerations, among others, led C. Vann Woodward of Yale, in his 1969 presidential address before the American Historical Association, to raise the unusual and upsetting question for historians of whether the study of the past has a future.[10] And in *The New York Times*'s annual education review of January, 1970, Stephen R. Graubard of Brown University suggested that during the 1970s knowledge of history increasingly would be confined to small numbers of experts, while becoming substantially meaningless for larger groups in the population. The idea of a Western heritage will be questioned, he felt, as well as the belief that the resolution of society's problems would be helped by greater historical understanding, or that the past may be consulted with profit as a guide to action. Graubard's conclusion was a challenge to all teachers of history: "Despite the booming sales of history books, the field itself is clearly on trial in a way that certain other academic disciplines are not."[11]

1

If history indeed is on trial, what can be done to bolster the defense? The worst possible course for history teachers would be to assume self-righteously that this hardy perennial among academic disciplines will survive and flourish because it always has, that it will be granted the court's indulgence regardless of what the witnesses say, for or against. Probably the single most effective testimony on its behalf would come from the effects of strong history teaching, at both the college and secondary school levels. But what can be done to strengthen the teaching of history? Both the American Historical Association and the Organization of American Historians dutifully have created committees on teaching. This worthy expression of organizational concern may be seen as yet another reflection of the widespread belief among teachers of history that the importance of their subject in American education is steadily being eroded. No one seems at all certain, however, what can or should be done to halt the process.

Most of us assume that the past is not on trial, but how historians deal with it. Therefore we teachers of history exert ourselves to do battle against the enemy—student apathy towards "news from the graveyard." As articles in *The History Teacher* and the American Historical Association *Newsletter* demonstrate again and again, historians exert themselves, sometimes frantically so, to develop new courses and methods designed to excite and provoke students into becoming more interested in the past—a past imaginatively searched in pursuit of meaningful analogies with the present, or seen as a road leading to the future, or the past used as a testing ground for value judgments, or considered, especially during the Bicentennial year, as a rich storehouse of human drama, especially so when put on film, or allied with a host of other variants.[12]

In the process of quite properly trying new ways to interest students in history, however, we run the risk of neglecting certain older concerns of our craft. A proper approach to teaching history should seek not the replacement of previous achievements but the renewal of a traditional conviction—that when studied properly, history offers such unique educational values that no generation can afford to neglect it.

In my view, history teachers should share certain assumptions. The first is that all generations tend to be present-minded. They will ask of the past questions that emerge from their own concerns. Frederick Jackson Turner's declaration, written years ago, should be considered a truism: "Each age will re-write the history of the past anew with reference to the conditions uppermost in its own time."[13] The growth during the 1960s of Latin American studies and history in the United States owed much to the rise of Castro and fear of communism in the western hemisphere. The inauguration of black studies emerged in the aftermath of the civil rights crusade, public concern with explosive conditions in black ghettos, and the impact made by strong black leadership. The striking growth of interest in urban history sprang from the long overdue discovery that American cities are plagued with problems of every sort. American historians of Germany have developed a new interest in the Weimar Republic as recent crises have given rise to doubts about the durability of democracy in the United States. Even American diplomatic history, which now seems to be such a "traditional" subject, actually has flourished in college curricula only since the late 1930s, when the United States first began to act upon its responsibilities as a world power.

Written history probably adjusts to changing contemporary interests more quickly than history as it is taught in most college courses. But Turner's truism means that few history courses will be meaningful for any generation of students unless to some extent they harness themselves to the purpose of helping the present understand itself better. Carl Degler's admirable survey of American history, *Out of Our Past,* takes its approach from the question: "How did Americans get to be the way they are (now) . . . ?"[14] Teachers of American or any other national history must keep this question constantly in mind as they plan their courses. Their students will in any case. Pondering that question may not lead all teachers, as it did Degler, to neglect the settlement of seventeenth-century colonies, presidential administrations between 1868 and 1901, and the War of 1812. But it will cause them to think through the reasons why they have selected these topics in their courses and neglected others.

To teach history courses that take into account the changing concerns of the present means a willingness to put aside old lecture and discussion notes, no matter how close the subject to the teacher's specialty, or how important it once seemed—the Thirty Years' War, Italian unification, the Oregon question, tariff struggles in the nineteenth century. The list of possible casualties in a European or American history course is both long and unpredictable. No matter how difficult, selection from the multifarious events of the past is a necessity. It should be made deliberately, perceptively, and ruthlessly.

To cultivate whatever awareness exists among students of what it is their forebears have done to them or for them should not lead either to a rejection or an imitation of the past. Instead it should encourage in them a realization that the actions of their own generation have lasting consequences, and that these will be judged by their descendants in the same manner as they are judging their ancestors now. When Abraham Lincoln asked Congress in late 1862 to amend the Constitution and provide for the compensated emancipation of slaves, he eloquently made just this case: "Fellow citizens, *we* cannot escape history. We . . . will be remembered in spite of ourselves. No personal significance, or insignificance, can spare one or another of us. The fiery trial through which we pass will light us down, in honor or dishonor, to the latest generation."[15] It may be true that no young person ever believes he will die. But maturity will begin for him when he realizes for the first time that the dead were once young.

Teachers of history ought to share a second assumption. Though contemporary values and interests inevitably will influence which history gets taught, how it is taught must not be so influenced. Instead historians must assume that it is possible, through an imaginative leap guarded by research, to put oneself in the past and deal with it in a way that seeks neither heroes nor villains, but an understanding of both. One of the most regrettable legacies of Turner's truism (attributable in part to the confusion engendered by one of Turner's most famous students, the late Carl Becker), is that the historian is like Mr. Everyman, trying to use the past to carry out some pragmatic task, such as paying his coal bill, by examining the historical particulars pertaining to it. Cushing Strout of Cornell effectively has pointed out that the historian does not use the past in this way: "imaginative understanding, which enabled Becker to see the past historian as part of the historical process, is itself destroyed if the present historian is *only* an illustration of his contemporary climate of opinion . . . to study history is always to attempt a self-transcendence that makes possible an imaginative grasp of men whose purposes are not our own and whose world at first seems alien and unintelligible."[16]

It is this *self-transcendence* that the teacher of history seeks to inculcate in his students. If he is successful, another value of the subject becomes apparent. To move beyond one's own times, to get outside oneself, is to become emancipated, that is to say, liberally educated. Historians must guard against the tendency, apparent at times in the work of present-minded social scientists excessively concerned with deriving "lessons" from human experience, to assign certain aspects of the past to obscurity. Parts of the past that seem recondite, alien, and remote may reveal most effectively the variety, the richness, the incredible adaptability of man, and thus provide vivid demonstrations of the glory of the species. As Hugh Brogan has written: "Historical literature . . . speaks directly to the reader's humanity. . . . It is for the reader himself to decide what relevance it has to his life."[17]

A little over a decade ago, in a fascinating and enlightening exchange that ranged beyond the subject matter of their discussion, the late David Potter of Stanford University and Kenneth Stampp of the University of California at Berkeley, two outstanding authorities on the pre–Civil War period, expressed somewhat differing convictions concerning the nature of the historian's quest.[18] According to Potter, "the supreme task of the historian, and the one of most superlative difficulty, is to see the past through the imperfect eyes of those who lived it and not with his own omniscient twenty-twenty vision. I am not suggesting that any of us can readily do this, but only that it is what we must attempt." To which Stampp responded: "In my opinion, that is one valid way to see the past; but having accomplished it, the historian's task is but half done. The other way to see the past is with all the wisdom and perspective that experience and hindsight can give us." Stampp did agree with Potter, however, that hindsight must be used "not to judge and condemn the men of the past, but to understand why their best laid plans so often went astray."[19]

If historians accept both these definitions of their task, as this essay does, it can readily be understood why the successful teaching of history generates considerable intellectual tension. The teacher constantly must shuttle mentally between past and present, doing the best he can to know a lot about both worlds, and not taking unfair advantage of either. Though he must not praise or condemn the past because to do so might interfere with his understanding, he cannot really avoid judging it, because all conclusions involve judgments. Though he cannot actually become self-transcendent in the sense of escaping his times and shedding his skin, he must constantly make the effort to do so. It is small wonder that historians disagree so often, for these intellectual journeys result in a good deal of bumping en route.

The dilemma created for the sensitive teacher of history as he tries to fulfill the dual tasks indicated by Potter and Stampp is a continuing one, never fully resolved. In times of social unrest and turbulent political change it becomes especially hard to resist the temptation to search for and draw "lessons" from a "usable past." During the agitation for reform in the pre–World War I Progressive era, for example, James Harvey Robinson, Charles A. Beard, and others launched their call for a "New History" that would spur the forces for change by revealing the "underlying historical realities"—the kind of search that often results in an exaggerated emphasis on economic motives and sordid, personal gain.[20] And out of the social stresses brought about by the depression and controversy over the New Deal in the 1930s there emerged a school of historians, whose influence is still pronounced, who tended simplistically to divide American political history into a Jefferson-Jackson-Roosevelt humanitarian-reformist tradition on the one side, and a Hamilton-Clay-McKinley-Hoover business-conservative orientation on the other.[21]

As Americans in the troubled twentieth century increasingly have felt the frustration of being captives of the past rather than the satisfaction of being its successors, they have wanted to learn more from history than how they got where they are, what their historical origins have been. Perhaps for this reason written history in this "age of analysis," as philosophers have dubbed it, has tended frequently to replace a genetic approach to the past, a search for origins, with what might be called a normative approach, a search through the past in order to discover and establish values for the present.[22]

A normative approach to history, not surprisingly, often finds fault with the past. The goals and values of previous generations turn out to be less idealistic than they should have been. Their aims, it is discovered, especially the most worthy ones, went unrealized for the most part. America's most renowned political heroes, it is contended, had distressing major weaknesses: Jefferson violated cherished civil liberties; Lincoln promoted white supremacy; McKinley and Theodore Roosevelt shared racist-imperialist views; Wilson and Franklin Roosevelt were grossly naive crusaders in world politics. The darker side of America's past—its violence, prejudices, and repressive aspects—having been neglected, it is charged, must now be emphasized. And voices that spoke for causes lost in their own time, such as those of W. E. B. DuBois, Eugene Debs, Emma Goldman, and Henry Wallace, are revived as part of a dissenting America that should be heard as guidance for the future. The mess of the present, attributed to the mistakes or villainy of the past, becomes the product of a history that took a series of wrong turns.

No historian or teacher of history should protect or enshrine the past. But if the normative approach results in isolating and concentrating upon history's transgressions and derogations as seen from the present, a likely result will be to spawn historical judgments that add up to a severe condemnation of the American experience. In recent years such condemnatory judgments have been growing. Examples are numerous: that "America, by history and by habit, has been a violent society;" that American slavery was "the most awful the world has ever known;" that Americans share "the hereditary belief that, *because* the United States is not like other nations but . . . exceeds them in virtue, all mankind are bound to accept its lead;" that the dynamic of American society has been its "continued commitment to the frontier-expansionist outlook," overseas economic expansion, and the defense of private property.[23] If such judgments filter into college textbooks and classrooms, as they seem to be in the process of doing, a litany of historical self-flagellation may overwhelm an unsuspecting American public even while it finds acceptance among students eager to believe the worst of the past because they are so unhappy with the present.

One result, suggested by Graubard, may be that the general American public will turn away from or repudiate their past, becoming disillusioned with history because it seems to be such a sorry and heavy burden.[24] No doubt counter judgments designed to "save" the American past will also emerge, to emphasize in unvarnished form stories that illustrate its lighter and brighter side. Something of this tone always has characterized many of the best-selling books on American history, and the popular articles, heavily spiced with personal anecdotes, that appear in magazines devoted to the "heritage" of the American past. Students, meanwhile, attracted by the voices of dissent in their history, will pay less attention to continuity than discontinuity, finding in the latter a key to hoped-for changes in the future.

The normative approach, then, is likely to confront the college teacher of history with a growing polarization of views about the past, especially our American past. It is not unlike the polarization which has developed among people in the present during crisis situations, whether in the South over civil rights, in the general public concerning Vietnam, or in the administrations of colleges and universities reacting to demands for drastic changes in policy and curriculum. Is it possible for the historian to cope with polarized views about the past and yet avoid taking an innocuous, middle course that weakly concludes there is something to be said for both sides?

One way is through more teaching of comparative history, a promising and relatively new approach to the past that is rapidly gaining favor.[25] To compare systems of slavery as they developed in the United States and Brazil, for example, is to broaden perspective and utilize more effectively the means by which historians traditionally have revealed the special angles of vision from which judgments of the past are often made. To study imperialism by placing the record of America's empire alongside that of Britain, France, Germany, or Japan will bring a fresh view to the much considered relationship between national character and foreign-policy making. A comparison of instances of racism, violence, and treatment of ethnic minorities as they have occurred, say, in the United States, Eastern Europe, and Latin America, may result in the reconsideration of value judgments derived from the standards of only a single culture.[26] A concern with comparative history clearly can be valuable for teachers confused by the normative approach, especially teachers who want to cultivate in their students what Winston Churchill considered to be a central value of studying the past: "to give one a sense of proportion about events."

The challenges coming from history students searching for values, in fact, offer the imaginative teacher an unusual opportunity to demonstrate that the historical approach has special importance in times of stress and rapid change such as our own. By insisting that the present is the product of a tradition, but being equally insistent that change is a constant in history, the historian reveals that his approach, which essentially has to do with the meaning of human events seen through the screen of time, yields unique dividends.[27] Where the dramatist may present Sir Thomas More as "a man for all seasons," the historian sees him as a temporal rather than universal figure, a product of one unique and nonrepeatable historical season, yet one with problems and conflicts that transcend his time and are meaningful to the present. When biography is written as the search for an individual's "identity crisis," called the key to character formation, the historian will accept the insight as valuable, but not as a substitute for his own emphasis on character development—a moving process—growing out of the constant interactions between a life and its times.[28] If behavioralists take seriously only measurable evidence about human experience and attach to it the timeless authority of mathematics, the historian reacts by pointing to important aspects of human behavior that cannot be measured, adding that much historical evidence seems to indicate that basic changes in human thought patterns occur over time. (Though when anti-behavioralists discount quantitative evidence, the historian is ready to agree that statistical analysis is helpful in answering certain kinds of questions about the past).[29] When the present falsifies the past by creating it in its own image, the historian has an obligation to sort out and reveal the anachronisms.

The historian or teacher of history, in short, is always suspicious of simple explanations, of hidden keys to understanding, of shortcuts to wisdom. He warns against the easy assumption, made in every age, that times do not change or that history repeats itself. In Woodward's view, "the historian is peculiarly fitted . . . to serve as mediator between man's limitations and his aspirations, between his dream of what ought to be and the limits of what, in the light of what has been, can be. There is no other branch of learning better qualified to mediate between man's daydream of the future and his nightmare of the past, or, for that matter, between his nightmare of the future and his daydream of the past."[30] For the usefulness of history lies to a considerable extent in its lack of immediate practical application by those who study it. It does not indicate solutions, even to the most pressing or directly related of today's problems, but endeavors to enlarge understanding of them. No one has put more eloquently in brief form this nonpragmatic purpose of studying history than Carl Becker: "The value of History," he once wrote, "is, indeed, not scientific, but moral: by liberalizing the mind, by deepening the sympathies, by fortifying the will, it enables us to control, not society, but ourselves . . . it prepares us to live more humanely in the present . . . and to meet the future."[31] Students who come to realize the implications in Becker's statement will appreciate the importance of the subject in today's college curricula.

2

To agree on the general aims of a college history course is one thing, how to accomplish them is another. Let me begin this portion of the essay by separating myself from the self-anointed, often self-appointed souls who pride themselves upon giving advice, a field perhaps properly dominated by marriage counselors, newspaper columnists, and schools of self-improvement. What follows represents some of the meat of my own teaching experience, which has been mostly in American history, plus what many valued colleagues have taught me about teaching over the years. Such meat may be another man's poison. So be it. Teaching is at its best when the teacher follows no prescription save that which enables him to develop his own strengths in the classroom. All the rules are made to be broken, and surely there are as many ways to teach effectively as there are ways of becoming an educated person.

At present the lecture method of teaching history is under attack from many students, for understandable reasons. Lecturing, a necessary form of teaching in medieval universities without books, seems to many in this era of the paperback revolution an outmoded form that epitomizes what is wrong with depersonalized, large-scale university instruction, and is a method whose defense is economic rather than educational. Surely all college graduates have shared the misery of listening to some professors teaching required courses who were "talking books" of the unpublishable sort, delivering their canned lectures from yellowing notes to an apathetic, captive audience that complained privately but seldom publicly. And if one (as a graduate reader) followed this dismal process through to the grading of essay examinations, he often discovered that the idea of education as self-enlightenment was distressingly absent—even very good students were content to repeat passively what they had heard, or could remember. In subjects where the teaching emphasis is on revealing usable knowledge of a cumulative sort, such as science and math, or is on providing orientation in the special discourse of a discipline, such as music and art, the lecture method is probably necessary, perhaps even preferable to other methods. But in history, where understanding is essentially noncumulative, and no special language is used, lecturing may seem to be a poor substitute for reading, or for an exchange of ideas with a professor that enables a student to sharpen or enlarge his own knowledge of a subject.

Yet the realities of higher education in America are such that the lecture method will continue in certain history courses to remain the indispensable means of dealing with large numbers of students. It also helps keep distinguished scholars in undergraduate classrooms. No doubt the lectures of some of these scholars will also increasingly be made available on closed circuit institutional television, or put on cassettes for national distribution and use by individual students in electronically equipped library carrels. In time students will be able to replay lectures by former great American historians brought back, as it were, from the grave, providing a personal record of the intellectual style and emphasis of another time, the lectures themselves having become historical artifacts. History teachers who fear that their lectures will become expendable as a result of television performances by their better-known peers are excessively worried. Nothing dates faster than lectures and lecture topics. Even the electronics world is unlikely to be able to keep pace with the rapid changes in historical subject matter, scholarship, and teaching approaches that shape courses taught by an able and energetic faculty. And most students still prefer a live professor, even when he is lecturing many yards away to hundreds in a large hall, to a picture on a screen; they recognize that involvement in the interaction possible between live audience and lecturer is a valuable part of the educational process. Selected television lectures from outside, or other audiovisual aids, may be a valuable supplement in a history course, but they are no substitute for the course itself.

A history lecture should be prepared with an awareness of the criticisms frequently made against the genre. It should avoid duplicating what is in the reading students are required to do in the course. This means that teachers regularly must refresh their memories by a quick rereading, or first reading, of assignments given their students. If the lecture course also requires discussions, the lectures should not be isolated pieces haphazardly placed in the syllabus, but parts of an integrated whole, useful in section meetings as well as helpful for students reading on their own.

Historical subjects especially worthy of exploration by the lecture method are those whose very nature makes them difficult to discuss —such subjects may involve so many diverse considerations that viable reading assignments are impossible; their focus probably will be diffuse without a strong organizing effort; comprehending them may be too difficult for beginning students on their own. Lecturing also offers an opportunity to sort out and comment upon the significance of changing historical interpretations, especially as they relate to major figures of the past every schoolboy thinks he knows. An excellent example of this type of lecture is the one David Potter delivered in 1948 as Harmsworth Professor at Oxford University, on "The Lincoln Theme and American National Historiography."[32] Its ambitious goal was to demonstrate to an English audience that "almost all of the important trends in American historical writing have been reflected in the interpretations placed upon Lincoln and his career." This impressive lecture not only traced the development of American history written on Lincoln from its stages of unbroken approbation to modern scholarly criticism, and from a parochial approach to a more worldly spirit that sought to transcend nationalism, but saw in this development an example of growing intellectual maturity, concluding, in a rare insight, that the more recent approaches actually represent a return to Lincoln's own recognition of the supremacy of universal human values over narrow nationalistic ones. It is the kind of lecture every American historian wishes he had given. Though no longer up-to-date on Lincoln historiography, the major theme certainly is still valid. It is convincing proof that listening to lectures can be a rewarding intellectual experience.

The lecturer's own angle of vision, his own interpretations and conclusions, should always be made clear. They should emerge directly from his remarks rather than indirectly from student guessing-games. No impression should be given, however, that final truth on the subject has been spoken, an impression exemplified by a nineteenth-century French historian, Fustel de Coulanges, misguided believer in "scientific" history, who once responded to his applauding students: "It is not I who speak, but history which speaks through me."[33]

Great care should be taken to provide a clear and steady focus to the lecture, so that it is not a shifting melange of considerations, trying to do so much that the listener becomes confused. One way to create a viable center for remarks, and to make them meaningful to students, is to challenge the views of an immediately recognizable, seemingly reliable authority. Samuel Flagg Bemis of Yale used to lecture on the background of the Monroe Doctrine by refuting the then popular thesis of Walter Lippmann, contained in Lippmann's best-selling book on American foreign policy, to the effect that the doctrine had originated as a tacit alliance between Britain and the United States, supported by the power of the British navy. Besides offering an illuminating contrast between the approach and evidence used by a scholar and a talented amateur, the lecture also demonstrated how tempting it is to read the historical record backwards: clearly what had led to Lippmann's bad history was his laudable desire in 1940 to stem Hitler's domination of Europe by the creation of a working alliance between Britain and the United States.

Every student recognizes that styles of lecturing vary greatly from one history class to another. From my own observations, all the following styles work: 1) a scholar immersed in his subject, deliberate in speech and precise in manner, carefully clearing a path through a thicket of ideas, and in the process convincing a class that it is witnessing thought in action; 2) a flashy, overwhelming personality, obviously enjoying himself, who attacks a historical problem with ferocity, overwhelms it with his own inspiration, information, and energy, and leaves his audience awed by his display of intellectual pyrotechnics; 3) the lecturer who seemingly coins arresting phrases as he speaks, scattering them like precious jewels along the path of his discourse, inviting students to pick them up, examine them, and speculate on their significance; 4) a brisk, confident, no-nonsense professional, whose carefully organized remarks have such clarity, substance, and logical structure that they are persuasive testimony to the power of his mind; 5) a witty performer, whose illustrative humor and personal anecdotes keep students alert and responsive to the points being made, but who restrains his natural gift for comedy short of wisecracking for the sake thereof; 6) the serious, obviously mature human being, whose students for the most part respond to the example of personal concern and commitment on display. Finally —in my list of successful lecturers—the casual, meandering informal commentator, whose observations, it suddenly becomes clear, contain insights that cause one to realize that he had never quite thought about the subject in that way before.

Given the variety of effective lectures, what conclusions can be drawn, or hazarded? In spite of the emphasis sometimes given to methodology, probably what is said about a historical subject is more important than how it is said. Of course, it is possible for a scholar to be a poor lecturer, to bore students with his presentation, to care nothing about teaching. But that is unusual. Historical scholars who care about teaching are usually much better than average teachers. For thoughtful preparation. breadth of interest, and depth of knowledge cannot be faked. They must be earned, and they will be recognized. It is never possible for a teacher to know too much about any historical subject, which by nature is open-ended.

Successful lecturing in any style begins with a conviction that the subject is important. If a teacher does not take it seriously, no student will do so. Stories are an important ingredient in history, but they must be used with restraint. The teacher who becomes known as a "great storyteller" will probably be dismissed by serious students as a dilettante, often with good reason. This is not meant to discourage the use of examples drawn from human experience—having men rather than forces march through a lecture—so that students will be brought to the realization, as one once confessed to me, that "for the first time . . . [he] understood that what took place before 1955 [the date of his birth] really happened." A successful act of self-transcendence had been performed by the student and he had seen living people, facing choices, making assumptions, having no more certain knowledge of their future, now our past, than we have of tomorrow.

Whenever possible a lecturer should refer to materials he himself has read from the sources. Nothing conveys a greater sense of contemporaneity and authority. Nothing makes clearer that the lecturer is speaking not merely as a teacher of history, but as a historian. He should speak if possible from notes and not read from a text. If self-confidence is lacking, especially at the beginning of a career, and the lecturer feels that he must write out what he wants to say, he should read it over so many times before delivery that familiarity with the contents leads to an informal presentation.

A lecturer in history should demonstrate the power of thought rather than the power of his own personality. The teacher of history, after all, is not trying to sell a product or win disciples. He is or should be trying to explain an intellectual point of view, to introduce students to a certain way of looking at human experience that they will find of value. In the only presidential address ever given to the American Historical Association on the subject of teaching (admittedly a shocking historical fact), Dexter Perkins, for many years a master teacher of American diplomatic history at the University of Rochester, summed up this emphasis: "A good teacher is an example of a man thinking, and somehow or other the example of a man thinking, may, by the grace of God, communicate itself to some of those around him."[34]

That this kind of communication does happen to students listening to history lectures has been attested to by a remarkable description of the teaching of Frederick Jackson Turner, written late in his career by one of his former students, Carl Becker:

> The lecture itself, if that is the word for it, seemed never "prepared," never studiously "got up" under the lamp. It seemed rather the spontaneous result of preparations always going on and never finished. The lecture was just informal, intimately conversational talk, beginning as might happen with this interesting matter, and ending as might happen with that; always serious without ever being solemn; enlivened with humor and wholesome infectious laughter, yet never falling to the level of the sad professorial joke; running off into relevant digressions occasioned by some student query; coming back again to the main point; coming now and again to the full stop while "notes" were eagerly searched for and found (oh, well, usually found), if not in one manilla envelope perhaps in another, notes containing some desired quotation from the

documents, with exact reference given, illustrating a point, clinching an argument. No, lecture isn't the word. . . .

An ordered body of information I could get, and did afterwards get, for myself; but from no other man did I ever get in quite the same measure that sense of watching a first-class mind at work on its own account, and not merely rehearsing for the benefit of others; the most delightful sense in the world of sitting there waiting for ideas to be born; expectantly waiting for secret meanings, convenient explanatory hypothesis to be discovered, lurking as like as not under the dullest mass of drab facts ever seen.[35]

Such a lecturer, it scarcely needs emphasizing, was a superb teacher of history.

To discuss history with students is quite different from lecturing and most teachers find it more difficult. It requires, first of all, listening to what students say. Many of us do not listen well. We prefer to teach by setting forth our own thoughts, not by reacting to what students have learned for themselves. Classes taught by the discussion method take such unpredictable turns that teaching them places a premium on an agile, flexible mind, quick to find expedients, and prepared intellectually for almost any eventuality, while at the same time deliberately leading verbal exchanges in a meaningful direction without seeming to be arbitrary. Students must have done their work, for the success of a class depends essentially upon them (though the teacher must also read the assignment, and constantly deepen his own knowledge of the subject). The right reading has to be selected. While experience helps in deciding on materials, what will work is uncertain until it has been tried. Classes must be small. While there is no magic in the number twenty, larger groups become more difficult to manage (though one extraordinary teacher of my acquaintance successfully used an informal method of give-and-take in a class of over 100!). But if a teacher does have the luxury of classes with twenty or so students, he should teach history by the discussion method. Provocative questioning in class has a power to evoke thought about history that is truly impressive. It is active education, closely related to that form of education which counts most, self-education.

Discussion can take a variety of forms in a history class. At one end of the spectrum are teachers who raise highly evaluative general questions about the reading ("What do you think of the author's treatment of John Winthrop?" "Is Winthrop a typical Puritan?") and encourage all members of the class to respond. The teacher's role becomes little more than that of a passive sounding board, the whole intention being to encourage students to talk. There are many dangers to this type of unguided discussion. Talkative but not necessarily able students may take over, and sensitive teachers soon discover that very little wisdom emerges from letting glib young tongues flap without restraint. Such a discussion does little for the quiet, introspective student, who proves on the first written test to have excellent comprehension of the subject, and who needs to be drawn out. In a misguided use of the word democracy ("all ideas are equal"), such discussion classes in history encourage excessive permissiveness. Passive teachers are as much to be regretted as passive students. The teacher who presides as the impartial arbiter of undifferentiated student opinion is not an educator; he is an irresponsible panel moderator.

At the other end of the spectrum some teachers use discussion classes to practice Socratic-like dialogue between themselves and individual students, chosen arbitrarily, with volunteers generally ignored. Questions tend to ask for precise understanding ("What is the difference between Arminianism and Antinomianism?"), a full answer, to be probed for, requiring detailed historical information. A skillful, wise teacher who knows how to develop questions out of student answers, without embarassing them, can make this into a highly effective method of education. For students the process becomes one of discovering how a sophisticated, better-stocked mind works, as well as the pleasurable thrill of occasionally keeping up with it. One of the method's drawbacks, however, is that students in fact do not learn very well listening to others while they are worried about being called upon themselves. Another weakness is that exchanges among students seldom occur. The value of general class involvement, of students helping to educate other students, is usually lost.

Probably a preferable method is one that attempts to guide the discussion in a way so as to involve larger numbers of students, which may at times use a Socratic-like dialogue with individual students, reserving some occasions for either a verbal free-for-all or student exchanges of opposing points of view. Questions ought to open up possibilities for student participation and move well beyond the obvious meaning of what has been read ("After reading about the background of Winthrop and the Massachusetts Bay Puritans, what is your reaction to the idea that seventeenth-century English emigrants to America were those who could not face up to difficulties at home?" "Why is it so important to understand the role of the covenant in Puritan theology?").

Discussions ought to vary in their emphasis, of course, depending on what is read. The more difficult assignments may necessitate direct explication by the teacher, who may even conclude that he needs to lecture briefly on occasion. The easier the reading, perhaps the greater leeway students should have in discussing it, though always with some guidance. The role of the teacher should be an active one, though not necessarily dominant, asking imaginative questions that reveal or illuminate the reading in a striking, unusual way. Much time in preparation needs to be spent on the making and phrasing of questions, at least those with which the class begins, or that deal with the important issues, for it cannot be overestimated how much depends on the way questions are asked. Nothing limps worse than the discussion class that consists of direct, categorical questions, calling for direct, categorical answers, without any opportunity for thoughtful, sensitive consideration. The historian's approach is to look first this way, then that, at the issues involved. The teacher's final responsibility should be not only to sum up in an orderly way what has happened in the course of the class. It should also be to judge the discussion and students' contributions to it, relying on his knowledge, experience, and training to point out what has been said of real quality.

The paperback revolution has profoundly enriched the possible reading assignments for class discussions in history. Every teacher should take full advantage of it by keeping informed, if possible, of the vast and continuous outpouring of publications that may be useful in his courses. The traditional textbook—a notoriously poor vehicle for encouraging class discussion because of necessity its coverage is thin, its approach usually a straightforward narrative—now may be supplemented, or even replaced, by a great variety of materials. Whether to use a textbook at all is much debated among college history teachers. History students, especially inexperienced ones, usually profit from having a convenient source of information, of chronology, of basic orientation. They may rely on it excessively, however, assuming naively that they know the subject being taught if they virtually memorize the text. Certain interpretive general accounts, containing selective but generally chronological coverage, such as Degler's previously mentioned *Out of Our Past,* are popular, highly readable, and successfully avoid the stigma of "text-book-itis." Whatever the decision regarding a text, all history courses should require students to read beyond it.

Among the most valuable types of readings for use in class discussions are well-written monographs that explore a limited subject in considerable but not exhaustive detail while also shedding light on a persistent theme in human experience. Such a monograph is Edmund Morgan's *The Puritan Dilemma: The Story of John Winthrop* (Boston, Little Brown, 1958). The central problem raised by the book—"what responsibility [does] a righteous man owe to society"—Morgan points out in his preface, "has concerned men of principle in every age, not least of all in our own." Students can and do return to the problem many times during the course of a semester, following it from a religious context to a secular one, and from domestic questions to issues of foreign policy.

All history courses should require some reading of source materials, or contemporary accounts, but these must be selected with special care. A steady diet of documents quickly leads to student indigestion, and becomes self-defeating. But a reading of Booker T. Washington's *Up From Slavery,* or sections from W. E. B. Du Bois's *Autobiography* will lead to an appreciation of these two remarkable black leaders that no secondary account can duplicate. A first-hand account written about a city boss, such as the amusing *Plunkitt of Tammany Hall,* re-creates late nineteenth-century urban politics in a way students find memorable. And there is no better introduction to late nineteenth-century farm life, its struggles with nature, its monotony, despair, and varied social types, than in the stories (created out of personal experience) of Hamlin Garland's *Main-Travelled Roads.* Selected sources containing diverse contemporary views on the same topic, if arranged imaginatively, can be used very effectively for discussion classes. One excellent example is *The Chicago Strike of 1894,* edited by Thomas Manning.

In many college courses it is currently popular to discuss selected historical topics rather than to follow a more strictly chronological approach. The emphasis has very distinct advantages—it allows for greater depth, more variety in materials, and the possibility of knowing a few subjects quite well. Yet a regrettable result may be to lessen students' understanding of the value and importance of time, which is, after all, the historian's medium. If a history class does not discuss such matters as the ripeness of time, the significance of contexts changing over the years, the conditions created by previous experience or lack of it, it will not be talking about a central concern of the subject. To give students the idea that the American Revolution was followed almost immediately by the Constitutional Convention, or that Jeffersonian democracy gave way to Jacksonian democracy, is to do a basic injustice to these topics. It wrenches them from their place in time and leaves them as flotsam on the narrative stream of events rather than an integral part of it. These periods will not be understood historically.

Some of the materials now being published in the form of "problems in history" seem designed to encourage the kind of uninformed exchange of random student opinion where anything goes, and intellectual discipline is soon gone. Lacking information and critical experience, students find themselves forced into the position of searching desperately for some kind of compromise conclusion. To be asked to decide, for example, as one popular series of problem books poses the question for students, whether John D. Rockefeller was a "Robber Baron or an Industrial Statesman" may cause students with a sense of humor to suggest, as one of mine once did, that Rockefeller was really a Baronial Statesman with the instincts of an Industrial Robber. The forcing of contrived value judgments, in short, may prevent or abort the real purpose of studying history, which is not to put the past on trial, but to understand and explain it.

The problems technique, if carried to extremes, also may encourage students to believe that all interpretations, or at least the latest ones, are of equal value in the intellectual marketplace, and that it is virtually impossible to distinguish among them except as a matter of individual preference or opinion. In the introduction to his *Pivotal Interpretations in American History*, Degler has issued the proper warning:

> Nothing could be more self-defeating to the critical study of history . . . all interpretations are not equal. Of all students of human behavior, historians are the least ready to talk of the "true knowledge" of their subject. . . . Yet [they] would be the last persons to say that "anything goes" in their subject. Otherwise . . . any fable would be indistinguishable from history. Far more than many will admit, historians recognize truth in their subject, and as all students know, penalize those who deviate too far from it.[36]

History is an empirical discipline. The validity of historical generalizations depends in the last analysis on how well they assess and use evidence. In discussing interpretations, students should be reminded that even though historians do not presume to pronounce final, absolute truths, they do say truthful things.

Let us carry through a sample discussion of the coming of the Spanish-American War, or, more accurately, the Cuban-Spanish-American War. Assume that the students have read a fairly sophisticated monograph without having the discussion "set up" in the form of a problem or conflicting interpretations—in a survey course, for example, H. Wayne Morgan's *America's Road to Empire,* or in a more advanced diplomatic history course, Ernest May's *Imperial Democracy.*[37]

To begin with the question, "What were the causes of the war?" will probably elicit an undifferentiated, non-chronological list, ranging from the effects of "yellow journalism" and the sinking of the *Maine* to publication of the Dupuy de Lôme letter and President McKinley's failure to reach a compromise with Spain. Sorting these suggestions will take time, and qualitative analysis will be difficult to achieve. Instead the first question must give the discussion a sharper focus. One might begin, for example: "With regard to Cuba, how did relations between Spain and the United States change in the six months or so *before* the sinking of the *Maine?*" Student responses should discern the importance of changing contexts—in the summer of 1897 McKinley hoped that a new Spanish cabinet would replace the harsh *reconcentrado* policies of General Weyler, and put into effect policies bringing an end to the rebellion—in short, that time was on the side of peace and hope. But by the middle of February, even before the *Maine* affair, most of the Spanish promises seemed unfulfilled, the conflict had continued, and clamor to bring it to an end had grown appreciably in Congress and among the public, making the president's position politically difficult.

One might then probe for an understanding of why the situation continued to worsen: "How did unanticipated incidents such as the *Maine* sinking and the de Lôme letter, plus the constant barrage of sensational journalism, worsen the situation?" Here students should be brought to see the importance of close reading and analysis. The de Lôme letter, for example, written by the ordinarily responsible Spanish minister to the United States, did not merely contain a gratuitous slur against McKinley, leading to an emotional reaction from an American public inexperienced in foreign affairs; it also seemed to reveal that Spanish diplomacy could not be trusted, and was deliberately trying to conceal its true intentions. The *Maine* tragedy not only cost 260 American lives and shocked the American public; it also apparently convinced McKinley and his Washington advisers that the war was out of control, that Spain could not end it, and that America was faced with a bloody, unrelenting, war of attrition on its doorstep. Many students will see in "yellow journalism," of course, a basic reason for the war, since the reputation of William Randolph Hearst (or his movie stand-in, Orson Welles) is difficult to downgrade. But at least the question may be raised whether in the Cuban crisis American newspapers did not reflect public indignation as much as they created it.

"On the eve of war," one might then ask, "that is, from the middle of March into April, what prevented diplomatic negotiations from succeeding?" This approach is designed to have students assess the chances for successful American mediation, given a situation in which Cuban leaders insisted upon independence and the Spanish government was unwilling even to consider it. McKinley, who believed that the war was steadily worsening, felt public and especially congressional pressures mounting on him to take decisive action. In the general discussion that should be encouraged here, perhaps the hypothesis will emerge that McKinley was too unwilling to sacrifice himself politically in ending the war, and that neither he nor the State Department was imaginative enough in devising proposals to bridge the diplomatic gap between Cuba and Spain. But the fact that a formidable gap existed cannot be denied. Students quick to condemn McKinley should be asked to elaborate on feasible alternatives under the circumstances. May's book is especially illuminating on the domestic situation in Spain which caused the queen regent and her government to cling stubbornly to Cuba even after it was clear that they could not put down the rebellion. And new scholarly emphasis on the enormous public and political pressures faced by McKinley has challenged the conclusion, widely accepted until fairly recently, that he was a weak president. Looking at diplomatic negotiations from all the sides involved is somewhat analogous to comparative history. It tends to put responsibilities for the failure of diplomacy and the use of force in greater perspective.

A final question might prepare for future considerations in the course: "Since a far-flung American empire emerged from this war, to what extent did an imperialistic urge lie behind it?" This should raise the broad question of whether preparations for empire in the preceding decades reached their culmination in 1898, or whether those who argue along such lines are expressing a *post hoc ergo propter hoc* argument. It is too big a subject to explore here. But what students should be brought to see (preferably for themselves) is that in the making of foreign policy there are always ambiguities the historian must keep in mind, contradictory facts hard to reconcile. There were men around McKinley then, such as Theodore Roosevelt and Henry Cabot Lodge, who wanted a big navy, possessions overseas, and an expanded role for the United States abroad, especially in the Caribbean. But they were *not* the makers and shapers of policy for the chief executive, and they were *not* much interested before 1898 in the Philippines as territory to acquire. Similarly, some American businessmen long had been interested in expanding foreign markets, but they did not want war or empire to be the means of achieving their goals. McKinley himself, certainly a reluctant imperialist before the war, found that the course of events during it changed many military and economic considerations in such a way that in the American interest acquisition of an empire in the form of the Philippines seemed more attractive than alternative policies. What should emerge from this discussion, a wide-ranging one, is a sense of that infinitely complex process by which great decisions in history are usually made, a process that challenges explanations by some overall theory or ideology. The late Princeton economist, Jacob Viner, once issued a warning to the effect that "theory is always simpler than reality."[38] Poised historical judgments emerge from comparing, analyzing, and testing the weight of evidence. Behind these judgments no amount of information is ever enough. Every discussion should end by making clear that the subject has not been closed, but remains open to future discussion, research, and scholarship.

3

How should a teacher of history respond to students who want to know the subject's structural concepts, to discover its underlying principles, or to search for the construction of models in understanding the past? He should not discourage such natural curiosity. But he also has the responsibility to warn that such searches may result in distorted and misleading responses. One such response is the overgeneralized generalization—once called historical laws, in a more hopeful age—such as the late E. P. Cheyney of the University of Pennsylvania outlined in his American Historical Association presidential address in 1923.[39] Cheyney's "law of continuity"—that "all events, conditions, institutions, personalities, come from immediately preceding events, conditions, institutions, personalities;" and his "law of impermanence"—that "unless nations, institutions, personalities *etc.,* adapt to altered conditions they cannot survive"—were broad-gauged tautologies (not unlike some of those more recently advanced by Arnold Toynbee) that invited students to think they knew something profound when they actually had heard something pretentious. Such generalizations continually crop up in new guises. George Orwell used to point out that James Burnham simply predicted the continuation of whatever was happening at the time of his writing. Orwell claimed that this tendency "is not simply a bad habit, like inaccuracy or exaggeration, which can be corrected by taking thought. It is a major mental disease. . . ." He saw it also in the defeatism of English intellectuals during World War II, remarking that "the quickest way of ending a war is to lose it, and if one finds the prospect of a long war intolerable, it is natural to disbelieve in the possibility of victory."[40]

Historical reality, of course, never lends itself to analysis in any meaningful sense through vague generalities. The habit of making relatively innocuous generalizations may lead to making harmful and misguided ones. The rest of Cheyney's "laws," as announced in 1923, indicate the dangers. They were: "the law of democracy," "the law of necessity for free consent," "the law of interdependence," and "the

law of moral progress." How do these sound in 1978? Courtesy demands a restrained response.

Another type of misleading response given to the questioner who
wants specific examples of historical concepts or principles is potentially as bad as the pious platitude, and is more prevalent today. It is
the generalization from insufficient, or insufficiently considered, historical evidence, often taking the form of at least mildly deterministic
theory. Bruner says, in his *Process of Education*:

> One teacher of social studies has had great success . . .
> through this approach: he begins for example, with the fact
> that civilizations have most often begun in fertile river valleys
> —the only "fact." The students are encouraged in class
> discussion to figure out why this is the case and why it would
> be less likely for civilizations to start in mountainous country.
> . . . This obviously is one kind of learning episode, and
> doubtless it has limited applicability.[41]

Indeed it has. It is going to confuse students no end to discover the
Inca civilization of highland Peru or the Minoan civilization of Crete.
And some may be alert enough to ask why it was that the American
Indians did not create a civilization of greater consequence in the
fertile and hardly mountainous Mississippi Valley. What has been
taught by this inquiry method—and in the name of improvement in
education—is in reality a form of geographical determinism. It tends
to ignore the challenges men and civilizations have overcome in environment, and at the same time to underestimate the impact of cultural level upon geography. What has been done is to narrow the
horizons of learning rather than to broaden them.

The teacher of history has an obligation to keep his students constantly aware of the way historians think about their discipline.
Bruner discourses most interestingly on the role of intuitive thinking
in education. In science and mathematics, he feels, intuitive thinking
is very important and should be encouraged under proper conditions
of control. He suggests, in a provocative passage:

> Surely the historian, to take but one example, leans heavily
> upon intuitive procedures in pursuing his subject, for he must
> select what is relevant. He does not attempt to learn or record
> everything about a period; he limits himself to finding or

learning predictively fruitful facts which, when combined, permit him to make intelligent guesses about what else went on. A comparison of intuitive thinking in different fields of knowledge would, we feel, be highly useful.[42]

What is being expressed here, in not very effective disguise, is that the historian should perform an "act of faith" to guide his researches. Now it is true that the historian and the history teacher have to select, that they work within limitations, and that they may have to make a number of intelligent guesses where the data are incomplete or difficult to interpret. But they do these things shamefacedly, not barefacedly. They do not exult about them; they apologize for them. For they know that they must always refrain from the tempting intuitive leap on the basis of partial, early evidence. Intuitive leaps in history tend towards dogmatic theories and a guided search for evidence to support them. Some evidence may be found to support any theory, including the most outlandish, as A. J. P. Taylor of Oxford University has demonstrated in his study of the *Origins of the Second World War,* holding Hitler no more responsible for it than his enemies. Responsible historians strive for judgments that weigh the accumulated evidence, keep an open mind in regard to it, and then try, given all the admitted weaknesses of human flesh, to explain and to assess past human behavior. Intuition cannot play an important role here. Perception, yes, imagination, yes, but intuition, no. In the teaching and writing of history there is no substitute for more knowledge, for new sources of information, for an understanding of details. The more students know in detail, the greater chance they have for sophisticated judgments, and the closer they may be able to give expression to the rich texture of historical reality.

Historians and nonhistorians, teachers and students alike, should rejoice that there is no royal road to understanding the past, or to teaching those who become interested in it. There is no structure of underlying principles; there are no basic laws. Let historians, at least, not be ashamed to admit this. Let them be proud to proclaim it, and to teach it. Their students will not suffer from its recognition, since the intellectual discipline of properly studying the past has its own built-in relevance. For every intellectual explanation of human experience, whatever its special mode of inquiry, must rely upon history for its content. There is no alternative.

NOTES

1. Martin Duberman, *The Uncompleted Past* (New York: Dutton, 1969), p. 355.
2. Henry Sigerist, ed., *Four Treatises of Theophrastus von Hohenheim called Paracelsus* (Baltimore: Johns Hopkins Press, 1941), p. 12.
3. Jerome S. Bruner, *Toward a Theory of Instruction* (Cambridge: Harvard University Press, 1966). p. 36. For a useful treatment of the subject, see Robert F. Berkhofer, Jr., *A Behavioral Approach to Historical Analysis* (New York: Free Press, 1969).
4. Three active centers for the production of materials and training of teachers along these lines are the Amherst Project of the Committee on the Study of History, Chicago; the Carnegie-Mellon Social Studies Curriculum Center, Pittsburgh; and the Social Studies division of the Education Development Corporation, Cambridge, Massachusetts. The guiding spirit of the Carnegie-Mellon project from its inception has been Edwin Fenton, whose book, *Teaching the New Social Studies in Secondary Schools: An Inductive Approach* (New York: Holt, Rinehart and Winston, 1966), should be consulted.
5. Quoted in John A. Garraty, *Interpreting American History: Conversations with Historians,* I (London: Macmillan, 1970), pp. 240–41.
6. Irwin Unger, "The 'New Left' and American History: Some Recent Trends in United States Historiography," *American Historical Review* 72 (July 1967): 1237–63; David Donald, "Radical Historians on the Move," *New York Times Book Review,* 19 July 1970.
7. Barton Bernstein, ed., *Towards a New Past: Dissenting Essays in American History* (New York: Random House, 1969), pp. ix, xiii.
8. Staughton Lynd, *Intellectual Origins of American Radicalism* (New York: Random House, 1969), pp. 9–10.
9. An American History Association survey of three hundred institutions of higher education, published in the *Newsletter* for September 1974, revealed that between 1970–71 and 1973–74 history course enrollments dropped 12.16 percent and the num-

ber of history majors receiving B. A. degrees declined 6.49 percent. Selective liberal arts colleges showed the least amount of decline; students in community colleges, which enroll approximately 50 percent of all American undergraduates, displayed alarmingly little interest in history. A more extensive AHA survey is now under way (1975–76) in cooperation with the Higher Education Research Institute: see AHA *Newsletter,* March 1976. To support the generalization that history teaching in the schools is in national crisis see the report by Richard Kirkendall, "The Status of History in the Schools," prepared for the Ad Hoc Committee, *Journal of American History* 62 (September 1975): 557–570. The tragedy of unemployment for the current generation of young American historians receives a sympathetic and sensible hearing in Frank Freidel, "Backlogging," *New York Times,* Op. Ed. page, 2 June 1976, excerpted from his April 1976 presidential address to the Organization of American Historians. See also AHA *Newsletter* for February 1975.

10. C. Vann Woodward, "The Future of the Past," *American Historical Review* 75 (February 1970): 711–726. Another expression of similar concern is reflected in the Winter 1971 issue of *Daedalus* titled "Historical Studies Today." In the Spring 1971 issue of *Daedalus,* "The Historian and the World of the Twentieth Century," the articles impressively demonstrate how robust historical scholarship is, but make no effort to analyze its impact on students and teachers of history.

11. Stephen R. Graubard, "The Present Puts History on Defense," *New York Times Annual Education Review,* 12 January 1970, p. 81.

12. *The History Teacher* 7 (February 1974), reflects all of these approaches. Since its September 1974 issue, the AHA *Newsletter* has contained a regular column inviting undergraduate teachers or departments of history to state what they have been doing to revive or to retain student interest in studying the past. The resulting columns have revealed a wide spectrum of so-called new teaching approaches, most of which emphasize ways to make history more appealing to students, and some of which have elicited concern that college history teaching may be in danger of becoming "hucksterism." See Michael Lodwick and

Thomas Fiehrer, "Undoing History; or Clio Clobbered," AHA *Newsletter*, May/June 1975.

13. Frederick Jackson Turner, "The Significance of History" (first published in 1891), in Fulmer Mood, ed., *The Early Writings of Frederick Jackson Turner* (Madison: University of Wisconsin Press, 1938), p. 52.

14. Carl N. Degler, *Out of Our Past: The Forces That Shaped Modern America* (1949; reprint ed. New York: Harper & Row, 1970), p. xi.

15. Philip Van Doren Stern, ed., *The Life and Writings of Abraham Lincoln* (New York: The Modern Library, 1940), p. 745.

16. Cushing Strout, *The Pragmatic Revolt in American History: Carl Becker and Charles Beard* (1958; reprint ed., Ithaca, N.Y.: Cornell University Press, 1966), pp. 42–43. The often quoted essay by Becker, which was his American Historical Association presidential address in 1931, appears as the title piece in a volume of his essays, *Everyman His Own Historian: Essays on History and Politics* (1935; reprint ed., New York: Quadrangle, 1966).

17. *The New York Times Book Review*, 29 November 1970, p. 5.

18. George Harmon Knoles, ed., *The Crisis of the Union, 1860–1861* (Baton Rouge: Louisiana State University Press, 1965), pp. 92–93, 108.

19. Ibid., p. 108.

20. For a perceptive analysis see Morton White, *Social Thought in America* (Boston: Beacon Press, 1949), especially chaps. IV, VIII, XIV.

21. The most conspicuous examples of writing with this orientation have been produced by the able Arthur M. Schlesinger, Jr. See his *The Age of Jackson* (Boston: Little, Brown 1946) and the first volume in his series, The Age of Roosevelt, called *The Crisis of the Old Order* (Boston: Houghton Mifflin, 1957).

22. For an extended consideration of the change from a genetic to a normative approach in history writing in America, see my article, "The New American History and its Audience," *Yale Review* 46 (Winter 1957): 245–59. John Higham, et al., *History: The Development of Historical Studies in the United States* (Englewood Cliffs, N.J.: Prentice-Hall, 1965), pp. 171–72, sees this kind of shift coming with the progressive historians,

around 1907, away from the conception of the continuity of history: "Whereas conservative evolutionists concentrated on the character of institutions, understood in terms of their origins, progressives focused on changes in institutions, explained in terms of a surrounding environment." In the series, Great Ages of Western Philosophy, the volume on the twentieth century, Morton White, ed., is titled *The Age of Analysis* (Boston: New American Library, 1955).

23. For the sources of these generalizations, in the same order as described, see Richard Hofstadter, "Is America by Nature a Violent Society?" reprinted in Michael McGiffert, ed., *The Character of Americans*, rev. ed. (Homewood, Ill: Dorsey Press, 1970), p. 398; Nathan Glazer's introduction to Stanley M. Elkins, *Slavery: A Problem in American Institutional and Intellectual Life* (1959; reprint ed., Chicago: University of Chicago Press, 1968), p. ix; Richard W. Van Alstyne, *The Rising American Empire* (1960; reprint ed., New York: W. W. Norton, 1974), p. 205; William Appleman Williams, *The Contours of American History* (1961; reprint ed., New York: Watts, 1966), pp. 464, 480, 483–88.

24. Graubard, p. 81.

25. See C. Vann Woodward, ed. *The Comparative Approach to American History* (New York: Basic Books, 1968); and the journal, *Comparative Studies in Society and History—An International Quarterly* (New York: Cambridge University Press, 1958–), ed. Sylvia L. Thrupp and Eric R. Wolf.

26. Slavery has been the subject of much work in comparative history, touched off by Frank Tannenbaum, *Slave and Citizen— The Negro in the Americas* (New York: Vintage edition, 1946, 1963), which maintained that slavery was legally, culturally, and actually so different in Latin America compared with North America that its history had a profound moderating effect on later race relations. Two recent studies that reveal the enormous profit to be derived from the comparative approach in making historical judgments, and which argue strongly against Tannenbaum's conclusions, are David Brion Davis, *The Problem of Slavery in Western Culture* (Ithaca, N.Y.: Cornell University Press, 1966), and Carl N. Degler, *Neither Black nor White: Slavery and Race Relations in Brazil and the United States* (New

York: Macmillan, 1971). Examples of materials for studying topics in comparative history in college classrooms are John J. TePaske, ed., *Three American Empires* (New York: Harper & Row, 1967); Laura Foner and Eugene D. Genovese, eds., *Slavery in the New World: A Reader in Comparative History* (Englewood Cliffs, N.J.: Prentice-Hall, 1969).

27. See Leonard Krieger, "The Horizons of History," *American Historical Review* 63 (October 1957): 62–74; Marc Bloch, *The Historian's Craft* (New York: Knopf, 1959), p. 27.

28. For illuminating brief treatments of the value and limitations of psychoanalytical approaches to the past, and consideration of what the historical approach has to offer psychologists writing historical biographies (i.e., Erik Erikson on Luther and Gandhi), see David Hackett Fischer, *Historians' Fallacies— Toward a Logic of Historical Thought* (New York: Harper & Row, 1970), pp. 187, 190, 213–15; Frank E. Manuel, "The Use and Abuse of Psychology in History," *Daedalus,* Winter 1971, pp. 199–202; and Jacques Barzun, "History: The Muse and her Doctors," *American Historical Review* 77 (February 1972): 36–64.

29. A central essay on the subject is William O. Aydelotte, "Quantification in History," *American Historical Review* 71 (April 1966): 804–825. See also Samuel P. Hays, "Quantificaton in History: The Implications and Challenges for Graduate Training," AHA *Newsletter* 4 (June 1966): 8–11. A valuable survey of the impact that quantification has on reasearch in American history is Robert Swierenga, "Computers and American History: the Impact of the 'New' Generation," *Journal of American History* 60 (March 1974): 1045–70.

30. Woodward, "Future of the Past," p. 726.

31. Carl L. Becker, "A New Philosophy of History," *Dial* 59 (1915): 148.

32. Reprinted in David M. Potter, *The South and the Sectional Conflict* (Baton Rouge: Louisiana State University Press, 1968), pp. 151–76.

33. Herbert J. Muller, *The Uses of the Past* (1952; reprint ed., New York: Oxford University Press, 1957), p. 28.

34. Dexter Perkins, "We Shall Gladly Teach," *American Historical*

Review 62 (January 1957): 294. Prospective college history teachers should read the entire essay, pp. 291–309.

35. Becker, "Frederick Jackson Turner," *Every Man His Own Historian,* pp. 197–99.

36. Carl N. Degler, ed., *Pivotal Interpretations in American History,* 2 vols. (New York: Harper, 1966), I: viii.

37. H. Wayne Morgan, *America's Road to Empire: The War with Spain and Overseas Expansion* (New York: John Wiley, 1965); Ernest R. May, *Imperial Democracy: The Emergence of America as a Great Power* (New York: Harcourt, Brace, 1961).

38. Jacob Viner, *International Trade and Economic Development* (Glencoe: Free Press, 1952), p. 12.

39. Edward P. Cheyney, "Law in History," *American Historical Review* 29 (January 1924): 231–48.

40. See Owen Harries, "Six Ways of Confusing Issues," *Foreign Affairs* 40 (April 1962): 447. Harries very astutely points out errors in thinking about foreign policy that frequently appear in public discussions; his article deserves wide reading.

41. Jerome S. Bruner, *The Process of Education* (New York: Vintage, 1960), p. 51.

42. Ibid., pp. 66–67.

EDWARD B. PARTRIDGE

Teaching English*

EDWARD B. PARTRIDGE (Ph.D., Columbia University) is professor of English at Newcomb College, Tulane University, where he was the recipient of the "Outstanding Teacher" award in 1969. He previously taught at Hobart College, Columbia University, Cornell University, Bucknell University, the University of Rochester, the University of Iowa, and California State University at Los Angeles. He is the author of *The Broken Compass: A Study of the Major Comedies of Ben Jonson,* the editor of editions of two plays by Jonson, *Epicoene* and *Bartholomew Fair,* and a contributor to various professional periodicals.

---

* Although this essay was orginally written for this volume, some of the material first appeared in the author's article "Representing Shakespeare," in *Shakespeare Quarterly,* vol. 25, no. 2 (Spring 1974): 201–8. Reprinted by permission of *Shakespeare Quarterly.*

I

First of all, what is "English?" What, indeed! Its shapelessness is part of my problem. If I were to define English in terms of the courses often taught by departments of English in the United States, I should have to throw a very loose line around phonology; grammar; semantics; the history of the English language; Old, Middle, and Modern English; American English; composition (creative writing, exposition, report writing); literary theory from Plato to the present; bibliography and research methods; the teaching of English; and, of course, the whole corpus of literature written in English (Old, Middle, Early Modern and Modern) since Caedmon (c. 657–680). The whole corpus means primarily English and American literature, but it could legitimately include and, in parts of the world, already does include Anglo-Irish, Scottish, Canadian, and Australian literature. And, oh, yes, certain classics from "World Literature" which are read in translation, if read at all, and are often taught by English teachers—classics like the Bible, *The Divine Comedy, The Odyssey,* and Greek tragedies.

Nor is the whole problem that "English" stretches all the way from the most delicate analysis of phonemes to the biggest problems of interpreting some of the most difficult literary works ever written. Consider just the problems of teaching literary works. What *are* we teaching? Absolutely discrete works? Forms? Genres? The history of ideas in dilution? The history of civilization? The pursuit of beauty? Values? Are we helping students discover themselves? Are we teaching them to think clearly, feel deeply, speak naturally, write imaginatively? Each of these has been offered as a reason for reading literature, and each is, to some extent, a legitimate reason. So is even the recent extravagant claim of Benjamin DeMott, who concludes, after saying that "English" is not centrally about poetics, metrics, the history of literature, the study of style or the majesty of Shakespeare, that the English classroom "is the place—there is no other in most schools—the place wherein the chief matters of concern are particulars of humanness—individual human feeling, human response, and human time, as these can be known through the written expression (at many literary levels) of men living and dead, and as they can be discovered by student writers seeking through words to name and compose and grasp their own experience. English in sum is about my

distinctness and the distinctness of other human beings."[1] Well, yes
—but no. True, "English" is about "the particulars of humanness"
as they are expressed in writing, but, on the same grounds, so are all
languages and literatures, and so are all humane studies, like history,
and some of the social sciences, like sociology and political science.
Professor DeMott would seem to be describing the function of most
classrooms, not just the English. Furthermore, the very things he
says are not central to English *are* central because they are the
uniquely literary means by which the intellect and the imagination
help to bring about the larger aim of educating human responses. We
must deal with form and technique in literary study because only
through them do we find out what the writer is saying.

How can one define "English?" From the point of view of linguistics, "English," like any other language, concerns itself with "speech
events," the constitutive factors of which have been explained by
Roman Jakobson in this way: "The ADDRESSER sends a MES-
SAGE to the ADDRESSEE. To be operative the message requires
a CONTEXT referred to ('referent' in another, somewhat ambigu-
ous, nomenclature), seizable by the addressee, and either verbal or
capable of being verbalized; a CODE fully, or at least partially, common to the addresser and addressee (or in other words, to the en-
coder and decoder of the message); and finally, a CONTACT, a
physical channel and psychological connection between the addresser
and the addressee, enabling both of them to enter and stay in communication. All these factors inalienably involved in verbal communication may be schematized as follows:

	CONTEXT	
ADDRESSER	MESSAGE	ADDRESSEE
	CONTACT	
	CODE	

Each of these six factors determines a different function of language."[2] His corresponding scheme of these functions is:

	Referential	
Emotive	Poetic	Conative
	Phatic	
	Metalingual	

These schemes can help us understand at least three aspects of "English." First, they explain why courses as diverse as creative writing, Old English, Restoration Comedy, and the principles of literary criticism can be taught by the same department: all deal with the making or the recording or the understanding, of speech events. Though English teachers devote most of their time to studying the "poetic" function of the message (which Jakobson points out is the dominant function of verbal art), they must be concerned with the interaction of all these factors in speech acts and not just the triad, addresser—message—addressee. For instance, they must care about the code they use—that is, the language spoken in everyday speech as well as the conventions and traditions it has gathered as it has been used by literary artists. Second, these schemes can be used to analyze the literary work, as René Wellek, sceptical of the usefulness of linguistics in literary study, and I. A. Richards, more sympathetic to linguistics than Wellek is, both admit.[3] That Jakobson's scheme can be useful in literary criticism does not mean that poetics should be seen as the wayward child of linguistics, or a child at all, as some linguists think. Poems and stories may be instrumental speech acts; they are never merely instrumental because their words become iconic rather than remain referential. Finally, the schemes picture the relationship between teacher and student in courses involving speech events. The contact is the class and the classroom. The context is the course with its texts, papers, and examinations. The whole exchange between teacher and student, each at times the addresser, each the addressee, constitutes the message. They exchange not merely ideas and speculations, but also all those exhortations, warnings, jokes, mockeries, and verbal gestures which occur when two or three are gathered together.

I had better admit straightway that I shall be writing about teaching poems, plays, and stories, and not much else. Properly, I should write about the whole immense business of English, but I simply do not have the time to deal with linguistics and writing here, nor have I had enough experience teaching them to make anything I should say worth listening to. Let me hasten to add that any English teacher must know a good deal about the history and the structure of his own language in order to teach anything about its use either in literary works or in writing done by students, and he must pay a great deal of attention to the way his students speak and write. A course in literature that does not draw on traditional philology or modern linguistics (preferably both) and that does not lead to some kind of careful writing by students is not being competently taught. No one can analyze or interpret even fairly easy literary works in English without having a sure grasp of the syntactical structures and the prosody as well as the diction of the English language. And one must not neglect any of these three—syntax, prosody, diction. If one confines one's analysis simply to the meaning of separate words and phrases and ignores either sound or syntax, then one is reading a literary work simply for raw information, as though it were yesterday's newspaper. Neglecting sound, one may miss the hypnotic pleasure of rhythm. Neglecting syntax, one may even miss the "information" itself or distort it cruelly. A simple example of how crucial sound and syntax are appears in the final lines of Yeats's "Byzantium":

> Marbles of the dancing floor
> Break bitter furies of complexity,
> Those images that yet
> Fresh images beget,
> That dolphin-torn, that gong-tormented sea.

What does "Those images" refer to? If one says "furies of complexity" because appositive phrases are attracted to the closest substantive, one gets one reading. If one says "Marbles of the dancing floor" because the rest of the poem suggests that images must here mean man-made images, one gets quite another reading. As for the effect of sound, Yeats himself has spoken of the way meter, by regularizing intonation, keeps the listener in a state of "perhaps real trance." On another occasion he spoke of "that subtle monotony of voice which runs through the nerves like fire."[4] In both prose and verse, sound and rhythm can focus and heighten the meanings of the words used and, by isolating the literary experience from the irrelevancies of everyday life, purify it and render it aesthetic. If one wants a longer look at more difficult problems in what Jakobson calls "the grammar of poetry and the poetry of grammar," one could scarcely do better than look at the analysis that he and Lawrence Jones made of sonnet 129, "The expense of spirit in a waste of shame" in *Shakespeare's*

Verbal Art (1970). Then one might read the review of this pamphlet by I. A. Richards in the *Times Literary Supplement*, May 28, 1970.[5]

To learn enough to describe with some accuracy even more difficult grammatical problems than Yeats poses (and some of Yeats's are difficult, indeed), we do not need to commit ourselves absolutely to the transformational version of generative grammar of Chomsky, Halle, and Lees as opposed to the older structural-descriptive approach of Bloomfield, Harris, Hockett, and Hill.[6] (I even feel a lingering fondness for traditional grammar, the loose old shoes in the back of my mind.) In fact, given the extraordinary flowering of linguistic studies since 1950, anyone who is not professionally engaged in teaching courses in linguistics had better keep an open, but not empty, mind on most linguistic matters lest he find himself defending a standard in a battle no longer fought. In the same way I think it unnecessary for most of us to commit ourselves unalterably to either of the two main theories of the nature of meaning—that is, the analytic approach of Stephen Ullmann and Ogden and Richards or the operational approach of Wittgenstein. Do words have fixed meanings which can be combined into larger units, as the former say (or as Richards once said; more recently he has moved closer to the operational theory), or is the meaning of a word in its use—its "field of force"—so that the separate elements of language derive their significance from the system as a whole, as Wittgenstein claims? For most of our teaching either theory works well enough.[7]

As for writing—we can only come to know, and know that we know about literary works or anything else for that matter by talking or writing at some length about them. Jerome Bruner makes this point with characteristic force: "I have often thought that I would do more for my students by teaching them to write and think in English than teaching them my own subject. It is not so much that I value discourse to others that is right and clear and graceful—be it spoken or written—as that practice in such discourse is the only way of assuring that one says things right and courteously and powerfully *to oneself*. For it is extraordinarily difficult to say foolishness clearly without exposing it for what it is—whether you recognize it yourself or have the favor done you."[8] This cruel truth ought to have two consequences, one for us, one for our students. We had better force our students not only to speak often and clearly and thoughtfully about the books they read and the ideas they have, but also to write about them with as much judgment and distinction as they can muster, lest they think they possess works and ideas which instead possess them. And we as teachers must keep on writing poems and stories and articles and books and book reviews throughout our professional careers, and try to get them published, not to keep from perishing, but to keep alive—which is not quite the same thing—or to have someone else tell us we're half dead.

II

Since the way one teaches a subject grows out of the nature of the subject, I ought to make clear what I think the study of literature to be. Most of what follows will be commonplace if you agree with me, and irritating if you do not, but it had better be said so that I can sensibly argue that, having this nature, English might best be taught in these ways. I have another reason for saying something big and obvious about literature here because what I say may suggest how to fill those sometimes empty classes at the beginning of a freshman course. Every teacher wants to say something breathtaking about the fascinating course that the students are going to share with him. How to do it? One way is to lecture with whirlwind eloquence on the nature of poetry. Another is to ask the students what they think the nature of poetry is—a dangerous and, on the first day, possibly disillusioning thing to do. They may think the teacher has been too lazy to work up a lecture, and he is certain they're stupid. A third, and the best, way is to hand the students a copy of a poem and, partly by making some of the points himself and partly by helping them discover the points themselves, to draw the nature of poetry from this concrete example of it. Something like the following paragraphs might be discovered. I shall summarize the various points that the teacher might want to make; the students, blast them, often have other things on their minds. I shall not try to duplicate the peculiar combination of lecture, discussion, and question-and-answer which might be used to make these points. If I had more time and talent, I might have the nerve to try to reconstruct such a class in all its messiness. But I haven't, and won't. So:

Literature, so everyone says, is imaginative writing. But what does this mean? Let us try to infer the nature of such imaginative writing from a poem by Robert Frost.*

> Nothing Gold Can Stay
>
> Nature's first green is gold,
> Her hardest hue to hold.
> Her early leaf's a flower;
> But only so an hour.
> Then leaf subsides to leaf.
> So Eden sank to grief,
> So dawn goes down to day.
> Nothing gold can stay.

What we see printed here is a set of black typographical signals which transmit to our brains a complex system of sounds. The printed words have meaning only in terms of the spoken language which Frost and his readers both know. Though literature now comes to us largely as something written down in books, rather than as something heard, it is still radically a "system of sounds," hence "a selection from the sound-system of a given language."[9]

This radical relationship to speech was, of course, much more evident in antiquity when three of the four standard types (epic, lyric, drama, and prose fiction) were properly rendered at all only when they were spoken or chanted or sung.[10] The epic poet or some "rhapsode" pretending to be the poet chanted or recited the *Odyssey* to a group of listeners who shared his joy in heroic exploits and his interest in the ethical bent of the hero. The lyric originally was, and still is, a cry of joy or grief, of triumph or despair, which the poet sings to himself. We who read a lyric become the poet or become the person the poet has pretended to be, and we sing to ourslves his joy or grief, his anguish or ecstasy, his triumph or despair, which then becomes ours. The drama—most obvious of all—must be heard to be understood. It too requires a speaker or speakers who do not merely recite or chant as the epic poet does or sing as the lyric poet

---

does: the words of a play are spoken by actors who play someone else. In short, by their very nature, epics, lyrics, and plays use words which must be "heard." We can read them silently, of course, but, unless we hear them in some inner ear as we read, we miss something of their essence.

Only prose fiction—that is, a novel or a short story—does not seem to require being heard in this fundamental way. The possibility of just reading novels and not hearing them can mislead people into thinking of all literature as something to be read silently and rapidly. This disastrous misconception may have begun five hundred years ago with the invention of movable type, that marvelous and dangerous invention which made it possible to read poems and plays and stories usually only heard before. By the seventeenth century the long story in prose written only to be read had begun to be the most popular of literary forms. Gradually since then, as the reading public grew, novels expanded in size and number, and the essentially "heard" nature of most literature was too often forgotten. We must always remember that literature uses words and that speech is finally the source and the criterion of language. As Sapir reminds us, writing is a substitute for phonetic language.[11] Underlying every poem, every play, every novel, every essay is the human voice—the speech of a human being.[12] That silence in which the music even of a novel is heard is the receptive silence of the inner ear. Lest I be understood as calling for "oral interpretation" of literature (though that can be rewarding in its own right), I ought to emphasize that I am insisting on the need to "listen" to a literary work, not on the need to read it aloud. I am insisting that the words, syntactic structures, and rhythms be listened to with our "auditory imagination" because they are prosodically—and thus aesthetically—meaningful. One great difference between literary and nonliterary discourse is that we must hear one and can scarcely endure hearing the other.

Literature is not just sound, but sound arranged artistically to make a pleasing or deliberately cacophonous musical effect. In other words, it is rhythmical. Rhythm, which comes from recurrence at equal intervals, as in walking or dancing, is pleasing in itself. Even rhythmically arranged words in a language you do not understand are pleasing; or in language which seems to have no meaning, as in

> Hickory! Dickory! Dock!
> The mouse ran up the clock.
> The clock struck one,
> The mouse ran down,
> Hickory! Dickory! Dock!

That's poetry on a fundamental phonetic and rhythmic level. If you don't respond simply and profoundly to those sounds and that rhythm, you probably can't respond on any other level that is going to have much effect on you. This poem about a mouse may have some meaning: there does seem to be a foreboding sense of time and change in it. But it doesn't need sense to make sense as poetry. The sound and rhythm of Hickory! Dickory! Dock! please the child who is not quite asleep in all of us.

Still, poetry often does make sense. It is not just phonetic and rhythmic, but also verbal. It uses words which, as linguistic signs, carry meaning. Let us look at the first line of Frost's poem—"Nature's first green is gold." Frost starts with one of the most complex words in the English language, but his opening words narrow and sharpen the meaning of "nature" by emphasizing three things about it— *first, green,* and *gold. Green* suggests what the third line reinforces: *nature* means the green things of earth—the trees, the grass, the bushes, the flowers. *First* suggests that he is talking about spring—the first green which the earth shows us after the long brown and white winter. We hear a man expressing, concretely and sensuously, one of those commonplaces about the brevity of spring which the seasons evoke from all of us.

But the end of the first line lifts this commonplace into a lie—that is, a metaphor. All metaphors are lies which pass for truths. They are ways of seeing something in terms of something it is not. "Nature's first green is gold." Nature is given life and color and in the second line, sex. The lie is doubled, and the metaphor becomes paradoxical when we hear its green is gold. How can green be gold? The next three lines reconcile us to this impossible identity by calling our attention, or recalling our memory, to that hour in early spring when the leaf first appears as a flower—a bud whose leaves are so light a green that, as they unfold, they seem gold. Note that Frost does not say yellow or light green or chartreuse—none of which would carry quite the suggestive effect that *gold* does. Words are not only descriptive, but evocative. Frost draws on the wealth of gold as the poem moves on.

This narrowing of nature down to a leaf illustrates another characteristic of literature: it necessarily uses synecdoche, that figure in which a part represents a whole concept or object. Here the leaf represents all green things, and its fate, as we shall see, is the fate of all. Frost himself has said: "Imagery and after-imagery are about all there is to poetry. Synecdoche and synecdoche."[13] He never explained what he meant by "after-imagery," and he certainly did not think figurative language is all there is to poetry, but a good many people would agree with him about the importance of synecdoche. One critic, Kenneth Burke, has even argued that synecdoche is the basic figure of speech. A poet can't talk about nature for very long or very profitably; he must talk about birches or stone walls or flowers or birds or girls. A poet is not a philosopher interested primarily in ideas, or a scientist interested in laws, or a historian interested in events, though he may use ideas, laws, and events for his own purpose. And the poet's purpose is to set a small world into motion in such a way that it suggests something true and memorable about the larger worlds we all live in or can imagine living in. Frost speaks about the leaf as a green-gold image of the earth in spring. The whole poem dramatically carries out the littleness of the leaf. The meter is small—three stresses to a line. The rhymes are in little couplets. The sentences are all short, the normal syntactical unit being five words. No phrase or clause runs beyond one verse of the poem. All but eight of the forty words in the poem are monosyllables. Everything seems small and precious and controlled.

Everything, that is, except the images which appear in the last half of the poem: Eden, dawn, and gold. Though the final lines preserve in meter and syntax the littleness we have noticed, the images widen the world of the poem. "So Eden sank to grief." "So" sets up a simple equation: just as the golden leaf subsides to the green, so Eden—the Golden Age—sinks to the grief of loss. Simply, almost artlessly, Frost here draws on what are now called archetypes—that is, age-old images which gain their power from countless experiences of our ancestors. "Eden," in a Hebraic-Christian culture like ours, is an archetypal image of Paradise, the garden where Adam and Eve lived until it and we came to grief. "Grief" is the first and only direct description of emotion in the whole poem. But its intensity is qualified by the second archetype—dawn. Dawn does not go down to night or even to twilight. Dawn goes down to day. The ironic tone saves the poem from being melodramatic or too simple. A tone is ironic when it suggests a discrepancy between what you expect to get and what you do get, or between what the words literally say and what they imply because of their context. Leaf subsides to leaf; dawn goes down to day. Green leaves and daylight are very good things in themselves. Neither is quite what it once was for one beautiful moment. The irony is paradoxical too: a leaf, in growing, subsides; Eden, the first of things, sinks; dawn, the going-up of the sun, goes down to daylight.

Simple as the poem seems to be, it dramatizes a complex experience economically. The very syntax of the sentences emphasizes the Fall which the images suggest. The pattern of the first two sentences is the same: a joyful observation is made, only to be immediately qualified:

> Nature's first green is gold,
> Her hardest hue to hold.
> Her early leaf's a flower,
> But only so an hour.

These sentences sink even as Eden does. But the fifth line almost reverses this movement. Leaf subsides to what? Leaf does not subside to nothing. Leaf subsides to leaf—a diminished thing, but a lovely diminished thing. Eden sinks not to chaos, but to grief—which, being human, has its own dignity. It isn't joy, but it isn't nothing either. Better to grieve than not to feel at all. Dawn goes down to a light less golden, but a light none the less. All of this ironic qualification prepares us for the final statement—"Nothing gold can stay"—in which gold, now no longer just a color, has gathered to itself spring and foliage, Eden and the Golden Age, dawn and childhood, innocence and joy: nothing gold can stay. But the verb suggests motion, as do *subside, sink, go down*. And these active verbs call up the immense archetypal image of nature herself, seasonally changing, her living bound up with her dying, growth necessarily following birth, and death inevitably completing maturity. The gold of spring can't stay, but it can come again.

As you can see, we have moved from the sound of words and their rhythmic arrangement to their meanings as metaphors and ironies and archetypes. This interaction of sound and rhythm and meaning creates the special tone of the poem—its pervasive atmosphere, its air, its unique voice. But we can not hear that tone accurately and fully unless we investigate the linguistic and stylistic details which compose it. Linguistically, these details are the phones, allophones, phonemes, morphs, and morphemes by which one person communicates with another. Stylistically, these morphemes or meaningful linguistic units are organized into words and word-groups which have multiple relationships and conceptual significance. A literary work is, as René Wellek describes it, "a stratified system of norms."[14] These norms are not necessarily normative statements or value-judgments (though they may be when they describe our moral and emotional reactions to a character or a situation). In general, I use "norms" to refer to established ways of speaking and acting. In literary study the norms can be classified as semantic or syntactic or prosodic, or as some combination of all of them. Frost can not speak to us unless we share such semantic norms as the meaning of words like "Eden" or "gold," or such syntactic norms as the parallel sentence structure of lines 6 and 7, or such prosodic norms as the scansion of line 2 into regular iambic feet. We can not fully experience Frost's poem or any poem unless we can interpret and properly evaluate both the linguistic norms which make up the discourse, and the social, moral, and literary norms which this discourse brings to our attention. Norms, like all standards, are artistic or social or moral conventions, not natural laws. As conventions, they are conditional and changeable, and therefore difficult to interpret even in a short poem. In a play like *Hamlet* the norms by which we even receive it, much less evaluate it, are so complexly organized that they are almost as endlessly interpretable as life itself.

The literary work, then, involves a speaker and speech, a context and an occasion, an imagined audience and a language by which one speaks to it—in other words, Jakobson's "constitutive factors in any speech event." There are, one must point out, at least two important differences between the speech events of everyday life and those which we can call literary works. One is that literary works are ordinarily recorded so that they can be repeated, and repeated not so much to transmit information or to influence behavior, as to give aesthetic pleasure. A second difference is that the audience of a literary work may be problematic in two ways. When the work is first written, its audience may not be exactly determined or it may be only the writer himself. Then, once it is recorded and thereby made public, it can be read by anyone lucky (or unlucky) enough to come across it. That poetic messages may be repeated at will and heard by audiences not interested primarily, if at all, in their referential truth makes aesthetic experience possible. Such experience is realized only when a reader or listener responds to the imagined world of a literary work for the joy it gives in itself. (Roman Ingarden claims that the reader must "concretize" the indeterminate areas of a work in his imagination before its "world" can be fully actualized.[15] I think that some such process of fleshing out must happen, but that the "concretizations" would vary enormously. For instance, what does Helen look like when one reads of her walking along the walls of Troy?) Once a work is experienced as a virtual world, it becomes an aesthetic system with its own integrity, coherence, and purpose. Yet, as a system of words, it is forever connected with the world outside itself because it uses the primary instrument of society—a language. So this "verbal contraption" (as Auden calls a poem) is both autonomous and connected.[16] Like the human being who wrote it, it is its own unique self and one among others. The classic statement of the autonomy of the literary work remains that of A. C. Bradley: "For its nature is to be not a part, nor yet a copy, of the real world (as we commonly understand that phrase), but to be a world by itself, independent, complete, autonomous; and to possess it fully you must enter that world, conform to its laws, and ignore for the time the beliefs, aims, and particular conditions which belong to you in the other world of reality."[17] Yet the literary work is not so purely independent as it seems to be. Though we must ignore the other world of reality in some radical aesthetic sense, we must draw on it continuously. All of the elements which a writer uses in a poem or a novel appear in other aspects of life: the language he draws on we speak day in, day out; the ideas and attitudes those words symbolize we believe in or fight against or speculate about; and the behavior he describes or presents we live through, dream about, run away from, or endure. A successful poem or novel pulls language, ideas, attitudes and behavior out of their contexts in what is quaintly called "life" and orchestrates them into a useless, but unforgettable, harmony. The details of Frost's poem are significant only because they point to, and draw energy from, a complex language, a long history of what Cassirer calls "symbolic forms," and a whole history of civilization. As we have seen, the poem calls for some experience of spring, trees, the cycle of the day and the cycle of the seasons, the Bible and—to be painfully obvious—joy, hope, grief, endurance. To understand even these eight lines properly, then, we must call on both literary history and literary theory.

Early in any English course the teacher had better remind his students that, properly speaking, he cannot teach them literature at all (they may have already suspected as much), but that he can only teach them how to study it. I say "remind," but reminding implies something already known and accepted, and I ought to admit that not everyone would agree with this point. For instance, that astute critic of the novel, Barbara Hardy, stated at the Anglo-American Conference in 1966: "Response is a word that reminds the teacher that the experience of art is a thing of our making, an activity in which we are our own interpretative artist. The dryness of schematic analysis of imagery, symbols, myth, structural relations, *et. al.* should be avoided passionately at school and often at college. *It is literature, not literary criticism, which is the subject.* It is vividly plain that it is much easier to teach literary criticism than to teach literature . . ." (her italics).[18] I think this complete distinction between literature and criticism is quite wrong as Mrs. Hardy states it. She is certainly right in saying that all of us must read books by ourselves. C. S. Lewis has written a superb chapter about "that inner silence, that emptying out of ourselves by which we ought to make room for the total reception of the work."[19] No one can "receive" a story or poem for anyone else. Everyone has to read a poem as though it were a love letter to him: slowly, alone, in full surrender to it. Yet even as one surrenders to a work or enters fully into it (either metaphor will do), some critical process, however unsystematic and even unconscious it may be, has already begun. Northrop Frye distinguishes between the direct experience of literature (Lewis's "receiving" it) and the study of it, which Frye calls "criticism." To him experience and study must reciprocally affect each other, the direct experience purifying literary study of pedantry, the judicious study purifying experience of stock responses.[20] So far as teaching is concerned, it is impossible to separate the experience of literature from the criticism of it. As soon as teacher and student come together, for better or worse, they begin to "study" literature. Each hopes the other has already experienced directly, recently, and lovingly the works they are going to study, and sometimes everyone is pleasantly surprised.

Quite early in any course the teacher should make clear that studying literary works involves a good deal more than explicating puzzling passages or analyzing patterns of imagery in them. I do not mean to say that such explication and analysis are bad things for students to do—far from it; they are absolutely essential skills to be learned, but literary study involves other kinds of critical ability than the skills of lexical analysis, and other kinds of knowledge than that brought by criticism. Here René Wellek's distinctions among theory, history, and criticism are useful. The criticism of a specific work begins with explication and analysis and culminates in evaluation. Even so stout a defender of historical scholarship as Helen Gardner agrees that the critic's primary task is "elucidation" or "illumination."[21] As a critic —and any reader is a critic—one tries to discover the unique experience of a work and to judge the value of that experience. Necessarily, both the analyzing and the judging depend on standards, and standards bring in literary theory. Literary theory, as distinct from literary criticism, concerns itself both with the kind of literature a work is and with the standards by which one ought properly to judge it. Literary theory asks: what qualities should we attend to in judging literary works—the lifelikeness of the events described, the truth of the themes presented, the vividness of the imagery, the complexity of the tone, the beauty of the formal structure? Literary history, as distinct from criticism or theory, studies works either in chronological series (the Romantic Movement) or in some kind of generic relationship (Shakespearean Comedy). For such study it must use the fruits of the critic's analysis and the theorist's concern with standards. Finally, literary history goes outside both the work and literature itself to deal with all the conditions—linguistic, cultural, social, and biographical —in which literary works and genres rise, flourish, and change. As Wellek points out, these three disciplines are closely interrelated.[22]

Let me offer an example. Do you remember in *Pride and Prejudice* when Lady Catherine de Bourgh speaks to Elizabeth Bennet of her upstart pretensions for thinking of marrying into the great Darcy family without having "family, connections or fortune"? Elizabeth, acutely aware of her mother's remorseless vulgarity, replies that, since her father is a gentleman, she is a gentleman's daughter and so far she and Darcy are equals. To explain this passage adequately to students in America where class lines are less rigid than they were in nineteenth-century England and where some students have never seen a "gentleman," the teacher would have to go outside the text and make use of his knowledge of English social history.[23] Of course, he'd have to draw on a good deal more than social history because two different meanings of gentility cut across this scene. One is based on a system of rank in which Lady Catherine is a lady because her father was an earl, and her husband a baronet, and Mrs. Gardiner, Elizabeth's beloved aunt, is not a lady because she married a man in trade. The other meaning is based on a code of gentle behavior, in the light of which the self-important and unfeeling Lady Catherine is not the lady that the "amiable, intelligent, elegant" Mrs. Gardiner is. Elizabeth's mother ought to be a lady because she married a gentleman (that is, a man who did not work with his hands), but, alas, she will never be gentle.

Necessary as a knowledge of the social structure of England is, it would not take one very far in responding to the novel. One needs to combine a good deal of experience in judging human conduct with a careful analysis of the structure of the plot if one is to understand the moral education of Darcy and Elizabeth justly. Like most writers of love stories, Jane Austen follows a simple plot: first, she brings her lovers close enough together to see each other, then drives them apart by circumstances, by society, by a misunderstanding or, best of all, by their own natures; then, gradually and painfully, she brings them together again.

First the lovers are driven apart by both their pride and their prejudice. Pride in his long family line and contempt for the inferiority of Elizabeth's family prevent Darcy from loving generously enough to awaken love in Elizabeth, whose own pride was piqued first by Darcy's comment on her unattractiveness at the ball, and later by his insolent proposal to her at Rosings. They are separated, too, by their prejudice. Wickham's slanders had poisoned Elizabeth's mind, and his attractiveness had blinded her to Darcy's own superior qualities. Darcy's judgment was so warped that he failed to see how Elizabeth or anyone could keep from admiring him no matter how reserved his manners were. The moment of greatest separation comes, ironically, when conventional lovers feel closest—at his proposal. At this moment, he is most insufferably proud, and she is most unrestrainedly prejudiced against him.

Pride and prejudice are thoroughly intertwined in both of them. Each takes great pride in his judgment, understanding, and intelligence. And each is, to some extent, justified in his pride. Elizabeth clearly deserves the admiration which, from the first, Darcy felt for the "liveliness of her mind." Darcy just as clearly has the finest understanding and the most mature judgment of anyone in the novel— except on one question: the effect he has on Elizabeth. But the pride each takes in his own intelligence is too great. When a character says, as Elizabeth says to Darcy, "I understand you perfectly" or to Jane, "One knows exactly what to think," he is in for trouble. Darcy's great pride in his judgment never allows him to consider that he might not know what is good for Bingley, either early in the story or—note that he does not change—late. Both Darcy and Elizabeth are revealed to be prejudiced. Elizabeth is blind both to Darcy's real love of her and to his real quality as a man. Darcy seems aware enough of Elizabeth's superiority to any woman he knows, but he is quite blind to her real feelings about him. "He spoke of apprehension and anxiety" when he proposed, "but his countenance expressed real security." No woman as proud as Elizabeth could stand such insolence.

We are given two people, each proud, each prejudiced. Perhaps Darcy has the more pride, and Elizabeth the greater prejudice. But both need to be mortified and gradually enlightened. The mortification and the enlightenment, which are as closely bound together as the pride and prejudice they eradicate, begin when the lovers are driven farthest apart. Darcy's pride is mortified when Elizabeth accuses him of not being a gentleman—the one count an aristocrat least likes to be criticized on—and begins to be enlightened about Elizabeth's thorough hatred of him: he is "the last man in the world" she could ever be prevailed on to marry. Darcy's letter the next day begins to educate Elizabeth. She begins the letter with "a strong prejudice against everything he might say" and becomes so angry on reading the letter that at first she has no wish to do him "justice." But justice is exactly what she begins to do him. Gradually, painfully, she disentangles the truth from her many preconceived notions about Darcy and Wickham. She deliberates judiciously on the probability of statements made by each of them and gains a second and truer impression of both. So educated, Darcy and Elizabeth are prepared to understand and love each other.

They are brought together again in four stages. First is the mortification already explained: each lover must undergo a withering of his egotism, which is the great enemy of real love. The second stage comes at Pemberley where they meet, each changed and each aware of the change in the other. In this stage a number of things combine to draw Elizabeth closer to Darcy—the woods and park and house, so well endowed by nature and tastefully arranged; praise of Darcy by those close to him; a sense that Darcy's manners may have softened because of her criticism of them and her power over him; the compliment of an introduction to his sister: any one of these by itself might make a man attractive. Elizabeth's emotions are analyzed by herself in a passage which Reuben Brower calls a "beautifully graded progress of feeling" in which each sentiment is defined with an exactness perfectly appropriate to Elizabeth's habit of mind.[24] The third stage centers on Lydia's elopement, which seems like a disaster for Elizabeth's growing attachment, but it ends by drawing the two closer together because Darcy proves his love when he rescues Elizabeth's sister from a fate she scarcely finds as reprehensible as society does. The final stage brings the lovers together, in part through the bad offices of Lady Catherine, whose very attempt to dissuade Elizabeth from marrying Darcy persuaded him he had some hope of winning her.

In short, to respond justly to *Pride and Prejudice,* one would have to know something about the social structure of early nineteenth-century England, understand the norms proper to honorable and happy marriage (as Jane Austen conceived them), and adopt, for the time being, the attitude appropriate to ironic comedy. In other words, the literary criticism of a work does not take place in the unique world of that work alone. Criticism must often go to history—social as well as literary—for help, and to theory for guidance.

Throughout his professional career an English teacher must keep a just and healthy relationship among these three, constantly refining his critical analysis and judgment, rationalizing his theory, and correcting and amplifying his historical knowledge. He will have to learn to steer a discreet course between the dogmatism of thinking he has found the only critical theory and method possible and the mindless acceptance of whatever theories and methods are currently fashionable. He had better accept, and urge his students to accept, the wisdom of R. S. Crane's claim that because "literature, by its very nature, admits a variety of responses," there must be, of necessity, a "plurality of distinct critical methods," among which a competent person can still discriminate judiciously.[25]

An inevitable and healthy plurality of critical systems appears as soon as we talk about even so small a lyric as "Nothing Gold Can Stay." It stuns us almost into silence as soon as we consider one of the larger literary forms—a play or a novel, for instance—or, worse yet, as soon as we read what other people think about them. Try reading for several weeks running what thousands of critics and literary historians have said about a large work like *King Lear*. It is enough to turn your wits. Yet it does not drive you mad exactly because so many different systems, so many diverse and even contradictory insights finally make or can make for sanity. Lear was driven mad by one obsessive idea and came back to his senses when he could accept the possibility that others could be right too. An object lesson for his critics.

But stunned as we may be by the size of the larger literary forms and the variety of responses to them, we had better ask ourselves how to teach—well, Shakespeare. It is much easier to say how not to teach Shakespeare:

1. We should not deal with Shakespeare's life any more than we absolutely have to, and we should especially steer our students away from fruitless research into the silly question of who, besides Shakespeare, wrote the plays. We can't ignore his life entirely because he led an interesting one, but we'll find ourselves speculating wildly, and uselessly.

2. We should never forget that a play is a play. I shall return to this point later.

3. We should not locate the play somewhere back around 1600 and leave it there. Our students are less interested in historical research than we are, though they should learn as much about the past as they need to. This may be a great deal.

4. Nor should we locate the play simply in 1977 and restrict our responses to what we can now naturally feel. The currently fashionable attempts of Jan Kott, Peter Brook, and Jerzy Grotowski to find in Shakespeare's plays problems that are relevant to our times, though often valuable as ways to keep the theater alive, can end by impoverishing the plays themselves. Patrick Cruttwell is right when he criti-

cizes Kott for going to Shakespeare for answers to problems: "If you ask Shakespeare the answers to problems, you ask him the problems you yourself are obsessed with and you find the answers you yourself have already found."[26] I suppose that books like *Shakespeare our Contemporary* touch on that sensitive nerve that screams, "We must be relevant!" But to go to the past only for what may be relevant to the present may be to search for an illusion, for by the time we find the relevance we are looking for it may turn out to be irrelevant to our latest urgent need.

5. We should avoid abstracting from the whole play any particular element that especially attracts us—ironies, paradoxes, patterns of imagery, characters, *topoi,* themes. Unless we are as subtle as A. C. Bradley at understanding dramatic characters, and even Bradley lost his way at times, we'll end by sentimentalizing, romanticizing, cheapening, or otherwise distorting the plays. The danger signal probably should be precisely our being attracted.

6. We should beware of Elizabethan World Pictures. Tillyard was not wrong to write the book, just a little too easy on himself when he gave it that catchy title. Hardin Craig's *The Enchanted Glass* and C. S. Lewis's *The Discarded Image* are more convincing to the extent that neither offers so neat and narrow a set of categories as chains of being, correspondent planes, and cosmic dances. G. R. Elton's warning against false emphasis on the notion that order and degree dominated all thinking in the later sixteenth century is, I think, apt: "Even commonsense suggests that commonplaces are repeated most insistently when they in fact encounter disagreement or hostility, and while no doubt there was much stress on order and all that in Elizabethan thinking, the trouble for many men lay in the increasing difficulty of maintaining that order."[27] The trouble with such commonplace notions is that they are painlessly easy to read back into the plays. Even if it were true that there was something like an Elizabethan world picture, we would still have to be very careful about handling ideas in plays because "unit-ideas," as R. S. Crane argues, represent not so much what the writer is thinking *about* as what he is thinking *with.*[28] Or, as Crane puts it elsewhere, ideas are means of constituting the characters, the purposes, and the states of mind of the dramatis personae.[29] In that sense, then, a poet or dramatist uses ideas; he does not either believe or disbelieve in them, at least while he is being a poet.

7. We should not spend too much time talking about "tragedy" or "comedy." These are fascinating questions which are worth a good deal of thought, but it is better for our students to know a dozen tragedies thoroughly than to construct an iron maiden called tragedy. If we want them to consider some profound theories of tragedy, we should send them to Aristotle, Hegel, Nietzsche, Bradley, Richards, T. R. Henn, Richard Sewall, and Northrop Frye, and of comedy, to Bergson, Freud, Susanne Langer, and, again, Frye. Any one of them can write circles around the rest of us.

So that's what we do not do. But what do we do? To repeat: we should never forget that a play is a play. Even now, with so many opportunities to see plays and after so many helpful books on theatrical production by Granville-Barker, Chambers, G. E. Bentley, Walter Hodges, Alois Nagler, Eric Bentley, J. L. Styan, and John Russell Brown (to name only a few), some of our best Shakespearean critics forget to remember about plays and many of our most earnest students have too little to remember. I cite Professor L. C. Knights's famous essay of 1933 (reprinted in 1964), "How Many Children Had Lady Macbeth?" In the process of justly taking Bradley and nineteenth-century critics to task for impoverishing the total experience of the play by their habit of regarding Shakespeare's characters as friends or actual persons, Knights claims that a "Shakespeare play is a dramatic poem. It uses action, gesture, formal grouping and symbols, and it relies upon the general conventions governing Elizabethan plays. But, we cannot too often remind ourselves, its end is to communicate a rich and controlled experience by means of words—words used in a way to which, without some training, we are no longer accustomed to respond. To stress in the conventional way character or plot or any of the other abstractions that can be made is to impoverish the total response." But describing dramatic response in this way seems an impoverishment too. Though he acknowledges action and gesture, he clearly thinks of words as the play's primary, if not sole, means of arousing a response. Later he goes so far as to say that "the only profitable approach to Shakespeare is a consideration of his plays as dramatic poems, of his language to obtain a total complex emotional response."[30] He has apparently never changed his mind about such an approach and—to show how not even dubious principles can ruin an intelligent critic

—has continued to produce excellent books on Shakespeare. Or John Holloway: after saying that he agrees with Knights's statement—"the total response to a play can only be obtained by . . . an exact and sensitive study of Shakespeare's language"—he asks himself: "Would this kind of approach, studying the language, exclude *anything* from our consideration of a play; or would it even tell us that some things were unimportant, others specially important? Certainly not: there is nothing whatever in a play—not plot, not characterization, not the Girlhood of Shakespeare's Heroines, even, which we could conceivably study in any way save by a study of the language of the play. There is nothing else to study. Whatever aspect of a play we study—relevant or irrelevant to true criticism—where we have to study it is in the language. If we study the language loosely and vaguely, our results are loose and vague; an exact and sensitive study gives exact and sensitive results. So this general principle gives no guide at all as to what things will be important in a play. It leaves every question completely open. In fact, it is a truism."[31] A truism? I can only say that though believing this principle may have allowed Holloway to write a good book on the tragedies of Shakespeare, the principle itself is neither a truism nor true in dramatic criticism. It is simply not true that in a play "there is nothing else to study" except language. There are—to refer only to obvious things—the expressive movements and the quite as expressive motionless presence of actors, the mise-en-scène and the costumes—in short, the whole visual aspect of the production. There are silences that can be as powerful as any speech, as an investigation of a Stanislavsky promptbook or any performance of a play by Harold Pinter can demonstrate. And beyond these separate elements is that synthesis of things said and done, that whole aesthetic experience of which words constitute a part, but only a part, and a part which has meaning only in terms of the whole synthesis. Jerzy Grotowski argues that, if one defines the theater as "what takes place between spectator and actor," then the theater can exist without a text.[32] I think it can, though not for one moment would I recommend that, because the theater can do without a text, we should get rid of Shakespeare's words (as sometimes has happened for whole scenes in recent productions). I am only trying to counter Holloway's assumption that there is nothing else to study except language.

Fastidious literary critics may find all this emphasis on the visual and the nonverbal so vulgar that, like Aristotle (or Aristotle in an unguarded moment), they may consider theatrical production the least important of all the elements of a play. Aristotle, apparently nicknamed the "Reader" inside Plato's Academy, may have believed the heresy that reading a play is as good as seeing it. And more than one writer might agree with Thomas Mann that the theater is too "sensual" to attract him. Still, any art that has attracted great writers for twenty-five hundred years must be something more than merely vulgar and sensual. Perhaps the impure combination of the inescapable sensuousness of theater, of actors there in space, their living voices arguing, cursing, pleading, questioning, and the whole movement and urgency of a plot pregnant with its own future, as Susanne Langer says, and embodying its life here and now, is precisely what attracts an artist interested in dominating so powerful a form of art. We must simply accept this impurity and remember that to *read* a play is a contradiction in terms, except as one speaks of reading a score in preparation for playing or listening to music. Plays are to be seen and heard and responded to as one responds to a rite or a spectacle. They can not be simply read as one reads a novel. Words are, first and last, signals from writer to director, actors, scene designers, costumers, and technicians. In a wider sense a play belongs to literature because it uses words as one means of representing its world. Sometimes, as in Greek and Shakespearean drama, words constitute a primary means; other times, as in some of Molière's plays and much of Lope de Vega's, words are subordinate to other means, such as physical action or scenic effect.

A consequence of this impurity is that two kinds of study are severely limited: the merely literary, because words are only part of the dramatic effect; and the merely theatrical, because words *are* part of the dramatic effect and must be subjected to the same kind of linguistic and semantic criticism that is given to any aesthetic use of words. The obvious answer is to fuse the literary and the theatrical, but that is easier said than done. The real reason for this difficulty is not, I think, the one usually given: that those who know literary analysis do not know the theater, and those who know the theater can not analyze words very well. The real reason is that the drama is a unique art which requires a unique kind of imagination. Something quite different—and more difficult—than merely adding literary analysis to theatrical experience is needed. A play uniquely fuses a number of arts and calls for a kind of imagination different from that required for enjoying ballet or oratory or painting or sculpture or architecture or music or poetry, though it draws, in some fundamental sense, on all these arts.

To respond fully to a play, we must understand these four aspects of it:

1. *The play as speech:* the verbal action of the play must be given the same kind of phonetic, syntactic, rhetorical, and semantic analysis that we give to any use of words.

2. *The plot:* the speech belongs to a series of organically related actions whose conflicts are finally resolved. This plot embodies various meanings; and its agents, being images of men and women, possess ethos. The ethos of the characters and the meanings which their actions embody require moral judgment and mature reasoning.

3. *Mimetic action:* the play moves not merely verbally but physically. The play is a mimesis by body as well as by voice.

4. *Mise-en-scène:* and all is represented as taking place in a certain (not always definite) space and at a certain (sometimes vague) time. Setting, color, lighting, and costume constitute another and valuable language.[33]

In short, we need to interrelate the auditory, the semantic, the architectonic, the choreographic, and the scenic elements of a play. Since every play is written for a particular theater for production in a particular style by a group of actors, a study of it would involve the analysis of the original stage and the original mode of production. Since every play has itself had a history, the analysis could—and, in certain cases, should—involve a selective history of productions from the first one. Such analysis, at once antiquarian yet fully in historical perspective, might seem only to render more complex, because it recognizes historical change, a subject complex enough at any time. But we must see the stage as an instrumentality and the drama as a form which have gradually gained and, once gained, never lost ritual, spectacular, artistic, and social significance, all of which must be attended to.

Now the question is: how are we and our students going to preserve the most intense linguistic analysis and, at the same time, gain some sense of the visual aspect of the play without actually seeing it and some sense of the auditory aspect without actually hearing it? The answer is that we must try to re-create by explication, analysis, and interpretation the play which we cannot actually or often see and hear. John Russell Brown talks about imagining it in the "theater of the mind,"[34] but I am not too happy with this phrase, remembering what Gilbert Ryle has to say about "in the mind"; still, it may not be too dangerous a catch phrase so long as we don't make too much of it and so long as we remember that our minds are in front of our eyes, not in back of them—that is, in the objects we attend to or the situations we are involved in, and not in some close corner of our brains.[35] Brown's theater edition of *Othello* is a fine example of the "representing" or "re-creation" I am calling for. I do not mean anything occult or even particularly unusual by this "re-creation." I only mean that we should systematically draw on whatever actors have told us about the roles they have created, directors about the plays they have directed, critics about the plays they have studied or the productions they have seen, scholars about the stages, the acting companies, the theatrical conditions, and the historical and literary sources of the plays they have learned about; and, then using whatever is significant, we should try to bring alive by our analysis and interpretation the play that is latently there in the text that has come down to us and in the theatrical history we have been able to recover. Good teachers, especially of history and literature, have been re-creating the past or some aspect of "reality" in this way for thousands of years.

Such verbal re-creation of a play is quite different from an actual performance of it. Even in our most imaginative moments we can never "see" the whole play being performed, or "hear" all its lines being spoken, or respond in class or on paper or in our study to the play we re-create as we would respond to the play as performed. What we can do to re-create the play is to draw on all that we can learn from history and previous literature, all that we can remember of our own feelings of pain and joy and hope and love and sorrow, and, fusing our learning and our memories, to call on our imagination for some significant response to the play. In one sense, no imaginative re-creation will be so good as even a bad performance of the play; in another sense, not even the best of performances quite embodies those ideal re-creations of the play we have seen in our inner theater where we recurrently enact our favorite plays. All of which means that we must keep on seeing and talking about plays the rest of our lives. The two feed on each other, the seeing keeps the talk aware of the concrete and sensuous life of a theatrical performance, the talk prepares us to see better next time and revives in words the past that may otherwise slip away.

I want to make clear that I am not suggesting that our students work out elaborate promptbooks or act out scenes in class or make lighting plots or scene and costume designs or write analyses of characters as though they were preparing to act them. All of these are valuable exercises which could lead to greater understanding and enjoyment of the play, but they eat up an enormous amount of the time that both teacher and student ought to spend on other plays. Besides, some of the work, such as the costume and scene designs, are fun to do, but of dubious value unless one is actually preparing for a production. But I do not object to such exercises so much because they take a great deal of time nor even because some of them return relatively little aesthetic good unless they lead to actual production. I object to even the best of them (such as Morris Eaves's excellent example of the workshop method of teaching Shakespeare) mostly because they misconceive the roles of teacher and student in courses of drama.[36] Our business is not to copy the work done in courses in acting, directing, scene design, and play production, though I'd be the first to grant that such courses or, better, some professional experience in the theater can lead to greater understanding of what a play is and of how one should respond to it. Our business is finally critical and scholarly and analytic, not technical or professional. We have to recover conceptually, in words, not actions, the experience of a play which we may have seen and heard, so we in part remember it, but which we may never have seen or even heard, so we must produce it in our imaginations. We recover it through long hours of critical analysis and long years of living with it as an object of contemplation until we see it in its total design and possess it—never finally, never completely—but possess it joyfully in so far as we are then able to.

Some brief examples. What should a teacher do with the last act of *Hamlet*? For one thing, he could begin his discussion of the play there and work both forward to the end of the play and backward to the scenes which prepare for this resolution. Whether he begins his discussion there or not, he will want to ask or answer such questons as these: Why does the comment on Ophelia's suicide come first from the gravediggers? Where have Horatio and Hamlet come from? What does Horatio's comment on "custom" echo? Why the allusion to Cain? What is Hamlet's attitude toward the skulls? Why is a special point made of Hamlet's being born on the very day that the elder Hamlet defeated the elder Fortinbras? What is Hamlet's attitude toward Laertes in the graveyard? Why is it important that we learn now what happened to Hamlet on the ship to England? What is Horatio's function in this scene? What is Hamlet's attitude toward "providence"? And so on. The questions are nearly endless. The answers offered will show that the last act is dominated by two powerful scenes, each of which draws together images, ideas, and emotional states rendered in previous scenes. One is the scene in the graveyard, the other the duel in court. The grave being dug for Ophelia concretely represents all those other graves in this death-ridden play, one of which had yawned to release a ghost early, another the grave into which Polonius had been cast "hugger-mugger," and those other graves to which Hamlet, Claudius, Gertrude, Laertes, Rosencrantz and Guildenstern are taken as the tragedy closes. We see and hear two gravediggers laughing and singing at their grim work and Hamlet standing on the edge of the grave, now capable of joking about the omnipresent leveler he has been haunted by. Then, the duel —the perfect resolution for a play which had been one long duel. It is apparently a courtly contest, but one rapier is deadly, and the wine is poisoned. The King, who had poisoned a brother, tries to poison his nephew, but succeeds only in killing his beloved wife. Laertes poisons the rapier which ends by killing him. Justice comes to Claudius by means of an inexorable and, to us, deeply satisfying ironic reversal: the poisoned rapier and the poisoned wine are used by the poisoned Hamlet to kill him. So Hamlet, the disinterested dueler, ironically achieves his revenge by means of a justice he does not try to bring about. Not even Shakespeare, fertile as he was in creating theatrical images, created more evocative images than the scenes of the grave and the duel, where word is wedded to action, and open grave and grinning skull, poisoned wine and poisoned rapier sum up the "bloody and unnatural acts," the innocent lives doomed, and the "purposes mistook/Fall'n on the inventors' heads."

Re-creating a play imaginatively is, of course, more than a matter of recovering the big scenes, such as Hermione, whose heart has turned to stone, gradually changing from a statue to a woman, or Othello giving himself, with both his heroic egotism and his greatness of heart, a court-martial, acting as defendant, prosecuting attorney, judge, jury, and executioner, all in eighteen lines.[37] It is very hard for even the most obtuse teacher to ruin these scenes. Sometimes what needs to be imagined is a passage that might not register at all unless it is fully realized. For example:

> *Fool.* Give me an egg, Nuncle, and I'll give thee two crowns.
> *Lear.* What two crowns shall they be?
> *Fool.* Why, after I have cut the egg i' the middle and eat up the meat, the two crowns of the egg. When thou clovest thy crown i' the middle, and gav'st away both parts, thou bor'st thine ass on thy back o'er the dirt. Thou hadst little wit in thy bald crown when thou gav'st thy golden one away.

(I.iv. 170–78)

On the surface this expresses a clear, straightforward analogy. Lear's kingdom is like an egg. Dividing the kingdom between Goneril and Regan is like cutting an egg in half. Even the only partly expressed parallels among the three kinds of crown is evident enough because "crown" was then a common term for the two halves of an eggshell, as well as an obvious term for head and king's crown. But at least three implications arise out of the passage because of its total theatrical context. First, an egg is the genetic bond between parent and child, carried by the female. To cut an egg in half is to destroy the possibility of the egg's being fertilized. In disowning Cordelia and cursing his other two daughters with sterility, Lear has ensured, in his own mind, at least, that he would not have the grandchildren any man wants. Second, "eating the meat of the egg" becomes an act emblematic of Lear's whole self-destructive egotism. "The act of eating," Freud reminds us, "is a destruction of the object with the final aim of incorporating it."[38] Lear denies his daughters, banishes Kent, and drives himself mad. Facing the nothingness of death, he obsessively moves toward it, destroying kingdom, family, sanity, and self. To the Fool he appears a "shealed peascod" (shelled peapod). Finally, "little wit in thy bald crown" is a clear anticipation of the madness which soon comes to him. The whole passage then gains a sharp visual point when the Fool introduces Goneril with "Thou hast pared thy wit o' both sides and left nothing i' the middle. Here comes one o' the parings" (ll. 204–6).

If I am right in thinking that a Shakespearean play, like any play, must be "re-enacted" by investing its several aspects—auditory, scenic, choreographic, and semantic—with whatever power our learning and our imagination can bring to this re-enactment, then our duty as teachers is painfully clear. What do we need to know? Everything: everything about the play—what our total dramatic experience of it may be; where its text came from; what editions are most useful; on what stages it has been produced and by whom and for what audiences; what actors and critics and scholars have discovered about it in the last three hundred years. What can we safely ignore? Nothing. Even wrong interpretations or idiosyncratic performances or apparently peripheral historical accounts may give us valuable insights. Is there no rest? No.

IV

In a famous defense of literature written nearly four hundred years ago, Sir Philip Sidney contrasts the "poet" (that is, any literary artist) with the philosopher and the historian. Specifically Sidney is concerned with the individual capacities of the three to lead men to the goal of a virtuous life. According to him, the philosopher, who necessarily deals with the abstract and the general, tries to win this goal by "bare rule" and precept, while the historian, tied not to what should be, as the philosopher is, but to what is, to the "particular truth of things," tries to win by examples. "Nowe dooth the peerelesse Poet performe both: for whatsoever the Philosopher sayth should be doone, hee giveth a perfect picture of it in someone, by whom hee presupposeth it was done. So as hee coupleth the generall notion with the particular example. A perfect picture I say, for hee yeeldeth to the powers of the minde, an image of that whereof the Philosopher bestoweth but a woordish description: which dooth neyther strike, pierce, nor possesse the sight of the soule, so much as that other dooth."[39]

Sidney's main points can be outlined this way:

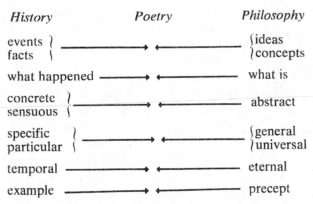

History	Poetry	Philosophy
events } facts	⟶ ⟵	{ideas }concepts
what happened	⟶ ⟵	what is
concrete } sensuous	⟶ ⟵	abstract
specific } particular	⟶ ⟵	{general }universal
temporal	⟶ ⟵	eternal
example	⟶ ⟵	precept

History, a chronological account of events and facts, deals with the specific and the particular in a concrete and sensuous world. It offers to its readers vivid examples. Philosophy, an exposition of ideas and concepts, deals with the general and the universal in a world of abstractions. It offers to its readers enduring precepts. Literature is superior to either history or philosophy because it marries "the general notion with the particular example," giving abstractions a local habitation and a name, charging events with ideal meaning. So Sidney claims. Let us use his distinctions without arguing about his debatable conclusions.[40] Before going any farther, I'd better say that not for one moment do I believe this preposterous poetic imperialism of Sidney, though I know more than one writer and teacher who does. I mention it because it brings out clearly some of the terms I have drawn on.

I have tried to show that a literary work does fuse the concrete and the abstract, the specific and the general, the image and the idea, as Sidney suggests (though I should not claim that, therefore, it is a better teacher than either history or philosophy). To put Sidney's point in more modern terms, we can say that a literary work creates a "virtual world" whose fictional life may bear some relationship to real life, but need not, because it is valuable in itself. Whenever we have a verbal structure whose words exist primarily for the sake of the structure and not for the sake of any instrumental use they might be put to we have a literary work.[41] A work is literary when its form has completely assimilated, and thereby aesthetically organized, its matter. This form not merely permits semantic and syntactic and prosodic analysis, but requires such analysis before it yields its full meaning and beauty.

Sidney's three kinds of discourse parallel the distinctions René Wellek makes among the three kinds of literary study (history, criticism, and theory) and define the poles between which English teacher and student must move and the center they must seek. Every teacher must decide for himself precisely how he is to draw on the historical and the philosophical in order to elucidate and evaluate the literary. To properly elucidate and evaluate literary works, one would have to consider all sorts of scholarly and critical questions that I should like to consider, but do not now have the time to consider—questions about point of view and characterization in fiction, or about prosody and metaphorical language in poetry, or about tone and theme in any genre. Nor have I time and still less the inclination to give any rules or even advice on housekeeping in class or out. Almost anything one could say about English as a subject to teach would have to be adapted to a specific context. Thus: Who is going to be taught? In what kind of course? What texts shall the students read? When during the course? What knowledge will they have of the genre the work seems to fit into? What knowledge do we as teachers have? And so on. The questions are nearly endless. So are the answers.

Every teacher has to keep his own house in order and work out his own methods for running courses, making out examinations, assigning and correcting papers. So long as he keeps alive a "current of true and fresh ideas" and an enthusiastic response to the works read, it doesn't matter very much how he runs a class—by lecturing all the time or by questioning and hoping for answers or by leading a discussion or by some combination of all of these. Good lecturing can be effective—if one is I. A. Richards; but too much passive listening by the student can drug his mind. Questioning is good if the questioner is Socrates, but endless questioning can be painfully unsettling for some students, and questioning an ignorant or timid person is tantamount to statutory rape. Discussion can be good if it is shaped, but shaping it requires saintly modesty in the teacher and quick intelligence in the students. Some days nothing works. In some courses nothing works right. Only rarely is teaching all that you once hoped it would be.

One last desperate question: how deeply involved are we going to get in the imagination, the intellect, the moral and emotional lives of our students? The safest answer is: not very—directly. We and they should meet in the works we all study, works which will be large enough worlds to live in without overcrowding.[42]

At the very center of literary study, then, are particular literary works, those isles of pure joy, our Capris to which we retreat when weary from our imperial cares. They are our stays in a bad world and refresh us even when we are exhausted trying to explain them. Everyone envies us for having them. Poor historians, what have they to hold on to? Only all of history, but no still points in the immense flux. Poor philosophers, homesick for the truth, they have found still points, but have lost movement. Language to them must be a machine only for telling truths, not for telling lies. Even poorer social scientists, who don't have history or truth. Only this dreadful moment, and they have to try to explain it! "There are two worlds," said Oscar Wilde—Wilde, that model English teacher, witty, charming, not too learned—"the one that *is* without one's speaking about it; it's called the *real world* because there's no need to talk about it in order to see it. And the other is the world of art; that's the one which has to be talked about because it would not exist otherwise."[43]

NOTES

1. Benjamin DeMott, *Supergrow: Essays and Reports on Imagination in America* (New York: E. P. Dutton, 1969), p. 143.
2. Roman Jakobson, "Concluding Statement: Linguistics and Poetics," in *Style in Language,* ed. Thomas A. Sebeok (Cambridge: M.I.T. Press, 1960), pp. 353–57.
3. Ibid., pp. 408–19; I. A. Richards, *Poetries: Their Media and Ends,* ed. Trevor Eaton (The Hague-Paris: Mouton, 1974), pp. 1–16. Frederic Jameson comments on Jakobson's model in *The Prison-House of Language: a Critical Account of Structuralism and Russian Formalism* (Princeton: Princeton University Press, 1972), pp. 202–5. See also Hayden White's re-working of it in "The Problem of Change in Literary History," *New Literary History* 7 (Autumn 1975): 106–11.
4. William Butler Yeats, "The Symbolism of Poetry" and "Speaking to the Psaltery," in *Essays and Introductions* (New York: Macmillan, 1961), pp. 159, 1–18.
5. Reprinted in *Poetries: Their Media and Ends,* pp. 39–42. See also the strictures of Jonathan Culler, *Structuralist Poetics: Structuralism, Linguistics, and the Study of Literature* (Ithaca N.Y.: Cornell University Press, 1975), pp. 71–74.
6. Peter S. Rosenbaum, "On the Role of Linguistics in the Teaching of English," *Harvard Educational Review* 35 (1965): 332–48, argues that transformational grammar is preferable to structural linguistics; reprinted in *Modern Studies in English: Readings in Transformational Grammar,* ed. David Rubel and Sanford Schane (Englewood Cliffs, N.J.: Prentice-Hall, 1969), pp. 467–81. Samuel R. Levin implicitly argues the case for structural linguistics in *Linguistic Structures in Poetry* (Gravenhage: Mouton, 1962). See also A. H. Marckwardt, *Linguistics and the Teaching of English* (Bloomington: Indiana University Press, 1966), and W. G. Moulton, "Linguistics," in *The Aims and Methods of Scholarship in Modern Languages and Literatures,* ed. James Thorpe (New York: Modern Language Association, 1963).
7. Stephen Ullmann, *The Principles of Semantics,* 2nd ed. (New York: Philosophical Library, 1957), pp. 300–304; L. Wittgen-

stein, *Philosophical Investigations,* trans. G. E. M. Anscombe (New York: Macmillan, 1968), pp. 6, 46–47, 151, 219.

8. Jerome S. Bruner, *Toward a Theory of Instruction* (Cambridge: Harvard University Press, 1966), p. 102.

9. René Wellek and Austin Warren, *Theory of Literature* (New York: Harcourt, Brace, 1949), p. 179.

10. For suggestive essays on the function of language, spoken and written, in classical and Christian culture, see Walter J. Ong, *The Presence of the Word: Some Prolegomena for Cultural and Religious History* (New Haven, Yale University Press, 1967), especially pp. 17–87, 111–91. See also Eric Havelock, *Preface to Plato* (Oxford: Blackwell, 1963), especially chaps. 3, 4, and 9.

11. *Language: Selected Writings* (Berkeley: University of California Press, 1942), p. 7ff.

12. See Francis Berry, *Poetry and the Physical Voice* (New York: Oxford University Press, 1962), especially pp. 3–26, 177–97.

13. Quoted by Gorham Munson, *Robert Frost: a Study of Sensibility and Good Sense* (New York: G. H. Doran, 1927), p. 97.

14. Wellek and Warren, *Theory of Literature,* p. 154. For different ways of describing the relationship of sound and sense see: Walter Sutton, *Modern American Criticism* (Englewood Cliffs, N.J.: Prentice-Hall, 1963), pp. 276–80; Harold Whitehall, "From Linguistics to Poetry," in *Sound and Poetry,* ed. N. Frye (New York: Columbia University Press, 1956), p. 135; Ullmann, *The Principles of Semantics,* pp. 30–31.

15. Ingarden, *The Literary Work of Art: an Investigation on the Borderlines of Ontology, Logic, and Theory of Literature,* trans. George G. Grabowicz (Evanston, Il.: Northwestern University Press, 1973), pp. 331–55.

16. Let me be dogmatic and say that no one should try to teach any poetry without having read W. H. Auden, "Making, Knowing and Judging," in *The Dyer's Hand* (New York: Random House, 1962), pp. 31–60.

17. A. C. Bradley, "Poetry for Poetry's Sake," in *Oxford Lectures on Poetry* (London: Macmillan & Co., 1963), p. 5.

18. Quoted by Herbert J. Muller, *The Uses of English* (New York: Holt, Rinehart and Winston, 1967), p. 88.

19. C. S. Lewis, *An Experiment in Criticism* (Cambridge: Cambridge University Press, 1961), pp. 92–93.
20. Northrop Frye, *The Well-Tempered Critic* (Bloomington: Indiana University Press, 1963), p. 145.
21. Helen Gardner, *The Business of Criticism* (Oxford: Clarendon Press, 1959), p. 14.
22. Wellek and Warren, *Theory of Literature*, Chap. 4; *Concepts of Criticism* (New Haven: Yale University Press, 1963), pp. 1–20.
23. See Anthony Wagner, *English Genealogy* (Oxford: Clarendon Press, 1960).
24. Reuben Brower, *The Fields of Light: an Experiment in Critical Reading* (New York: Oxford University Press, 1968), p. 179.
25. R. S. Crane, *Critics and Criticism: Ancient and Modern* (Chicago: University of Chicago Press, 1952), pp. 5–12.
26. Patrick Cruttwell, "Shakespeare is not our Contemporary," *The Yale Review* 59 (Autumn 1969): 49.
27. G. R. Elton, *England, 1200–1640* (Ithaca, N.Y.: Cornell University Press, 1969), p. 207. See also John Holloway, *The Colours of Clarity* (London: Routledge and Kegan Paul, 1964), pp. 17–23; Herbert Weisinger, *The Agony and the Triumph* (East Lansing: Michigan State University Press, 1964), pp. 71–91; Wilbur Sanders, *The Dramatist and the Received Idea: Studies in the Plays of Marlowe and Shakespeare* (Cambridge: Cambridge University Press, 1968), especially pp. 1–19, 61–71, 110–20, 194–204.
28. R. S. Crane, *The Idea of the Humanities* (Chicago: University of Chicago Press, 1967), I, p. 176.
29. R. S. Crane, *The Languages of Criticism and the Structure of Poetry* (Toronto: University of Toronto Press, 1953), p. 186.
30. L. C. Knights, "How Many Children Had Lady Macbeth?" in *Explorations: Essays in Criticism* (New York: New York University Press, 1964), pp. 18–29.
31. John Holloway, *The Charted Mirror: Literary and Critical Essays* (London: Routledge and Kegan Paul, 1960), pp. 220–21.
32. Jerzy Grotowski, *Towards a Poor Theatre,* ed. Eugenio Barba (London: Methuen, 1969), p. 32.
33. See J. L. Styan, *The Dramatic Experience* (Cambridge: Cambridge University Press, 1965). Also, Styan, *Drama, Stage and Audience* (Cambridge: Cambridge University Press, 1975), es-

pecially chap. 2; Maurice Charney, *How to Read Shakespeare* (New York: McGraw-Hill, 1971); Bernard Beckerman, *Dynamics of Drama: Theory and Method of Analysis* (New York: Alfred A. Knopf, 1970), especially chaps. 4 and 6; Brownell Salomon, "Visual and Aural Signs in the Performed English Renaissance Play," in *Renaissance Drama,* N.S. 5, ed. S. Schoenbaum and A. Dessen (Evanston, Ill.: Northwestern University Press, 1972), pp. 143–69.

34. J. R. Brown, "The Theatrical Element of Shakespeare Criticism," in *Reinterpretations of Elizabethan Drama,* ed. Norman Rabkin (New York: Columbia University Press, 1969), pp. 177–95.

35. See Gilbert Ryle, *The Concept of Mind* (New York: Barnes & Noble, 1949), especially pp. 35–51. Also the whole chapter on imagination (pp. 245–79) is the kind of de-mythologizing that English teachers often badly need.

36. Morris Eaves, "The Real Thing: a Plan for Producing Shakespeare in the Classroom," *College English* 31 (February 1970): 463–72.

37. For a brilliant chapter on teaching *Othello* by Ephim Fogel, see *Teaching Shakespeare,* ed. Arthur Mizener (New York: New American Library, 1969).

38. Sigmund Freud, *Complete Psychological Works,* trans. James Strachey (London, 1964), 23: p. 147.

39. Philip Sidney, "An Apologie for Poetrie" (1595), in *Criticism: the Foundations of Modern Literary Judgment,* eds. Mark Schorer, Josephine Miles, Gordon McKenzie (New York: Harcourt, Brace, 1958), p. 413.

40. Sidney's ideas have been elaborated on by Northrop Frye, "Levels of Meaning in Literature," *Kenyon Review* 12 (Spring 1950): 246–62, and by Donald Davie, *Articulate Energy* (London: Routledge and Kegan Paul, 1954), pp. 130–36.

41. Northrop Frye, *Anatomy of Criticism* (Princeton: Princeton University Press, 1957), p. 74; Wellek and Warren, *Theory of Literature,* pp. 17–18, 140, 154, 198.

42. For another answer see David Holbrook, *The Exploring Word: Creative Disciplines in the Education of Teachers of English* (Cambridge: University Press, 1967).

43. André Gide, *Oscar Wilde* (London: William Kimber, 1951), p. 18.

ROBERT H. GURLAND

Teaching Mathematics

ROBERT H. GURLAND (Ph.D., New York University) is professor of philosophy and chairman of the department at New York University. He previously was associate professor of mathematics at C.
W. Post College of Long Island University, where he was the only
faculty member in the college's history to be twice named "Teacher
of the Year." He is the youngest person ever to win New York University's "Great Teacher" award. He taught mathematics at San Jose
State College, Adelphi University, Hofstra University, and presented
a course in logic on the CBS Television Network program, "Sunrise
Semester." Currently he is a visiting professor in the humanities at
The United States Military Academy at West Point. He is a contributor to *Mathematics Magazine*.

It is a widely held and often articulated view that mathematics owns the dubious distinction of being both the most difficult and most poorly taught subject in the curriculum. The pervasiveness of this attitude has resulted in the evolution of a mystique which envelops the discipline and has had decidedly negative effects on the entire enterprise of mathematics education. The widespread acceptance of the essential difficulty of mathematics has resulted in a conscientious effort by students to avoid the subject at all costs and to treat any other discipline dependent for its expression or understanding upon mathematical methods as fatally touched with the plague. Thus the fearful attitude towards statistics expressed by students of education, psychology, and sociology; the failure of biology students to study biometrics and genetics which are heavily dependent upon statistics and probability; the attempts by chemistry students to avoid differential equations; and the chagrin expressed by business administration and economics majors over the inclusion of statistics, probability theory, linear programming, and game theory as seminal theoretic tools in the study of decision- and policy-making.

As one might imagine, this fear has resulted in an unwarranted reverence for those who have mastered its intricate and elusive concepts. The homage paid the mathematician has served to kindle an attitude within the mathematics establishment itself that tends to treat the mathematically competent as the intellectual superiors of those who have proven themselves in other disciplines. Such academic chauvinism (not unique to mathematicians) has the damaging effect of insulating the mathematical community, thereby alienating the uninititiated, perpetuating the attitudes of awe, hostility, and fear commonly directed towards the discipline, and impeding efforts to generate communication between those who know and those who do not.

Every distinct subject presents a special set of pedagogical problems arising from its particular character. The problems may be regarded as particularizations of the general pedagogical considerations that must be treated by any teacher who seeks to discharge his educational responsibilities efficaciously. The complexity of the teaching relation becomes apparent when one attempts to dissect it in order to isolate its component elements: the teacher, the material, the student, and the variety of possible instructional methods, all considered within the framework of a particular institution at a given time embedded within a particular social context. No single constituent can be stressed at the expense of the others, nor can any element be ignored without a loss in quality of the total process. In analyzing the teaching situation on the college level, I have found that all too often the student and his interests, attitudes, needs, and problems are given only cursory consideration by those involved in structuring and presenting a course. But such factors are crucial to the development of a sound educational experience.

If we accept the thesis that the three key issues to be treated in the presentation of any given course are (a) who is to be taught, i.e., the particular category of student involved, (b) what is to be taught, i.e., the nature of the material to be presented, and (c) how the material is to be presented, i.e., methodological considerations, then I maintain that the questions of what and how are secondary to, or must be answered in terms of, the who-question. The purpose of the entire educative process is to communicate material or content to persons; we educate people. To ignore the recipient in the process in favor of some single-minded dedication to the content or subject material can only serve to create the deadly, unrealistic, and qualitatively poor education that prevails in so many of our college classrooms today.

I

The systematic alienation of the student which results from a failure to place his role in proper perspective has become characteristic of higher education and is to a great degree responsible for the upheavals which have swept through the groves of academe. This shortcoming is neither oversight nor accident. Rather its roots lie in the philosophical position that regards the college and university as the playground of the faculty, an academic community formed for the expressed purpose of affording the faculty the opportunity to pursue its scholarly interests within a milieu which provides all that is necessary for success in these endeavors, e.g., libraries, contact with other interested scholars, subsidized attendance at scholarly conventions, contracted or light work loads, and sabbatical leaves. Such a view often results in the relegation of teaching responsibilities to a secondary status. The student is then treated as a necessary evil, his presence on campus merely providing the financial wherewithal to allow the institution to sustain itself and to permit the faculty member to "do his own thing," which "thing," all too often, fails to include a studied attempt to sharpen and improve teaching techniques.

Little constructive effort has been expended by the college community at large toward raising the level and increasing the efficiency of classroom communication. Whereas great care has been given to the preparation of the prospective elementary- or secondary-school teacher, no wide-scale attempt has been made to ensure that a neophyte college instructor is capable of consistently producing a high level of classroom teaching. This tendency to eschew any systematic program for the heightening of teaching competence on the college level by instituting apprenticeship programs or developing seminars concerned with methodology seems to follow from treating two theses as axiomatic: (1) good teachers are born, not made; and (2) if an individual has demonstrated academic competence in a subject area, then he will necessarily be successful in communicating his knowledge in the classroom.

Although teaching skill is to a degree a function of the teacher's personality, wit, dynamism, and ability to relate to groups of students, nonetheless central skills in good teaching, such as selecting appropriate motivational devices and examples, employing sound methodology, testing and evaluating competently and realistically, apportioning classroom time, and anticipating student difficulties, can be acquired and should not be regarded as innate.[1] Similarly, although knowledge of the material on the instructor's part is a necessary condition for good teaching, it is not a sufficient one, since teaching involves a mastery of communication skills which are independent of any particular academic discipline.

The narrowly traditional conception of the dynamics of higher education has viewed the student's role in the classroom and the college community as passive. His presence at the college is the result of a free choice. He must be self-motivated and possessed of a sufficient degree of natural interest, desire, and tenacity to cope with the vicissitudes inherent in the attempted mastery of any sophisticated subject matter. He must be willing to delve into subject areas prescribed by the educational establishment as indispensable to the development of the "educated man," regardless of his interest in or appreciation of such material. In short, the student comes to the college or university of his choice in order to enjoy the privilege of sitting at the feet of the masters, eagerly gathering pearls of wisdom. His is not to reason why, but to accept the dictates of the institution in an uncritical and obeisant fashion. The absurdity of this role—its lack of insight into the position of the educational institution within the framework of modern society, and its failure to assess realistically and consider seriously the student as an active force—was certainly a contributing factor in the students' chaotic undermining of higher education.

To attribute the campus unrest of the sixties entirely to a deteriorating classroom environment would be to oversimplify the case, since student activism represents a reaction to political and social issues as well as educational ones. One may view the student movement as a rebellion against authoritarian and *in loco parentis* positions assumed by the university, but recent campus ferment is largely a result of total disenchantment with the quality and kind of education disseminated by institutions of higher learning.

Student complaints have focused on a variety of issues. First, the depersonalization of classroom processes due to increased class size and faculty indifference has resulted in a breakdown in student-faculty contact on an individual level. Second, the sacrifices made in the quality of undergraduate education in order to further and finance graduate programs has often resulted in the use of adjunct personnel and graduate students as instructors, particularly in elementary and core-required courses where fine teaching is essential. Unfortunately, such individuals are too often inexperienced, less competent academically, and less committed to the aims and needs of the institution and its students than full-time faculty members. Third, the compartmentalization rather than the integration of course content in the liberal arts program and the failure to tailor the core requirements to the nature and interests of the students taking these courses has often made them seem irrelevant, arbitrary, and without justification. Finally, the lack of concern with the quality of classroom performance on the part of the faculty and administration has resulted in boring classes that fail to communicate an appropriate selection of material so as to reveal its relevance to other areas within the given discipline as well as within the total framework of human knowledge and concern.

It is probably inaccurate to argue that the degeneration of the classroom situation is a result of a depreciation in the quality of teaching in general; rather, the maintenance of the status quo in terms of method and attitude has become less valid, hence more glaringly ineffective, within the rapidly changing social structure. In a technological society that demands both the education of a greater number of individuals for a longer period of time and the commitment to provide universal educational opportunities, the role of the institutions of higher learning must change to meet these needs. The teacher is now confronted with a cross section of students whose basic preparation, abilities, interests, and needs are exceedingly diverse. As the ranks of students swell and faculty ranks diminish or just remain constant due to financial exigencies, the university becomes more bureaucratic; contact and communication between the administration or faculty and the student body is diminished.

The problem of inadequate teaching is equally the responsibility of administrators. The policy of college and university administrations to award faculty members promotion and tenure primarily on the basis of their research and publications has encouraged the faculty to concentrate on these activities at the expense of energetically dedicating themselves to their teaching duties. Hiring practices have taken into account only the need to balance the composition of the various departments in accordance with the specific areas of academic competence and interest exhibited by their members, but not the need to mix liberally those whose prime concern is teaching with those who effectively and consistently publish. I am not, however, forwarding the fallacious tenet that teaching skill and the interest and ability to carry on significant research are mutually exclusive.

One result of such policies has been the disenfranchisement of the faculty from the sphere of curriculum determination. The students have now usurped the role of the faculty, resulting in the possible destruction of the liberal arts curriculum. The students have coerced schools either to eliminate entirely or drastically reduce requirements outside the student's major. Such actions enforce changes in the nature of the higher degree, reducing its value and failing to produce any positive effects on the quality of education. The surrender to student demands for greater voice in curriculum determination is unfortunate and ill-advised, for it delegates to the student body and its representatives a right which they are incapable of exercising competently.[2] The academic establishment is paying the piper for not responding to the needs of the student. Acquiescence to student force is not the appropriate means of redressing the wrongs perpetrated upon the students in the name of good education. Although such concessions may appear to be the most effective means of soothing the savage beasts, they will prove a temporary expedient, for they meet a student demand that is essentially misdirected.

The students, reacting to a dismal classroom situation and in many cases mistrusting the ability and desire of the university to respond to their complaints, concentrated their energies in a thrust which missed the mark, not meeting the real problem, the need to improve the teaching-learning condition. Rather than demanding a new emphasis on teaching performance and more interrelation between disciplines, while attempting to decrease class size and improve other aspects of the educational process, the students chose to strive for the elimination of entire courses, rejecting the material of certain disciplines as irrelevant to the pursuit of their educational goals. The courses were not irrelevant, however, although the way in which they were presented made them appear so. Stress upon the wrong concepts, failure to relate concepts to other ideas that transcend the bounds of the discipline, and failure to motivate the students rendered courses sterile and uninteresting, isolating them from the total schema of human concern.

Academicians, meekly succumbing to misdirected student pressures, abdicated their responsibilities to both the student and the society at large by removing valuable courses from the required core instead of retooling the courses, revising the material, and coming to grips with the problems. The result has been that the student, who usually lacks the competence to judge what is of genuine benefit to his own intellectual development, has been left to his own inadequate devices in the determination of the content and structure of his academic program. Abolishing required courses does not upgrade the quality of education by improving courses and teaching procedures, but rather permits the student to choose freely from an essentially unchanged and still inferior potpourri of courses. The quality of the product has not improved. The student has merely won the privilege of choosing his own poison, where it was once forced upon him by prescriptions in the catalogue.

The foregoing position may appear to smack of the very authoritarianism, elitism, and paternalism that the students attempted to combat through confrontation tactics. An argument from competence, however, neither constitutes nor entails an affirmation of the authoritarianism or elitism that the students find so repelling. Most students come to the university seeking the guidance that will enable them to discover their interests, develop their talents, and ultimately actualize the greatest possible proportion of their potential. They seek honest and competent advice from individuals whose abilities, skills, and motives they both respect and trust. They crave identification with an educational community that recognizes their contribution as active agents in the educative process.

Students cannot help but be disillusioned with the university as it presents itself to them: a monolithic gristmill, grinding all the students down to some common grain, insensitive to individual needs and differences, and devoid of personal contacts with teaching faculty. Furthermore, the students feel subjected to a quality of teaching which provides stimulating and provocative classroom experiences only as the exception rather than the rule, where material is presented in a fragmented and disconnected manner, and where no raison d'être can be discerned for the requirements imposed by the university's intolerably impersonal authority.

Students do not genuinely want the responsibility of academic self-determination, for they realize that they are not in a position to make vital decisions about which courses are needed in order to pursue certain goals. But students do want the administration and faculty to be responsive to their complaints and needs, and to consult with them in good faith. They must feel that their recommendatioins will be considered seriously and have the potential to move the institution to positive action. In short, they recognize the distinction between authority competently exercised and authority that is abusive. Their unrest represents a protest against the latter and should be construed as a plea for the former.

II

The challenge of college teaching consists of the concerted effort of every faculty member to reveal the organic relation between the material of his subject and the seminal concepts of both his discipline and others. This kind of teaching should be done without compromising the standards of the institution or the nature of the material and should consider the level of competence of the students involved, as well as their interests, aims, and needs. The teacher must recognize his own responsibility in presenting material that will serve to stimulate the intellectual appetites of his class. As a teacher of mathematics

I have always felt that mathematics deserves a place within the liberal arts program, that it is a subject to which nonscience majors should be exposed. With the disappearance of core requirements and the unfavorable attitude of students developed through a host of negative experiences suffered at the hands of academically incompetent lower-school teachers, mathematics is losing its foothold in the liberal arts program. This displacement is occurring at a time when mathematical techniques are becoming necessary tools in all areas of human inquiry, and where the failure of students to be exposed to mathematics and the physical sciences results in unhealthy and unreasoned fears of the growing influence of technology. A central portion of the challenge of teaching mathematics on the college level is to dispel these fears, to dissolve the confusion that has accompanied the attempts to understand its content, and, in effect, to save mathematics as an integral part of the liberal arts program and maintain its place in the intellectual toolbox of any individual who wishes to be well-educated.

The unique character of mathematics creates special pedagogical problems. Although no two mathematicians define their subject in precisely the same terms or stress the same characteristics, nonetheless few fail to make reference to its exclusive reliance upon deductive methods. Such reliance is intimately connected to the axiomatic structure of mathematics, the necessity of its conclusions, and its essential similarity to linguistic systems. In addition, its remarkably dualistic nature is seldom overlooked in discussions aimed at laying bare its essence; the Janus-like character of mathematics allows it to be viewed as both a pure and an applied science.

As a pure and totally abstract discipline, it can be pursued completely divorced from any considerations of reality and viewed as self-contained and independent of any experiences. As an applied discipline it serves as the language of the sciences, capable of providing both the models that serve as explanatory devices for the understanding and interpretation of physical phenomena, and the conceptual framework and media of expressions needed to capture, formalize, schematize, and communicate complex relations that link phenomena in an ordered cosmos.

To a degree, a teacher's presentation of a subject reflects both his conception of what he considers the nature of his discipline to be, and his own particular areas of interest within that discipline. Nevertheless the effective presentation of most undergraduate courses depends upon a certain neutrality in approach. Whether a mathematician is philosophically a logicist, a formalist, or an intuitionist with respect to the essential nature of his subject, or whether his interest lies exclusively either within the domain of pure mathematics or applied mathematics, these leanings should not affect his pedagogy in most elementary courses, save those which call for a particular slant in their very composition. The teacher must resist the natural temptation to proselytize, not allowing his own prejudices to interfere with presenting a pedagogically sound course.

The mathematics teacher who views the subject in its purest and most formalistic terms is in danger of presenting elementary courses, particularly those in elementary analysis and the calculus, as an endless string of formal proofs, deriving theorem upon theorem, proving lemma upon lemma, without deigning to provide the models, analogies, examples, and problem applications necessary for the student to grasp the significance of the statements resulting from these formal demonstrations. Unless the course is designed primarily to present the purely axiomatic development of a given area of mathematics, the tendency to prove the obvious, to demand exacting rigor, and to develop material in an excessively abstract and formal manner invariably destroys interest, obscures ideas, and fails to provide the necessary concrete touchstones needed by the unsophisticated mathematics student if the concepts under consideration are to be grasped in all dimensions. There is a point where rigor generates rigor mortis. The measure of the creative teacher is his ability to concretize the abstract, to provide the appropriate set of examples and models that reveal the nature of an idea couched in the unfamiliar and often complex symbols which characterize the language of mathematics. The student craves the visual model or diagram, the analogy, and the situation in which a given concept is operative in order to create the frame of reference required to achieve understanding. Effective comprehension is invariably tied to our capacity to devise a schematization or representation of a given concept. Such models serve to breathe life into the abstract by providing a concrete element of association which aids in the unraveling of the abstraction, supplying a real peg upon which the student can hang an abstract hat. If teachers persist in operating in the classroom at a level of abstraction that emphasizes the apparent lack of relatedness of mathematics to the concrete and that accentuates the abstract nature of the subject by failing to generate the necessary concrete explicatory models, analogies, and examples, then they can rest assured they will continue to preserve the secrets of mathematics.

Whether or not one relies heavily on the use of formal techniques in the development of a mathematics course, proving theorems and logically deriving particular statements raise serious pedagogical problems which are often ignored by teachers of the subject. One cannot teach mathematics and preserve the integrity of the discipline while completely ignoring its deductive nature. Students must appreciate that unlike the inductive forms of reasoning employed in many other subjects, the conclusions and theorems of mathematics follow with inexorable necessity from its initial assumptions. However, the student's ability to grasp the necessity of a conclusion in a deductive context and to follow the intricacies of a particular proof is dependent upon his understanding of the rudiments of symbolic logic, including canons and inference rules, criteria of validity, and specific methods of proof employed impartially within a given system to sanction certain symbolic manipulations and forbid others. The tendency of mathematics teachers to presuppose such understanding of logic on the part of their students has proven fatal to the successful communication of proofs.

Teachers have mistakenly subscribed to the thesis that the student will grasp the methods of deductive inference by exposure to proofs within a system. Others argue that one can develop the necessary logical tools as they are needed. These assumptions have played an instrumental role in generating the difficulty so commonly experienced with Euclidean geometry on the high-school level, a difficulty which results in widespread failure and the abandonment of mathematics after the tenth year by many who could potentially succeed in mastering its content. If logic were carefully and coherently developed prior to its employment as a tool in the axiomatic presentation of specific areas of mathematics, the student would be able to concentrate on the specific content of the material without having to struggle with the underlying logic as well. He would recognize a logical contradiction when one appeared, understand a *reductio ad absurdum* argument, be able to determine whether a given statement can be legitimately introduced as a hypothesis, grasp the fact that from an inconsistent premise set anything can be proven, and be alert to the dangers of assuming what he sets out to prove or of assuming a special case where generality is required. Only the rare student can penetrate particular arguments and proofs in order to distill out and comprehend the specific set of logical techniques employed in the context. The piecemeal development of logic as it is needed often results in fragmented understanding which is ineffective because it lacks cohesiveness and continuity.[3]

Even students who are quite mathematically sophisticated and capable of following a proof often cannot themselves prove a particular theorem they have never seen proven, because they do not know which logical strategy to employ in the given situation. Understanding of logical techniques cannot be assumed, and a teacher presenting a course dedicated to the development of a given area of mathematics cannot be expected to devote the time necessary to delve into the theory of proof in any depth. Thus the teacher must verbalize carefully the proof strategy before he covers the board with symbols. By discussing in everyday language the proof technique he is going to employ, clearly revealing the sense and significance of the conclusion, how the given will be manipulated to reach the conclusion, the value and need for each step in the process to arrive at the desired conclusion, the reasons for injecting each assumption, the sanctions for each move, and the reasoning behind the selection of the particular strategy chosen, the instructor may enable students to achieve a level of understanding that could never be realized by merely formalizing the proof. By constantly verbalizing the sanction and significance of each step, the instructor may transform a usually imposing mass of symbolism into a coherent and comprehensible argument whose meaning and importance are more easily seen by the student.

In addition to having difficulty with mathematics because of its high level of abstraction and logical rigor, students encounter many problems generated by the extensive use of unfamiliar symbolism. The language of mathematics is characterized by its economy and its precision, but these virtues are purchased at the expense of rapidly introducing a great many strange symbols which serve to represent complicated and sophisticated concepts. The blackboard or textbook page covered with mathematical symbolism is psychologically imposing, and it causes many students to turn off and give up at the very start. I have often heard students remark while thumbing through a calculus text, "Ugh!" It looks (a) "impossible," (b) "terrible," (c) "like Greek to me." This attitude can be overcome only by carefully explaining each symbol as it is introduced and frequently and persistently verbalizing the sense of mathematical statements, employing them until familiarity is achieved. Students should be made aware of the linguistic problems of mathematics and be prepared to exert the sort of concerted effort necessary to incorporate these symbols into their basic vocabulary, recognize them immediately, and conceptualize in terms of them.

Definitions in mathematics also present a special problem, not only because they are packed with symbolism and are frequently quite involved but also because they must be regarded as functional. They are often employed directly in proofs, either as given statements or as the rational backing for the introduction of hypotheses, and students are required to be capable of utilizing these definitions in a constructive manner. They must be prepared to substitute for the variables contained in the definition or to employ the definition in conjunction with other statements as a means of drawing inferences in the context of a formal proof. Many teachers of mathematics erroneously assume that merely stating a definition or writing it on the blackboard suffices to communicate its meaning and import to the student. Difficulty in comprehending certain key definitions can often result in a failure to understand the central concepts of an entire course.

The teacher must be prepared to spend extra time on such critical concepts, time which is won at the expense of other concepts judged less crucial. The teacher must learn to anticipate the trouble areas and, robbing Peter to pay Paul, make value-judgments as to the relative importance of the material in the syllabus. When he encounters a seminal concept he must be prepared to produce the examples, preferably concrete and drawn from the realm of the student's experience, in order to highlight the content and significance of that concept and communicate the essence of the particular definition. The usual model for communicating the limit concept, that of the secant slithering along a curve to a point of tangency, may not be sufficient to do the job. Use of Zeno's "Achilles and the Tortoise" paradox to motivate a discussion concerning the limit concept and the problems of dealing with the infinite in mathematical terms seldom fails to generate interest. Where all else fails, a simple example culled from every student's elementary-school experience may lay bare the essence of the definition of a limit, for every sixth-grader encounters an infinite series with a finite sum when he meets the decimal expansion for certain common fractions such as one third ($\frac{1}{3}$). A detailed discussion of the series $.3 + .03 + .003 + .0003 + \ldots$ will serve to clarify the meaning of that "epsilon-delta business" which students of the calculus find so mystifying.[4] Teachers should not fail to look to the history of mathematics as a source of material to motivate students, provide examples, and place the ideas of the course in historical perspective. Quite frequently, valuable and useful examples and models can be gleaned from relatively primitive mathematical notions and from the content of elementary- and secondary-school mathematics as well.

Unfortunately, mathematics presents itself to the student as the paradigmatic instance of an absolutistic and completely objective discipline, one in which answers are essentially right or wrong; mathematical truth, once the system is specified, cannot be made up as one goes along, and students cannot argue that the correctness of a problem is subjective, i.e., a matter of opinion. The teacher represents the ultimate authority on the true and the false, the correct and the incorrect. This apparent authoritarianism and lack of flexibility with respect to the evaluation of a student's output tends to mitigate against the popularity of the subject and, more seriously, generates student passivity. This attitude is manifested by a belief in the omniscience of the professor, a tendency to copy uncritically whatever is uttered or placed on the board, and the absorption of material in spongelike silence, the student contributing little or nothing to the procedings.

The instructor must consciously attempt to involve his students actively in the learning process by employing methods which require the student to shed his spectator stance and view himself as a participant. Socratic techniques which encourage dialogue between individuals and the instructor and which serve to challenge the collective mind should be used wherever and whenever possible. The student must be made to see the value of thinking along with the instructor, of anticipating his moves, of formulating conjectures, and of suggesting alternative methods of solution. The student should not consider himself an onlooker, one who pays his tuition as a price of admission to view a show where his instructor performs mathematical calisthenics and "chalks around" on the blackboard. The student will not voice his conjectures and openly articulate his ideas and problems unless the teacher has proved himself receptive to participation, tolerant of mistakes, and generally patient rather than brusque and overbearing in his approach. The responsibility for creating a healthy atmosphere for learning in a classroom is essentially the teacher's, and it is usually established by the enthusiasm he shows for his material and the warmth, sincerity, and genuine concern which he extends towards his class.

In addition, the instructor should encourage student participation for his own benefit. Besides enabling him to familiarize himself with the students and use their efforts and mistakes as an aid in teaching (a great deal can be learned from the analysis of intelligent mistakes), the instructor will find that he too will grow from such exchange of ideas. He will grow as a teacher, for by learning how students at a particular stage of mathematical development handle certain concepts, he will better be able to anticipate student difficulties and gear his future lectures accordingly. He will also grow mathematically, for students are often capable of original and creative insights which may be suggestive mathematically as well as pedagogically.

The need to appeal to the intuitive faculties of the students cannot be overemphasized and is frequently overlooked by excessively formalistically oriented professors. The students, in applying their natural abilities to a given problem or concept, often relive or recreate the entire history of the central idea involved, with the result that solid insight is achieved. The student must be presented with material that will motivate him sufficiently to sustain him when his learning curve reaches a plateau. A professor who walks into his classroom, sketches an irregular blob on the blackboard, and asks his class, "How do you think we can go about finding the surface of this amoeba?," may well be on his way to generating a discussion that will lead to a clear grasp of what the definite integral is, and what integral calculus is all about. On the other hand, the professor who marches into the class and states, "Today we will define the definite integral," while slathering a definition on the board that involves least upper bounds, greatest lower bounds, Riemann sums, limits, convergence, and so on, will more likely than not leave all but the best students in limbo. The first professor will get to the definition presented by the second, but not before he has his class playing with the problem of finding the area of irregular closed figures and the area under a continuous curve. Invariably, through exercise of their intuition and through open dialogue involving surmise and conjecture, the students will evolve a method of exhaustion similar to the techniques for solving such problems developed by Eudoxus and Archimedes. The professor may then derive the formula for the area of a circle using a method related to Riemann summation, or he may use Archimedean techniques to calculate the value of pi, but whatever paths he chooses to follow he will have created enthusiasm, actively involved his class, and developed the concept with maximum understanding.

One must not omit, in any discussion of the teaching of mathematics, some recognition of the pedagogical difficulties generated by the activity of problem-solving, the central concern of those whose interest lies in the area of applied mathematics. Just as there are courses whose content requires the axiomatic approach of pure mathematics, there are also those courses whose content demands a stress on application. Teachers in such courses, however, should resist the pressures and temptation to ignore entirely the axiomatic and theoretic underpinning of the applied methods employed in their courses. Failure to do so leads to "cookbook" courses in which the student learns to match the correct recipe to the problem at hand. Often he just memorizes a technique related to a particular model example and then uses it as a paradigm. He classifies future problems in terms of these paradigms and solves them by employing the suitable methods, i.e., the methods employed in the solution of the paradigm. Unfortunately, if the theoretical backing for the methods is ignored (as, for example, is suggested by engineering students who argue they should be spared the need to suffer the proofs related to the techniques they must learn to employ), then the depth of understanding needed to solve problems containing some new wrinkle and not neatly falling under a familiar heading will be absent. The student who can think well mathematically can handle both the proof and the problem, and he is operating under an illusion if he thinks them to be completely disjointed.

The student who has difficulty in following the logical development of a proof is usually unsuccessful in the business of solving problems, not because he cannot drop problems in their appropriate pigeonholes, but rather because he cannot set the problems up. This process involves translating the problem from the verbal context within which it is presented into the language of mathematics so as to insure that the sense of the problem is correctly captured in the mathematical statements which will be manipulated according to the rules that define and govern the relevant operations and relations. Most students become adept at blindly pushing symbols; it is knowing which symbols to push and correctly formulating the problem in mathematical terms that offers the real test of a student's ability to solve problems. Contrary to the opinion of many, problem-solving, like the techniques of generating proofs, can be taught. The professor would do well to consult the work of George Polya who has, with consummate skill and insight, analyzed the dynamics of problem-solving and made many valuable concrete suggestions along these lines.[5]

A last word with respect to teaching problem-solving in general concerns the selection of problems. Too commonly textbooks fail to provide the kind of problems that students find interesting. The absurdity of the content of the problems of elementary algebra did much to destroy interest on that level (nobody really cared how far apart the boy who was rowing upstream was from the hat he had dropped in the water flowing downstream, after three hours of frantic paddling against a four-mile-an-hour current). The failure to produce meaningful and relevant problems can be fatal, for not only does it destroy interest on the part of the students but, in addition, it can cause a mathematics department, which functions as a service department to some degree, to lose the jurisdiction over courses that really belong within its domain. In teaching a statistics course, for example, an instructor should make a careful study of who is in his class. If it is composed primarily of education, psychology, or economics students, then the professor would do well to present problems from these particular areas that employ the statistical methods under consideration. Failure to do so can result in a belief on the part of the students that statistics has no application to their field of study, and hence is irrelevant. Usually this dissatisfaction is expressed in complaints to faculty advisors or chairmen of major departments which seek to have the requirement removed. Departmental reaction to such appeals has often been the creation of courses, taught by their own personnel, who, though usually not as competent mathematically, are aware of the various applications of the material in their discipline. Such courses encroach upon an area legitimately within the bounds of the service responsibility of a mathematics department. The result is a chaotic proliferation of courses that fail mathematically to measure up to standards.

The situation can be easily remedied through increased interdepartmental dialogue. By discussing his course with interested members of other departments, the mathematics professor can obtain suitable examples and problems that will serve to motivate his students and show where and how given mathematical concepts operate within the disciplines of their interest. The fact that interdepartmental dialogue is minimal within the college community has a strongly negative impact, fostering compartmentalized, disjointed, and irrelevant education. Whether or not this is the case due to academic chauvinism, lack of mutual respect for one another's interests and talents, or sheer laziness, if professors and departments cannot exchange ideas, rather than merely competing for a bigger share of the academic and monetary pie, then courses will continue to lack meaning for students, a disastrous situation for higher education.

III

As I stated at the beginning of this essay, the kind of student to be taught is the primary factor in deciding what is to be taught and how it is to be taught. The pace of the class, the specific content to be stressed, the amount of time needed to motivate the students, the balance between proof and application, the choice of problem material, the use of Socratic vs. lecture methods, and other such pedagogical issues must all be weighed in terms of who is being taught. The mathematics teacher will find himself confronted by three basically different categories of student: (1) the mathematics major, (2) the student who is studying mathematics because it provides tools and techniques that he needs in order to understand and gain competence in some other discipline or task which employs them, and (3) the liberal arts student who is studying mathematics in order to understand its special relation to other disciplines and its role as a distinctively human achievement and crucial factor in the development of human thought.

The mathematics major is committed to the subject and, therefore, represents the least challenge to the pedagogical skills of the teacher. Such students are usually highly motivated, and although at an advanced level they may challenge and drain the intellectual resources of the teacher, the actual teaching skill of the instructor as a critical factor in the classroom situation is minimized; the student with natural ability and interest seems to learn even in spite of the teacher. This is not to say that good methods and a sound approach to the subject are either undesirable or unappreciated. Poor presentation may serve to destroy the interest already kindled within such students or may fail to entice the student who is merely considering the possibility of pursuing mathematics seriously and is in the process of making up his mind. As a rule, however, students in this category have mastered the difficult technique of reading a mathematics text with comprehension (having discovered that one must "read" a mathematics book with a pencil). The student who chooses to undertake the study of mathematics as an end in itself has already enjoyed some degree of success in his previous work in the discipline and, hence, is not hindered by the fears which fetter other students' ability to learn. More often, he looks to the teacher as an advisor, one who will provide him with guidance, direction, source materials, and so on; only with regard to this student is it at all valid to use scholarly competence as the sole relevant ground for academic appointments. Most neophyte teachers of mathematics view the business of teaching in terms of this category of student. This misconception lies at the source of a great many of the difficulties that such teachers will ultimately experience once they become actively involved in undergraduate education, for, in fact, these students comprise a relatively small percentage of those taught.

The teacher will most frequently be in contact with students for whom the study of mathematics represents either a means to some other end or a mindless, arbitrary, and unjustifiable requirement imposed by the college or university with an eye to creating impediments that mitigate against acquiring the coveted sheepskin. Thus, rather than being confronted with students who regard the structured development of a mathematical thought as the ultimate aesthetic experience, the teacher is more often faced with the task of presenting mathematics to students who view it as another hurdle in an educational obstacle course. Rather than dismissing these students in some a priori fashion as unworthy of concern, the teacher must view this prevalent attitude of fear and hostility as a challenge to his abilities, not as a mathematician but as a teacher of mathematics. He must understand the basis of this fear and hostility as the result of repeated failures to master the subject. He must be prepared to encounter a student who is heavily "teacher dependent," whose ability to learn from the text is minimal, who has not mastered the proper study techniques necessary to learn mathematics,[6] who has been subjected on the elementary level to teachers whose academic qualification to teach mathematics is questionable, and whose preparation to handle many concepts central to the course under consideration is inadequate. He must be prepared to face these students in awkward situations, in classes which are often so large that active student participation on a wide scale is nearly impossible, in classes where the pressures of covering a great deal of material in a relatively short amount of time are often present, and in classes where the lack of homogeneity with respect to background, preparation, and ability is so glaring that the determination of a common ground from which to launch the material is most difficult (a problem compounded by open enrollment policies now in effect in many schools).

The teacher of mathematics must also understand the especially critical nature of his confrontation with the student who is himself aspiring to become a teacher. Teachers tend to reproduce or recreate their own educational experiences within their own classrooms and, as a result, tend to perpetuate the bad as well as the good from their own conceptual development. The college instructor who teaches the future teacher must not only relate the material he teaches to the business of teaching but must also employ sound pedagogical techniques himself for the neophyte to emulate. The only way real progress can be made in the improvement of mathematics education is to provide more teachers competent to deal with the content on the elementary and secondary levels.[7]

The elementary school teacher who is forced into the unenviable position of being jack-of-all-trades is often least secure in teaching mathematics. Great care must be taken to impress these teachers with the difficulty of their task and the nature of their responsibility in teaching the young. They must understand that their obligation lies in presenting mathematics as competently and as enthusiastically as possible, no matter what their own disposition towards the subject may be. The elementary student represents virgin terrain; he is unclouded by fear and prejudice towards material, and the attitudes of the teacher towards the various subjects presented are quite contagious. The college teacher of mathematics must realize the importance of producing an elementary-school teacher who is free of mathematical neuroses and who is prepared to pursue the teaching of mathematics with competence, enthusiasm, and dedication. Success here represents the sole opportunity for those seriously concerned with mathematics education to effect a significant change in the attitude of students toward the discipline and break the vicious circle which serves to perpetuate the mathematical mystique.

The problems of teaching mathematics become magnified and intensified when the liberal arts student is involved, for he is the least receptive and the most antagonistic towards any attempt to force-feed him any mathematics beyond the required dose administered in the secondary schools. Unlike the student who can be convinced of the need to study mathematics once the instructor succeeds in demonstrating how the mathematical methods under consideration function in contexts that are obviously within the discipline of the student's concern, the liberal arts student must be convinced of the relevance of mathematics to his intellectual growth. Rather than present the usual smorgasbord of disconnected and unrelated mathematical ideas, the instructor must adopt the point of view that sees as the aim of a liberal arts mathematics course, not the development of mathematical power in discontinuous and arbitrarily chosen areas of mathematics, but rather the transmission to the student of what a math man does when a math man does do math. Courses directed towards such students must treat the historical, social, and cultural dimensions of mathematics. Topics and material must be selected with an eye toward presenting the distinctive nature of mathematics as well as the various ways it impinges upon other areas of study. Teaching such a course involves great expenditure of time and energy on the part of the teacher, for in order to present such a course creatively the teacher will have to consult many sources in diverse disciplines. He will have to compile material, problems, and puzzles to motivate his class, selecting carefully ideas and concepts that best do the intended job, for no single text satisfactorily provides such materials. He must build a significant course that presupposes little or no background knowledge beyond the barest rudiments of arithmetic, algebra and the geometry of the Euclidean plane. He must set a pace and generate exercises in such a manner as to maximize the possibility of success on the part of these students, for nothing can serve to dissolve their fears more effectively than the sweet smell of success.

Many approaches, if handled imaginatively, may capture the interest of the class while communicating the flavor and significance of the subject. A discussion of statistics may be based on a consideration of pollsters and the projection of election results. The study of logic may relate mathematical proof theory to the general problems of argumentation. The study of set theory may be motivated by a discussion of the concept of infinity, actual and potential (which in turn can lead to treating the nature of calculus by reference to an illuminating source such as W. W. Sawyer's *What is Calculus About?*). A study of axiomatics may spring from a historical discussion of the genesis of non-Euclidean geometries and from consideration of the nature of mathematical models and their use in the sciences. A unit concerned with the nature of computers serves to generate understanding in an area of concern for the modern student. Questions such as "Can machines think?" "Is a man a machine?" "How do we communicate with a machine?" lead to treating linguistic problems in general as well as the development and nature of machine languages, the ways in which machines function, the capabilities and potentialities of machines, and the differences between thinking machines and men.

Often a puzzle can serve to initiate interest in an entire unit. For example, the famous problem about linking three houses to three separate sources of gas, electricity, and water without having any of the necessary ducts leading from the homes to these power sources intersecting any other of the ducts at any point can successfully embark a class upon an excursion into topology. The students are asked to see if the problem is solvable on a Euclidean plane, then on a spherical surface, and so on, ultimately arriving at the problem of what it would be like to live on a bagel (bagel = petrified doughnut = torus). The possibilities for the teacher with creative insight are unlimited, as long as he is willing to shed tradition and experiment with material along lines that transcend the usual well-traveled and well-worn routes.[8]

A teacher in the colleges and universities today faces a challenge which tests his mettle, his conviction, his dedication, his commitment, and his pedagogical acumen. For many students college represents no more than an extension of the dehumanizing, compartmentalized, discontinuous, unintegrated, pedagogically inept, and irrelevant educational processes to which they have been subjected from the lowest level of primary school. When the student reaches college age, he understands his plight sufficiently, realizes his power in the educational complex, and is mature enough to formulate and articulate his discontent. Rather than succumbing to student pressure by conceding to demands that fail to improve the quality and tone of higher education, the academic community must rethink its position. It must shift the emphasis of its concern to the classroom situation in order to cut to the heart of the problem and regain the faith and confidence of the student by providing him with an organically interrelated curriculum rather than a conglomeration of inert and lifeless ideas, a curriculum implemented by a dedicated and competent faculty in a physical environment conducive to learning.

The teacher of mathematics, if he wishes to preserve the subject as a vital component of the liberal arts program, must be prepared to extend himself to generate the kind of enthusiasm for the discipline that can only be attained through an integrated and meaningful approach to its material, presented in a setting which respects the integrity of the subject while recognizing the needs, attitudes, and dignity of the student.

NOTES

1. I am not trying to minimize the positive advantages that accrue to the teacher possessed of a charismatic personality. Showmanship may be overly important in the current classroom, a fact which may be attributed to the TV syndrome, an affliction which has transformed the "now generation" into a voyeuristic group who more often than not see themselves as an audience rather than a class and, as such, expect to be entertained. The instructor is now rated not only upon the content of his lectures but on his delivery as well. The inability to present material in a theatrical manner may result in a low Nielsen rating. Mathematics has been said to attract the introvert, the self-contained and inner-directed personality; hence, as a group mathematicians tend to possess traits that, as a rule, do not characterize the effective classroom teacher.

2. I am holding the view that the students should be consulted, that their opinions on matters of curriculum revision and degree requirements be solicited, that they serve in an advisory capacity, and that their suggestions be acted upon in good faith. I do not think, however, that students should exercise voting power in these matters, not only because of a lack of competence but also for a reason not often forwarded, namely, that those who act as spokesmen for the student body are often selected in a random manner (the procedures which govern student elections are grossly inadequate), and they seldom reflect the position and attitudes of the major portion of the students they purport to represent.

3. I should like to see more experimental programs instituted on the early secondary level that would include a self-contained course in logic (both formal and informal) prior to the presentation of any axiomatic development of some aspect of mathematics. If this were done, then a course like Euclidean geometry could be developed, presupposing these logical skills. The result would be greater understanding of Euclidean geometry and the possibility of considering alternative geometries in order to place the nature of mathematical truth into a more realistic and accurate perspective. If a student is expected to learn simultaneously both the content of geometry and its underlying logical structure, it is obvi-

ously more reasonable to expect him to gain success if he focuses his energies upon one of these factors at a time. Since the logic is more basic and is used as a tool in the axiomatic construction of geometry, its study should precede that of the particular geometry. In addition, the course can be justified on its own grounds, independent of its persistent application in mathematics, for its relevance and value are obvious when linked to the general problems of argumentation, reasoning, and inference-making which cut across disciplines. I would even venture the speculation that the student who fails to grasp its concepts will likewise fail to succeed in his attempt to master any axiomatic mathematics, and second thoughts should be given to his continuing in the study of mathematics until his problems are rectified.

4. I have often felt that high schools should eschew courses in the calculus during the senior year in favor of courses that serve to prepare a student more adequately to succeed in the study of calculus once he enters college. Such courses should demonstrate the need and value of the calculus, thus motivating its study, and present a careful development of the mathematical tools that are essential to mastery but which, due to time pressure, cannot later be treated adequately. Such courses could include work with inequalities, absolute value, the limit concept, sequences, mathematical induction, the field axioms, and analytic geometry.

5. See *How To Solve It* (Garden City, N.Y.: Anchor Books, 1957); *Mathematical Discovery,* vols. 1 and 2 (New York: John Wiley & Sons, 1962, 1965); *Mathematics and Plausible Reasoning,* vols. 1 and 2 (Princeton: Princeton University Press, 1954).

6. The sequential nature of the development of mathematical concepts is not conducive to the cramming method of study so frequently employed by college students. The successful mastery of mathematics usually requires disciplined day-to-day effort. I make every effort to convince my students that thirty minutes a day is preferable to an eight-hour study day on some weekend or holiday. Lack of discipline rather than lack of intelligence is the cause of failure in mathematics on the high school as well as the college level. Failure to study or do an assignment usually means, at the very least, a lack of familiarity with a concept or technique necessary to comprehend the material presented on the following day. Ignoring assignments for a time span as short as a week has

a snowballing effect which can result in a course being irretrievably lost, especially since most students are not adept at learning from the text, and a saturation point with respect to the ability to assimilate mathematical material is reached quite quickly.

7. A radical solution for the improvement of mathematics education which presents itself to me involves the elimination of all formal presentation of the subject below the seventh-grade level. The elementary-school student would be subjected only to a leisurely and empirical development of the most intuitive concepts of number and space. Then, at an age when the student is more likely to succeed, he would be exposed to a sophisticated treatment of the subject by a teacher who is a specialist. Removing formal mathematics from the elementary school would eliminate the deadly exposure of the embryonic student to a teacher whose mathematical training is minimal and whose enthusiasm for the subject is nonexistent.

8. A sampling of source materials that provide the sort of topical development and examples which are easily incorporated into a viable liberal arts mathematics course might include the following: W. W. Sawyer, *What is Calculus About?* (New York: Random House, 1961), vol. 2 of eighteen, all of which are pertinent, and published as The New Mathematical Library; Edward Kasner and Joseph R. Newman, *Mathematics and the Imagination* (New York: Simon & Schuster, 1940); Thomas L. Saaty and F. J. Weyl, *The Uses and the Spirit of the Mathematical Sciences* (New York: McGraw-Hill, 1969); R. L. Wilder, *Evolution of Mathematical Concepts* (New York: John Wiley, 1974); Sherman K. Stein, *Mathematics: The Man-Made Universe* (San Francisco: W. H. Freeman, 1975); Morris Kline, *Mathematics: A Cultural Approach* (Reading, Mass.: Addison-Wesley, 1962); Anatole Beck et al., *Excursions into Mathematics* (New York: Worth Publishers, Inc., 1969); J. R. Newman, *The World of Mathematics*, vols. 1–4 (New York: Simon & Schuster, 1956–60); *Mathematics in the Modern World* (San Francisco: W. H. Freeman, 1968); Charles S. Ogilvy and John T. Anderson, *Excursions in Number Theory* (Oxford: Oxford University Press, 1966); Bradford Arnold, *Intuitive Concepts in Elementary Topology* (Englewood Cliffs, N.J.: Prentice-Hall, 1962); Irving Adler, *Thinking Machines: A Layman's Introduction to Logic, Boolean Algebra, and Computers* (New York: John Day, 1974).

Teaching
Science*

ARNOLD B. ARONS (Ph.D., Harvard University) is professor of physics at the University of Washington. He has served as president of the American Association of Physics Teachers and in 1972 was awarded the Association's Oersted Medal for notable contributions to the teaching of physics. He previously taught at Stevens Institute of Technology and Amherst College. While at Amherst he developed a general education physics course which became well-known throughout the country. At the University of Washington he has developed a physical science program for pre-service and in-service elementary school teachers and received the University's Distinguished Teaching Award in 1973. He is author of *Developments of Concepts of Physics* and *The Various Language, An Inquiry Approach to the Physical Sciences,* co-editor of *Science and Ideas,* and a contributor to various scientific journals.

* Although this essay originally was written for this volume, a shortened version appeared in the *American Journal of Physics*, 41 (June 1973): 769. Reprinted by permission of the *American Journal of Physics*.

In the voluminous literature on the teaching of science, authors invariably agree that science is not just a string of names, facts, and classifications to be committed to memory or of routines of problemsolving to be mastered as a salutory mental discipline. There is much eloquent discussion of science as a cultural enterprise, a structure of concepts and theories created by acts of human imagination and intelligence, giving man the power to grasp elements of order and predictability in what would otherwise be a chaotic, capricious, incomprehensible flux of phenomena impinging on every aspect of his being. "It stands to the everlasting credit of science," wrote Albert Einstein, "that by acting on the human mind it has overcome man's insecurity before himself and before nature."

Yet in actual practice, despite valiant, scattered efforts by a small number of articulate teachers and textbook writers, H. J. Muller's observation is all too valid.

> Although all students of the humanities have had a course or
> so in some science in which they picked up some technical
> knowledge together with probably fallacious notions about
> "the" scientific method, most know little about the history,
> philosophy, and sociology of science, or about how and why it
> has revolutionized thought and life. They have no clear idea
> what questions science can and cannot answer, why its answers
> are always partial and dubitable, why its triumphant advance
> may make the humanities all the more important, or why these
> are not living merely on left-overs. They have a legitimate
> excuse in that introductory courses in science are usually
> taught as technical courses, a basis for more advanced work,
> not as humanistic studies for nonspecialists, or even as
> introductions to the fundamental question—the nature of
> scientific inquiry. . . . Students of literature in particular may
> share the traditional attitude reflected in T. S. Eliot's "Notes
> Toward the Definition of Culture," in which he completely
> ignored science. . . .[1]

The ignorance that Muller deplores pervades the outlook of most students of science as well as of students of the humanities. As he points out, science curricula are generally barren of the intellectual content he defines, and the relevant humanistic insights do not automatically penetrate the walls of the nonscience compartments to which the "humanities requirements" are confined.

Similarly, the vast majority of so-called "general education science courses" or "courses for nonscience majors" have no more cultural impact than the introductory courses for majors—the recent plethora of " _____ for Poets" books notwithstanding. (Put any science you like in the blank space.) I submit that most of these efforts founder—and will continue to founder—because they almost invariably confront their victims with little more than an incomprehensible stream of technical jargon, not rooted in any experience accessible to the student himself, and presented much too rapidly and in far too high a volume for the assimilation of any significant understanding of ideas, concepts, or theories. The pace precludes the development of any sense of how concepts and theories originate, how they come to be validated and accepted, how they connect with and elucidate experiences other than the particular ones glibly and superficially asserted in the text—much less allowing reflection on the scope and limitations of scientific knowledge or its impact on our intellectual heritage and view of our position in the natural universe. The "stream of words" approach has not solved and will not solve our educational problem—even if it is loaded with handsome illustrations and salted with allusions to pollution, energy crises, black holes, and Kafka.

It seems to me that, at the present moment, there are two major channels through which positive educational attainments of the kind advocated by Muller could be promptly and widely injected into college-level science teaching. I shall discuss these in sequence without attempting to deal with many other undeniably important elements of curricular structure or with the horde of operational facets of teaching. One of these channels resides in giving students time to study and develop a genuine understanding of a limited number of significant scientific ideas by synthesis of their own experience and thought rather than through a rapid, unintelligible, verbal barrage of names and asserted end results; the second resides in bringing a more articulate historical, philosophical, and sociological content directly into all science courses—particularly those at introductory levels.

ELEMENTARY-SCHOOL SCIENCE CURRICULA

The finest, liveliest, and pedagogically most effective curricular materials currently available for teaching concepts and subject matter of science are to be found not at college or secondary-school levels but among some of the new materials being released, after long periods of trial, development, and revision, for use in the elementary schools.[2] The groups that developed these materials worked directly with the children they sought to teach and met the latter on their own ground and at their existing verbal and conceptual starting points rather than in some never-never land of unchecked, untested hypotheses and assumptions about children and learning. In these materials, concepts are developed through experience, induction, and synthesis, with the teacher as guide and pilot rather than verbal inculcator. Ideas are developed *first*—out of direct experience, in terms of prior, familiar vocabulary, regardless of how cumbersome the latter might be—and technical terms are generated operationally only *after* experience has given them sanction and meaning.

The essence of instruction with these materials, whether the subject matter is physical or biological, is to give the children *time*—time to explore, to test, to manipulate, to suggest hypotheses, to follow trails to dead ends and to retrace their steps, and to make mistakes and to recognize and correct them on their own initiative without being punished for being "wrong." In other words, children learn from experience rather than from verbal inculcation. This is not to suggest that they are expected to be Newtons, Faradays, Agassizes, and Darwins who independently rediscover the structure of science *de novo* by the age of ten; they are ordinary, lively, curious, fun-loving children who react to the opportunity to learn from perceptively guided experience and observation. They retain what they have learned because they are synthesizing genuine experience and not just memorizing a jumble of unfamiliar words. They know where their knowledge comes from, on what evidence it is based, and they are capable of addressing the very sophisticated questions: "*How* do we know . . .?" "*Why* do we believe . . .?" "*What* is the evidence for . . .?"

But these materials are by no means "teacher-proof." They can be handled effectively only by teachers who hold a deep enough understanding of the subject matter to possess the security and flexibility to lead investigation rather than to dictate end results; to accept incorrect suggestions or hypotheses, recognize the misconception in the child's mind, and guide him into revision and correction of his ideas rather than rejecting them by assertion and insisting on a memorized conclusion.

Were these new materials (together with existing new curricula in middle schools and high schools) suddenly effectively implemented throughout our schools, we would have an entirely different problem of science education in the colleges—one that we are *totally* unprepared for, but one that might, at this level, be somewhat more successfully handled with the verbal methods we now use. This millennium is still very far off because, among other reasons, we have not generated a corps of teachers prepared to handle the new materials effectively. We—the college-university community—"educated" the teachers and the condition in which we have left them is depressing evidence of the total inadequacy of what we are now doing.

Since the envisaged millennium is not immediately at hand, we might, for the time being at the college level, profit from the example set by the new elementary school teaching materials and follow their mode and pattern (at an appropriately adult level). Were we to do this, I am convinced that we would induce a discontinuously sharp improvement in the understanding acquired by our students, eliminate the fear and hostility that many hold toward science, and at the same time start producing what does not yet exist: a corps of school teachers competent to handle the elementary science materials.

THE FAILURE OF VERBAL INSTRUCTION

As we look for improved effectiveness in college science teaching and for the sources of our failures, experience makes it increasingly clear that purely verbal presentations—lecturing at large groups of students who passively expect to absorb ideas that actually demand intense deductive and inductive mental activity coupled with personal observation and experience—leaves virtually nothing permanent or significant in the student mind. The procedures that have been found necessary to generate real learning in the elementary school child are equally necessary for the college student (if he has not yet had the given learning experience); hence the significance of the pedagogical patterns set by the new elementary science materials.

In the last few years I have had occasion to work with college students (many of them future elementary teachers) who come to take some physical science late in their academic careers. I find that all of these students have, somewhere in their school experience and elsewhere, heard the term "electrical circuit," seen diagrams of circuits in books or on blackboards, listened to descriptions of facts and concepts concerning current electricity.

When these students are given a dry cell, a length of wire, and a flashlight bulb and are asked to get the bulb lighted, they almost invariably start by connecting the wire across the terminals of the battery and holding the bottom of the bulb to one battery terminal. They have no sense of the two-endedness of either the battery or the bulb; few of them notice that the wire gets hot when connected across the battery terminals and almost none infer anything from the observation; it takes them up to twenty minutes to half an hour to discover, by trial and error, a configuration that lights the bulb. Seven-year-old children when confronted with this situation go through exactly the same sequence at the same pace. In the absence of the synthesis of actual experience into the concept of "electrical circuit," the college students, despite the words they "know" and the assertions and descriptions they have heard, have no more understanding of the ideas involved than the seven-year-old approaching the phenomenon *de novo*. Purely verbal indoctrination has left essentially no trace of knowledge or understanding.

These results are confirmed repeatedly by my colleagues and can be documented over and over again with other illustrations. In having the same group of students carry out a very basic and unsophisticated investigation of the behavior of pendulums, I brought them to the point where they simultaneously started swinging two pendulums of equal length but unequal weight of bob. They were astounded that the pendulums swung together in synchronism despite the fact that one bob was of lead and the other of wood. When I asked whether they were aware of any other instances in which two very different bodies moved together if released simultaneously, a few students responded that they had "been *told* that such bodies would fall together if dropped from a window," but that they had "never really believed this." Purely verbal inculcation uncoupled to experience and unrelated to any additional context or phenomenon, had left no trace of knowledge or understanding and had not even attained credibility, much less awareness or expectation of a connection between free fall and the swinging pendulum.

It is easy to get students to repeat the statement of a law or principle perfectly correctly. This is, however, no assurance that they have any understanding whatsoever of the principle being enunciated. Take, for example, Newton's first law of motion (the law of inertia): A body moves in a straight line at uniform velocity unless a force acts to change either the magnitude or direction of the velocity. This statement was the seventeenth-century declaration of independence from Aristotelian science. An understanding of its implications is essential to the transition of each one of us from the Aristotelian view of motion with which we are born to the far less obvious view that lies at the heart of modern science. Without an understanding of this conception, one cannot begin to comprehend why we hold the view that the earth and planets revolve around the sun.

An understanding of Newton's first law resides not in the ability to repeat the words of the statement but in the ability to recognize its relevance or applicability in simple, everyday phenomena. If the reader has never done so, I suggest that he take a group of students who have become verbally familiar with this principle, who can talk glibly about the frictionless puck moving at uniform velocity on a smooth tabletop, and ask them about the forces acting on the puck while it is in midair, in a trajectory resulting from having sailed off the edge of the table. He will be shocked at how many of these students insist on the sudden appearance of a horizontal force in the direction of motion, a force they did not invoke while the puck was moving along the table. These students can give a correct statement of the law of inertia, but they have no real understanding of its meaning. The idea is subtle; it takes time to assimilate from a sufficiently wide context of laboratory experience and thought experiments, but students are rarely afforded this luxury; all too frequently they are expected to be purged of their natural Aristotelianism simply by listening to a lecture, working a few sterile, end-of-chapter examples (not problems) that contribute neither insight nor understanding, and then to regurgitate the verbal statement memorized as Newton's first law.

If one gets students to think through the problem of the force exerted by the floor of an accelerating elevator on a person standing inside and carries the reasoning step by step in the direction of increasing the downward acceleration, he can lead them into a perception of what happens when the acceleration approaches that of free fall; the force exerted by the floor on the person becomes zero; all objects in the elevator are falling freely side by side; this is the condition referred to as "weightlessness." Then suggest the following thought experiment: Suppose the elevator cabin is now catapulted upward; it leaves the catapult, moving upward with decreasing velocity. During the period of upward motion, what will conditions in the cabin be like? What force will the floor of the cabin exert on the person inside? Relatively few students recognize that the situation is again one of weightlessness—in this sense, just another instance of free fall, even though the motion is directed upward.

Only after such questions have been raised and the thought experiments digested, do many of the students begin to recognize orbital motion of a satellite or the coasting of a space ship toward the moon as additional instances of a condition of weightlessness, conceptually identical with those cited above. All this takes time, contemplation, freedom to think incorrectly and then retrace and adjust one's line of thought. Not given such an opportunity, students desperately try to memorize what the lecturer tells them about the end results. They gain nothing in knowledge and understanding. They see science as a mystery totally impenetrable to them and harden their feeling of hostility toward an enterprise whose irrelevance is magnified by exactly this impenetrability.

If you have students perform a simple experiment on the electrolysis of water, collecting oxygen and hydrogen in separate tubes, stop and ask them how much liquid water disappeared in order to form the gases in the tubes: Was it a volume of water equal to the volume now occupied by the gases? Was it more? Much more? Less? Much less?

Regardless of what has previously been said verbally about densities of liquids and gases, regardless of what calculations have been made in sterile, end-of-chapter numerical exercises, you will find that many students say that the volume of water used up was equal to the volume of gas formed. Few have noticed that the water level has risen in the surrounding container or by how much; and even if they have noticed, they have not thought to interpret the effect. A few leading questions can now send them back to some pencil and paper work with volumes and densities; the inquiry has become motivated by a challenge and a question related to experience. When, through their own calculations, they realize how tiny an amount of liquid water has been used up and begin to comprehend what was meant by all the talk about density differences, the astonishment on their faces is well worth seeing. It is a lucid demonstration to the teacher of how little knowledge or perception of connections among disparate events has penetrated from verbal indoctrination and how necessary both experience and time are to the development of genuine comprehension.

I have been drawing illustrations from very elementary levels of college instruction, but the same problems pervade more specialized levels. I was recently asked to devise a question on atomic physics for a preliminary examination for first-year graduate students. Seeking a question that would probe for understanding of some very simple and basic aspect of modern physics, I chose to present reproductions of the emission and absorption spectra of sodium vapor. Calling attention to the fact that those lines that were present in the absorption spectrum exactly matched corresponding emission lines but that many lines present in the emission spectrum were totally absent in the absorption spectrum, I asked how these facts were qualitatively explained by the quantum model of the atom. Out of fourteen students, one gave the simple and straightforward answer that, in the case of absorption, electrons would have to be raised from ground states and that only those lines corresponding to such transitions could be present; several students launched into elaborate, irrelevant quantum mechanical formalism, liberally sprinkled with inapplicable jargon about selection rules; the remainder made no attempt to answer. This dismal failure is not the fault of the victims of the examination; these were highly selected, bright and able students. It is the fault of a system that forced them into becoming equation-grinding automatons who had never had the time to contemplate the *physics* into which the analytical techniques give us such deep and elegant insights.

Understanding Ideas vs Memorizing End Results

Virtually any student can tell you, with an ingenuous smile, that the Earth is spherical and that it and the other planets revolve around the sun, but if you ask how he knows these assertions to be true, on what evidence we believe such statements, his smile turns to dismay and embarrassment—in all cases except, perhaps, for a very few physics majors. In terms of our vaunted goals for "higher education," do these students really hold any significant knowledge? Are they in any way better educated than their medieval counterparts who would have given what we now consider the "wrong" answer on exactly the same basis that modern students give the "correct" one—an end result received from authority? If we wish to do more than render lip service to excellence, if we are indeed serious about cultivating capacities to think and to understand, to have our students see science as a comprehensible product of imagination and intelligence rather than as an assembly of "facts" and names, it is absolutely essential that we give them a chance to follow the development or growth of several significant concepts and theories—to address themselves to the questions "How do we know . . .?" "Why do we believe . . .?" For example:

Why do we believe the earth revolves around the sun? In what context of concept and theory is this statement "true"?

Why do we believe that matter is discrete in structure; i.e., what is the evidence for the atomic-molecular theory?

What do we mean by the concept of "electrical charge"? How does the concept originate? Is "charge" a kind of substance? On what grounds do we believe there are only two kinds of electrical charge? What (hypothetical) experience would force us to conclude we had discovered a third variety?

Why do we believe that atoms themselves have discrete structure on a subatomic scale? What are some simple, intelligible pieces of evidence? (Bland assertion of the existence of an entity named "electron" is not evidence of anything at all; yet much teaching is done in this style.) What experiences lead to and reinforce the creation of the concept of "electron"? What is the evidence that such an entity is a universal constitutent of matter? What is the evidence that it has subatomic mass?

PACE AND UNDERSTANDING

If we are serious about cultivating some measure of the kind of understanding I have been defining above, we must give the students time to learn; the pace must be slow enough to let them confront evidence, to think and contemplate, to relive some of the steps by which the human mind first achieved these insights. This means we *must* cut down on "coverage." It is futile and fatuous to drown students in a stream of names and jargon, to throw at them in one quarter or one semester all of physics from Galilean kinematics to the uncertainty principle, not to speak of adding meteorology and geology on the side. It is equally fatuous to submerge them in verbal assertion of the end results of chemistry or molecular biology as is so frequently done.

In a well meaning "science methods course" in a school of education, I have seen future elementary teachers reading a text which, among other things, discussed the nature of scientific law and theory, making correct but casual allusions to the "Copernican Revolution" and the "Newtonian Synthesis," to thermodynamics and the kinetic-molecular model. The same text discussed Piaget's investigation of conservation reasoning in children at different age levels and discussed concept formation and the way in which concepts, which we invent by acts of our own intelligence, give us an insight into deep relations among apparently unrelated phenomena. The students reading this text were the ones who shorted the battery and set the bulb on one terminal hoping against hope that it might light; they were completely innocent of any genuine scientific knowledge, having satisfied their "requirements" by memorizing names in "easy" science courses. They did not have the remotest conception what was meant by "Copernican Revolution" and "Newtonian Synthesis"; they had no idea of what "conservation reasoning" was; they could not give an example of a concept, much less point to a case in which a concept revealed deep relations among disparate phenomena.

These students dutifully read the text and tried to memorize words and phrases they might recognize on a multiple choice test. They had no idea that they had no understanding of what they were reading; all of their other 'learning" experiences had been of the same variety, and they assumed that this was the way of all "knowledge."

When I tell fellow members of the scientific community about this travesty, many of them sneer patronizingly (or contemptuously) and ask me what else I would expect of the "educationists." Yet when I look at what these same scientists are doing in their own courses I find numerous examples such as the following:

> Students are being told about the "fascinating" particles of
> high energy physics, with jargon about interactions, angular
> momentum, mass-energy relations, quantum transitions, and
> the uncertainty principle, while they have yet achieved no
> conception of what is meant by velocity, acceleration, force,
> mass, energy, or electrical charge, much less of how we
> obtain evidence regarding the structure of matter on a scale
> that transcends our senses.

Students, who are still intrinsically Aristotelians, and have no significant understanding of the law of inertia, are invited to toss around phraseology about Coriolis effects in meteorology and oceanography.

Students, who have no notion how to define "local noon," midnight, or the north-south direction, who have no idea of the origin of the seasons cr the phases of the moon (they believe the unilluminated part of the moon to be the earth's shadow), who are unaware that the stars have a diurnal motion, are subjected to lectures on stellar nucleo-synthesis, quasars, pulsars, and black holes in courses called "astronomy."

Students are conned into reading and talking about DNA, the molecular nature of genes, nerve and muscle action, while they have no idea why we believe in atoms and molecules; how we come to know anything about molecular formulas, size, or structure; what is meant operationally by "oxygen," "nitrogen," "carbon"; what is meant by "electrical charge" or "potential difference" and how we know that these concepts have anything to do with nerve action.

Among the students being debilitated in this way is a major fraction of our future elementary teachers. Is it any wonder they emerge totally unable to handle the new elementary science materials? Students exposed to such incomprehensible jargon and end results are being bludgeoned with a noneducational experience not one iota different from the debilitating one I described in the methods course—this time inflicted not by educationists but by scientists so wrapped up in their beautiful, up-to-date words, names, and insights that they have lost all awareness of how impenetrable the whole miasma is to a newcomer—how long it takes to develop some understanding of necessary prior concepts; to follow at least a plausible line of evidence, even if it is incomplete and not perfectly rigorous; to see at last what we know and how we know it.

When I urge, as I do here and continue to do at every turn, that we back off, slow up, "cover" less, give students a chance to think and understand, someone invariably demurs: "But if we stop way back here, if we do not cover our subject, the students will never *know* about this matter," or that, or the other "which is so profoundly important," or which is so "fascinating" because it happens to be modern or topical!

To this I can only respond that the demurral constitutes a terrible prostitution of the word "know." What did the students reading the methods text "know" as a result of having read it and memorized the phrases? What do students coming out of the similar science instruction I have just described "know"? I submit that they "know" absolutely nothing; that the jargon they have acquired is not knowledge or understanding but is useless, irrelevant baggage that evaporates immediately after the course examination; that even when the jargon is remembered in bits and pieces, students cannot put it together into meaningful statements or insights of their own.

To the interested or doubtful reader I suggest the following experiment: Ask any group of students, including ones who have had a conventional introductory physics course, to write a one-page statement of what the term "electron" means to them—where the idea comes from, why we believe in such an entity, where and how electrons occur, and what properties they have. Virtually everyone has heard and used this term, but the papers, in the majority of cases, are either a string of meaningless gibberish with words juxtaposed in random sequence, or just a plaintive, more honest, confession of complete ignorance: "I was told that such things exist; I have no idea of what they are or how we know anything about them." Reading such papers is a traumatic but salutary experience; I urge others to share it with those of us who have tried the experiment. (I wish to make it clear that I am not objecting to exposing students to the concept of "electron." I only make the earnest plea that, if we elect to do so, we give the exposure sufficient time, breadth of context, and connection to relevant ideas and experiences to make the concept meaningful in terms of the questions raised above—not just produce a meaningless verbal assertion.)

The time is long past that we can teach our students all the things they must know. It is hardly an original assertion that the only viable and realistic function of higher education is to put the students on their own intellectual feet: to give them conceptual starting points and an awareness of what it means to learn and understand something so that they might then continue to read, study, and learn, as need and opportunity arise, without perpetual formal instruction. Instead of just rendering lip service to this ideal, let us implement it by teaching science in an experiential, moderately paced way such that students have a chance to understand and master a limited number of important ideas instead of staggering breathless through a verbal marathon.[3]

FACETS OF SCIENTIFIC THOUGHT

When in the *Two New Sciences,* Galileo confronts the problem of describing the change in the velocity of a moving body (the idea to which we give the name "acceleration"), he points out that there are at least two alternatives: (a) we observe that the object changes its velocity from one value to another while it traverses a distance of so many feet, and we might then elect to describe this motion by means of the number which indicates how much the velocity changes for each successive foot of displacement; (b) the same velocity change, however, occurs over a measurable interval of time, and one might also characterize the process by the number which indicates how much the velocity changes in each successive second. Which mode of description should be adopted? The choice is not trivial.

Galileo selects the second concept: change of velocity per unit time. His objective is to create a description of "naturally accelerated" motion (free fall), and he has a deep intuitive conviction that free fall is *uniformly* accelerated in this sense, but not in the sense of change of velocity per foot of displacement. On the basis of a hypothesis, an inductive guess, he selects the concept that will yield the simplest and most elegant description of free fall and proceeds to test the hypothesis by deducing consequences that can be tested by experiment.

Here are lucidly displayed several significant facets of the scientific enterprise: the roles of inductive and deductive reasoning; the fact that scientific concepts are created by acts of human intelligence and are not material objects stumbled over and described by their discoverer like a new continent or a new animal species; the fact that an element of choice may enter into the sequence and that there might be room for essentially aesthetic criteria such as elegance and simplicity.

I do not invoke this well-known story to make a claim to new or profound insights into the philosophy and history of science. I only wish to point explicitly to a set of significant ideas that young college students can comprehend and appreciate—ideas that lie just below the surface in any introductory study of physical science but that students are rarely given the opportunity to discover, articulate, and savor. To discover these insights, students must have the opportunity to stand back and examine what happened, to relive some of the intellectual experience, to analyze and assess the line of thought, recognizing the elements of its logic, its strengths and its limitations.

In most texts and courses, however, students are not afforded this opportunity. The standard definitions of velocity and acceleration are asserted as though they were inevitable, rocklike formations that have existed for all time, while deference is paid to "history" by mention of the name of Galileo and by a few pompous, unsubstantiated cliches about his invention of "The Experimental Method" and his paternity with respect to "Modern Science."

Students can indeed acquire mature and intelligent intellectual perspectives toward the methods, processes, successes, and limitations of science, but such perspectives are not automatically conveyed by training them to calculate how high a stone rises when it is thrown up into the air or how much an electron beam will be deflected by a given electrical field. The intellectual perspectives can be developed only by coupling conceptual understanding of the kind defined earlier in this paper to an articulate discussion of how the concepts or theories originate and evolve, how they are validated, what limitations they have exhibited, what connections they have revealed among apparently unrelated phenomena, what role they have played in social or intellectual history and in our view of man's position in the universe.

FURTHER EXAMPLES OF HISTORICAL AND PHILOSOPHICAL IDEAS

Opportunities to examine these facets of the cultural phenomenon that is science literally abound at almost every turn as can be illustrated by a few specific examples:

From the didactic manner in which scientific concepts are forced on students in early schooling, it is understandable that they acquire the notion that scientific terms are rigid, unchanging entities with only one absolute significance that the initiated automatically "know" and that the breathless student must acquire in one brain-twisting spasm. It comes as a revelation and a profound relief to many young people that scientific terms go through a sequence of evolution, redefinition, sharpening and refinement as one starts at a crude, initial, intuitive level and, profiting from insights gained in successive applications, develops the concept to its later sophistication.

For example, the concept of "force" is legitimately introduced by connection with the primitive, intuitive, muscular sense of push or pull, but, in the law of inertia, we quickly redefine it to apply to *any* effect that imparts an acceleration to a material object (the action of an electrically charged rod on bits of paper). We endow completely inanimate objects with the capacity to exert forces on other objects [the charged rod exerting a force on the bits of paper, the table exerting an upward force on the book that rests upon it, the Earth exerting a downward force on us (our weight) and an upward force at our feet]. Following Newton, we then extend the concept even further and create the idea that when the table exerts an upward force on the book, the book simultaneously exerts a downward force on the table. By this time we have come a very long way indeed from the original use of the word "force" for an animate, muscular push or pull on another object.

Similarly, starting with the crude idea of "velocity" as a measure of how fast (as an average over a finite time interval) an object travels along a straight line, we refine this primitive notion into a concept of *instantaneous* velocity; we endow the concept with additional properties of direction in space and with rate of change of both direction and magnitude.

At each stage in this sequence of evolution and redefinition, the same original word ("force" or "velocity" as the case may be) denotes a new and more sophisticated concept; its meaning has been changed in significant, intrinsic ways; it no longer denotes only the first intuitive idea to which it was applied. Modest self-consciousness about the process of definition and redefinition enormously increases the confidence of students in their own grasp of the new sequence of thought, opens their eyes to similar shifts and extensions in the subsequent generation of concepts such as "energy" and "electrical charge" and alerts them to watch for similar semantic shifts that are rarely pointed out to them in their study of social sciences and humanities.

During the 1830's and 1840's, Michael Faraday's beautiful and elegant experimental investigations of electricity and magnetism caused him to raise some very deep questions about these phenomena, and students can be led to articulate a few of these themselves: Is there a *process* by which one electrically charged particle exerts a force on another? If one of the particles is suddenly displaced, does a finite time interval elapse before the force on the second changes? Does a finite time interval also elapse between the instant an electric current flows in a wire and the instant a neighboring compass needle begins to swing in response to the magnetic effect of this current? If a finite time interval does elapse in each case, what happens in the intervening space between the interacting objects? To answer these questions, Faraday invented a model, a visualization that completely transcended any direct sense experience—the famous concept of "lines of force" that stretched, contracted, spread apart, and pulled together, propagating electric and magnetic effects through evacuated space—the concept that Clerk Maxwell subsequently elaborated into the sophisticated modern notion of "field." Almost apologetically, Faraday writes about his highly speculative model:

> It is not to be supposed for a moment that speculations of this kind are useless or necessarily hurtful in natural philosophy. They should ever be held as doubtful and liable to error and to change, but they are wonderful aids in the hands of the experimentalist and mathematician; for not only are they useful in rendering the vague idea more clear for the time, giving it something like a definite shape, that it may be submitted to experiment and calculation; but they lead on by deduction and correction, to the discovery of new phenomena, and so cause an increase and advance of real physical truth, which unlike the hypothesis that led to it, becomes fundamental knowledge not subject to change.

Not only is this a beautiful description of the point and function of a theoretical model, but it simultaneously reveals a characteristic facet of the thinking of many nineteenth-century scientists: They were indeed convinced that they were stockpiling "real physical truth" and "knowledge not subject to change."

After the students learn something of the conceptual revolution associated with the elements of relativity or after they have seen some of the failures of Newtonian and Maxwellian physics in the atomic realm, it is interesting to ask them to contrast with Faraday's statement the sadder and wiser one by Oppenheimer:

> We come to our new problem full of old ideas and old words, not only the inevitable words of daily life, but those which experience has shown fruitful over the years. . . . We love the old words, the old imagery, and the old analogies, and we keep them for more and more unfamiliar and more and more unrecognizable things.

In the light of such perspectives, students spontaneously begin to articulate some sense of why most scientists now view scientific knowledge as mutable and provisional rather than permanent and final. They anticipate limited ranges of validity to successful theories and are fully prepared to find a deeper regression of unanswered questions behind every answered question.

In still another sequence involving models that transcend direct sense experience, one can get students to follow and examine the evidence that led to our belief in the atomic-molecular structure of matter as well as in a structure of atoms themselves. They must be allowed to doubt with the early participants, to articulate uneasiness about the interpretation of some of the evidence—not just to be stuffed with a few disconnected and, in themselves, unconvincing arguments, followed by assertion of the end results. (After all, the original doubters were a goodly and far from foolish company.) Many illustrative gems line the way through such a sequence. Dalton, for example, in his original attempts to develop a quantitative atomic-molecular theory, confronted chemical data in the form of percentage composition by weight of various compounds. The only regularity that had been noted in these data was the so-called "law of definite proportions"—the fixed percentage composition of any definite chemical compound, and even this was still a matter of some controversy and uncertainty.

Dalton's preconceptions concerning corpuscular constitution of matter led him to give particular consideration to cases in which a given pair of elements (say carbon and oxygen) form more than one compound, and it occurred to him that if 1.0 g of carbon combines with 1.3 g of oxygen in one compound, then for the same 1.0 g of carbon in the other compound one should find perhaps 2.6 or 0.65 or 3.9 g of oxygen—or some other quantity that bore a small whole number ratio to 1.3. One would expect just such simple numerical relations if compounds did indeed consist of molecules made up of small numbers of atoms of the combining elements. The data had never been examined this way; this particular orderliness lay hidden behind the unrevealing percentage compositions. Dalton looked, and the order was there; he *predicted* what is now glibly known as the "law of multiple proportions." (In most modern courses this law is presented as though it had been known initially and provided *a priori* evidence for the atomic theory.) The point here, of course, is that very frequently "facts" do *not* speak for themselves. In this instance the facts had been available for a long time, but they were not even seen until looked for through the lenses of a theory; then suddenly their presence fed back as a dramatic confirmation of the theoretical conception that revealed them.

An inverse illustration of this idea resides in the story of the famous Piltdown hoax which was exposed in the 1950s. Many paleontologists accepted the spurious "Piltdown Man" fossil with a man-like skull and an ape-like jaw because their theoretical preconceptions led them to expect an evolutionary sequence in which brain development led the way and changes in other parts of the body followed. They accepted the forgery for almost forty years, even though it was well known that it did not fit any known niche in the humanoid fossil sequence. Here again facts did not speak for themselves; they were viewed through the lenses of a theory, and the theory led many astray.

Very few students have any conception of the revolutionary thrust of seventeenth-century science: the discarding of the notion that the heavens and heavenly bodies were made of a different substance and obeyed different natural laws from those of the terrestrial sphere; the subsumption of the entire universe under one system of humanly comprehensible natural law; the extension of the universe to infinity and the concomitant removal of the literal, sheltering heaven from close overhead. Here was a profound turning point in our intellectual history; the personal outlook of every individual toward himself and toward his place in the universe is deeply conditioned by this heritage from Galileo, Newton, and the other seventeenth-century natural philosophers. An educated man should be aware of such a heritage in historical and intellectual terms, not in the mere assertion of end results.[4]

A similar revolution in intellectual history is associated with man's growing awareness of mutability in the heavens, in the earth, and finally in living species—his grasp of the extent of geological time which so vastly transcends his own temporal experience. Through what groping, what steps, what transitions were the insights won? How do we come to hold the view of evolutionary processes that we now hold? There are fine educational experiences to be gained in following at least some of the pieces of this story, particularly as they are traced in works such as John C. Green's *The Death of Adam*.[5]

VARIATIONS ON THE THEME

The preceding illustrations of epistemological, philosophical, and historical aspects of science happen to be personal favorites of mine; I present them for the purpose of being specific in my illustrations and not to advocate them above the host of other possibilities. Each teacher must select ones that appeal to him and that he can articulate to students in the most stimulating and compelling way. There is the whole array of aspects that James Conant referred to as the "tactics and strategy of science." There is the fascinating, partly scientific, partly sociological, problem of validation and acceptance of scientific theories. There are the philosophical problems of positivism and the questions concerning the "reality" of entities that transcend our senses: atoms, molecules, electrons.

There are also, of course, the topical, pressing, social problems that stem from the energy crisis in general; the release of nuclear energy in particular; the application of science to warfare; the possibility of synthesizing living matter and of controlling the genetic development of human beings; the problems of controlling and limiting abuse of our terrestrial environment. I have no intention of minimizing the significance of these vital problems, but I do have reservations about launching into analyses or discussions of them on a level not significantly different from that which I objected to in another context earlier in the paper: that of encouraging students to be glib with words such as "strange particles," "accelerators," "mass-energy relation," "atomic structure," and "uncertainty principle" when they have no idea of what they mean, much less have any significant comprehension of force, mass, energy, gravity, or electrical charge. I see the two contexts to be quite analogous. If one takes the trouble to lay an adequate background for intelligent, critical discussion, a look at the problems mentioned above is fair game; otherwise, it is nothing more than trivial, superficial chitchat which does the damage of allowing students to think they have mastered profound levels of knowledge.

It is necessary to give students an adequate frame of reference, and that means it is essential to study enough of the relevant substantive scientific subject matter to make such discourse and discussion meaningful. This does not mean that it is necessary to follow every historical dead end in exhausting detail, nor is it necessary to become involved in mathematical analysis that is excessively formidable and time-consuming, especially for nonscience students. Each teacher must seek an optimum balance that will vary with the particular group of students addressed; they should be exposed to enough scientific subject matter to make their involvement genuine but not so much as to bury them. The essential criterion is that they must not end up regurgitating secondhand pronouncements about the nature and processes of the scientific enterprise without ever having articulated any such insights out of their own intellectual experience. Without at least some participation in comprehension and interpretation of scientific concepts, theories, and philosophy, second hand statements about science have no more educational value than a commentary on poetry without a reading of the poetry, or a dissertation on the philosophy of history barren of any knowledge of the history of anything.

Given a chance to comprehend scientific ideas on the level and in the manner I have been trying to define, students will begin to express a variety of significant intellectual insights. To illustrate, I quote some passages from student papers. Some are term papers in a science course, others are from papers submitted in entirely different courses, unrelated to science. These are all eighteen- or nineteen-year-old freshmen. The ideas they develop were deliberately planted in the learning experiences to which they were exposed, but the final articulation and synthesis are their own:

> "concepts such as simple harmonic motion show us
> similarities in a clock pendulum, sound, and light. The
> description in terms of new language is a powerful weapon in
> ordering the flux of impressions. We see our concepts bringing

order out of chaos. Concepts are used to form new concepts. From ideas such as velocity, force, and energy have been compounded more complex descriptions such as gravitation, atomic energy, electricity, magnetism."

"It is the hope of education that from working through a problem like the Millikan experiment, aided by a guiding outline which breaks the problem up into a series of smaller steps and shows me where I want to go in the end, that I will learn techniques that will at some time enable me to tackle a problem that hasn't been attacked before, without an outline or a knowledge of the final result."

"my actions begin with the use of language to form relationships. This is the essence of 'homework.'
By relating the terms 'electron,' 'nucleus,' and 'photon,' my ability to use them is increased, and I can form even more relationships. . . . My problem . . . [is that of] . . . using and relating various languages my teacher has presented to me and *not* regurgitating the specialized cases which we say the teacher has 'taught' me."

"I. . . create a means of describing motion in terms of concepts already defined. . . . I select 'time' and 'distance' as the physical concepts which I will use to effect my description by inventing the concept 'velocity.' . . . It is something I have *created* not something that is intrinsic in the car or the motion. Similarly 'weight,' 'mass,' 'density,' 'magnetism' are all conceptualizations that have been created by man."

"*Student.* If the centripetal force acting on the moon is really terrestrial gravity, the centripetal force acting on the planets must be the gravitational pull by the sun.
Angel. That's reasoning by induction.
Newton. It may work for all bodies.
Angel. That's more induction.
Student. Actually we have not defined any new concepts, nor do we have an empirical law.
Newton. We have a theoretical law based on the assumption that gravity is the force that causes the centripetal acceleration

of the planets, and that by induction this same force acts
between all objects.
Student. What causes the force?
Angel. I've heard that before.
Newton. I frame no hypothesis."

"Finally, we have seen the necessity of changing existing
models and theories to fit new evidence (in particular we
notice the photon and quantum theories.) In all that we have
done this year, perhaps this lesson is the most important:
Science is not static and definite. New things are seen, new
relationships found as our tools and eyes become sharper. Our
ability to adjust the theories we have proves two very
important aspects: the orderliness of Nature and our
understanding of what our previous theory implied and of
what its limits were."

I have never known a colleague who had the temerity to offer a
course under the rubric "Wisdom 402. 3 lectures, 1 laboratory session per week." Yet we all aspire to contribute to the wisdom of the
human beings we strive to educate. We do so by dealing with rather
modest and tractable elements of knowledge and insight that constitute our intellectual heritage and matrix of current inquiry. Rather
than step into a classroom and beat our breast about the quandaries
into which the release of nuclear energy has precipitated mankind,
rather than pontificate about the still undefined ethical and moral
problems that will descend on us with synthesis of living matter and
control of genetic mechanisms, it seems to me far more effective and
rational to get our students to confront science through some of the
more modest insights and experiences I have tried to illustrate above.
I am convinced that such studies contribute to the development of
better educated individuals and more intelligent citizens in exactly the
same way as do an awareness of history and sensibility to literature.
As educated human beings, they must then, together with all the rest
of us, confront the grave problems that are not yet material for the
classroom.

WAYS AND MEANS

There is neither space nor time for a lengthy discourse on the
logistics of teaching in the vein advocated in this essay; my intent is

only to inject a few cursory remarks on what seem to me to be particularly crucial matters.

I cannot conceive of a truly effective science course that does not contain a tightly integrated laboratory experience as a vital and intrinsic component. This is not to imply, however, that the rigidly structured, step-by-step directed, *ex post facto* tests and "verifications" so prevalent in many existing laboratory courses constitute an educationally viable structure. These are almost invariably reduced to sterile busy-work that further antagonizes students and reinforces their sense of the artificiality and irrelevance of the effort required of them.

A viable laboratory is one in which the student must make some decisions of his own, profit from his mistakes, and retrace his steps if necessary. It must be one that allows the student to carry over his activities from day to day and does not compel him to "finish something" within the confines of a straight jacket. It must be one designed to generate learning by induction from experience rather than from *a priori* verbal indoctrination.[6]

Laboratory work is admittedly costly in space, time, and facilities. Some cost-conscious administrators are pressing science teachers to abandon laboratory work (basing their pressure on legitimate criticism of the sterile laboratory instruction so prevalent in our colleges and universities) and to concentrate on lecture presentations to huge classes. This pressure should be articulately and vigorously resisted if we still wish to strive for any measure of excellence and effectiveness in science teaching, but the resistance must be accompanied by cultivation of stimulating and effective laboratory experiences such as those I have attempted to define above. Much current practice is simply indefensible; attempts to maintain it without drastic change are probably doomed to defeat; and such defeat is bound to have a weakening impact on support of good instruction wherever it may be struggling for survival.

I urge teachers to experiment more widely and more courageously with individualized, open schedule, laboratory-oriented science courses, in which most of the work takes place in the laboratory from day to day, and in which lecturing is limited to occasional pulling together of concepts and subject matter *after* students have encountered them in laboratory experience and to the discussion of historical, philosophical, and sociological ideas *after* the students have learned enough subject matter to make the discussion meaningful. In other words, the verbal presentations and analyses, if they are needed, should come *a posteriori* and not *a priori*.

TESTS AND PROBLEMS

One of the weakest links in our chain of instruction consists of the questions and exercises that are embalmed at the ends of chapters, purportedly to guide students in thought and study. Although there do exist a few texts that maintain a high intellectual standard, the great majority (particularly introductory texts for nonmajors) confront the student with little more than debilitating chaff—chaff for which he has no respect and to which he has no motivation to respond.

The "problems" consist of routine drill in calculations, vocabulary, or identification (such drill is indeed necessary but, with a little more ingenuity, can be incorporated in broader and more interesting context), or they consist of sterile demands that the student calculate some final resulting value of a particular parameter under conditions in which all other relevant parameters have been preselected and specified. In other cases, eager authors have generated rather more interesting problems, but, wittingly or unwittingly, they have written for the eyes of their colleagues rather than for students, and the results are problems far beyond the readiness or immediate comprehension of the students being addressed.

We are desperately in need of collections of questions and problems that. sensitive to the obstacles that arise in student minds, lead the student through the difficulties and subtleties in thinking and reasoning that he must face and overcome. We need questions that challenge his curiosity and ability to perceive relationships but that he can encompass and deal with successfully a reasonable fraction of the time. We need problems that lead him to make his own choices of relevant parameters, simplifying assumptions, or boundary conditions. We need problems that lead him into exploring extreme, special, or asymptotic cases in order to test his own reasoning for internal consistency. We must cultivate his habit of testing and checking the results of his reasoning in every possible way, so as to sharpen his own sense of when he is right or wrong and lessen his childlike dependence on confirmation from the teacher. Above all, we need questions and problems that, gently and gradually, lead the student into extending, inventing, perceiving questions of his own. This is, of course, the highest and most sophisticated skill, but it is quite possible to initiate such activity at very humble and unsophisticated levels and to see students develop steadily and rewardingly as they gain confidence in their own intellects.

Few aspects of a course do more to set its tone, cultivate the respect or contempt of students, and determine its overall effectiveness and reputation than do the tests and term-paper requirements. It is essential that our testing be consistent with the educational principles we articulate. If we render lip service to reasoning, thinking, and understanding relationships, but then concentrate our test questions on memorizable end results, names, or procedures, we might as well forget the grandiose objectives. The students, just as human as all the rest of us, will concentrate on the memorizable end results and forego the "intolerable labor of thought, that most distasteful of all our activities"—to borrow Justice Learned Hand's phrases.

Writing good tests and fruitful term-paper assignments is a demanding, challenging, brain-twisting chore, but when it is well and conscientiously done, it wins the respect and confidence of students and becomes one of the firmest underpinnings of a viable and successful course.

LARGE COURSES

After discussion of the educational modes I have fervently advocated in this essay, I am frequently asked, "But what would you do if you have to teach science by lecturing three hours per week for one quarter to a class of five hundred?" Although my emotions respond with "a plague on all their houses," my intellect knows this to be a legitimate question. I can only say that no one—least of all I—possesses a magic wand with which to turn this pumpkin into a royal coach. This view *must* be firmly and repeatedly conveyed to presidents, deans, curriculum committees, trustees, legislators—any and all who influence policy, educational and financial. Unavoidable concessions will be made to expediency (the individual teacher cannot fight this alone), but the institutional authorities must not remain unchallenged when they simultaneously make specious claims about excellence of instruction.

What might one do in this case? I would proceed to lecture, taking a very limited number of topics or concepts: go very slowly, limiting the pace to that which students set themselves in an individualized course, with many illustrative questions and problems, discussed after students have had a chance to think about them; use many demonstrations (not spectacular show pieces, but the simple fundamental experiences, deeply relevant to concept formation, that I would have used in the laboratory); use as many "take home" or "do at home" observations and experiments as I could contrive. If the course is enthusiastically and carefully done, with stimulating articulation of humanistic insights beyond the scientific content itself, I think it can be useful and respectable, but its effectiveness should not be overrated.

In summary, I make a plea for literate, sensibly paced, experience-oriented, courses of study that are firm and challenging in asking students to shape up to high standards of comprehension of concepts, soundness of reasoning, and clarity of expression in their mother tongue—courses that, by virtue of these very requirements, show respect for the intellect and capacity of the students.

(N.B. It is clear that throughout this essay I have been writing as a physicist. I can only ask the indulgence of non-physicist readers. My aim has been to provide very specific illustrations to back my contentions and advocacy; these illustrations, to be vivid and meaningful, had to come from personal experience. I am deeply convinced, however, that what I have had to say applies to virtually all college science teaching. Readers will certainly be able to connect their own analogous experiences with mine and extrapolate relevant aspects of this commentary to their own fields.)

NOTES

1. H. J. Muller, *The Children of Frankenstein*: *A Primer on Modern Technology and Human Values* (Bloomington: Indiana University Press, 1970).
2. Educational Development Center, *Elementary Science Study* (St. Louis: McGraw-Hill, 1968); AAAS Commission on Science Education, *Science—A Process Approach* (Cambridge, Xerox Education Division, 1968); Science Curriculum Improvement Study, SCIS *Materials* (Chicago: Rand-McNally, 1968).
3. It would be very satisfying to be able to point to specific curricular materials that might help a teacher construct a course of the kind advocated above. A very few such materials do exist in the area of science for the nonscience major, and I mention them below with brief commentary. In the area of instruction for science majors and engineers, however, I feel that the situation is very bleak: there are many texts in all subject areas, but the presentations are purely verbal, encompass far too much material presented far too rapidly, and give very little consideration to the obstacles that arise in student minds. We get away with this only because so many science majors are already committed to their choice of subject; enough of them persist and survive the pedagogical abuse intrinsic to introductory courses so that we remain satisfied and worry little about those who drop by the wayside. The time will come when this cavalier attitude will have to change, and we will be forced to give attention to more competent instruction for our future majors. For the present the college teacher must intervene with the courage of his own convictions and apply judgment and restraint in his use and pacing of existing materials—many of which are at least competent in their treatment of the subject matter even though they leave much to be desired as vehicles of instruction.

   As remarked above, in the area of instruction of nonscience majors, there do exist some materials that can help a teacher implement a laboratory-oriented, individualized course giving students a chance to breathe and learn:

   (1) A prototype version of such a course is IPS Group of

Educational Development Center, "College Introductory Physical Science" and "Physical Science II" (Englewood Cliffs, N.J.: Prentice-Hall, 1969–1972). This program focuses on why we believe in atoms and molecules and then proceeds to deal with electricity, heat, and energy concepts. All ideas are carefully developed and motivated. High sensitivity for steps of concept formation. Essentially no historical or philosophical content. At least a one-year course. Parts would have to be carefully selected for a one-semester course.

(2) PSNS Project Staff, "An Approach to Physical Science" (New York: John Wiley, 1969). A full year course, laboratory-oriented, focusing on structure of matter. Concepts of physics are developed much too rapidly, glibly, and with little sensitivity for linguistic and conceptual obstacles arising in student minds. The overall treatment and pace, however, are far superior to those of conventional physical science courses and can make a good program in the hands of a discriminating teacher. No historical or philosophical content.

(3) The secondary school physics courses, "PSSC Physics," 4th ed., Heath, 1976; and "The Project Physics Course," 2nd ed., 1975 (New York: Holt, Rinehart, and Winston) lend themselves to use in laboratory-oriented, individualized programs. They contain far too much material for a one-year course, but judicious pruning and selection of material can lead to a possible program. "Project Physics" has a strong historical-philosophical content. "PSSC Physics" is particularly careful about "How do we know . . .? Why do we believe . . .?" questions.

4. Gerald Holton, *Introduction to Concepts and Theories in Physical Science* (Reading, Mass.: Addison-Wesley, 1952), gives a fine development of this episode in the history of ideas and an excellent version is contained in the "Project Physics" materials.

5. J. C. Greene, *The Death of Adam* (Ames: Iowa State University Press, 1959; reprinted, New York: Mentor Book, 1961).

6. For prototype examples of laboratory work of this kind, I suggest referring to the elementary science materials cited earlier (note 2) and to the *College Introductory Physical Science Course*

(Englewood Cliffs, N.J.: Prentice-Hall, 1969). There is also a voluminous and useful literature on college laboratory work to be found in the various journals devoted to problems of teaching physics, chemistry, biology, etc. Useful documents emanate from the Commission on College Physics, the Commission on Under-graduate Education in the Biological Sciences, and other such groups; the reader is urged to refer to the appropriate organs in his own field of science.

Teaching
Social Science

RITA W. COOLEY (Ph.D., New York University) is professor of politics at New York University, where she received the "Great Teacher" award in 1967. She was Visiting Fulbright Lecturer in American Government and Politics at the University of Innsbruck, Austria, during the academic year 1965–66. She is co-author of *Government in American Society* and has contributed to various periodicals, including the *American Political Science Review, Western Political Quarterly, American Journal of Legal History, Journal of the American Judicature Society,* and *New York University Law Review.* During the academic year 1975–76 she served as chairwoman of the New York University Faculty Council, which represents all schools and colleges of the University.

Social scientists share with natural scientists a desire to render the world intelligible and to obtain knowledge about reality. But social science is characterized by certain ineluctable qualities and all teachers, whether fledgling instructors or veteran professors, are confronted with intrinsic teaching difficulties growing out of the nature of the discipline.

What Is Social Science?

Social science is a body of knowledge and thought pertaining to human affairs as distinguished from physical objects such as sticks, stones, or stars. The subject matter is man and the basic data are the ascertainable facts about the four billion men, women, and children who inhabit the earth and those from whom they have descended. The social sciences treat all the manifold activities of human beings from their helpless beginnings to their involuntary ends and, as Robert Merton puts it, "from the brain cortex to entire societies." In the broadest sense social science includes all that men on this planet have said, done, felt, and believed.

In the academic world, the social sciences embrace those disciplines that deal primarily with man as a social being—anthropology, sociology, geography, psychology, economics, and political science. These subjects are a counterpart to the life sciences which focus on nonhuman living creatures. Botanists and zoologists investigate life in the natural world while social scientists study the creature who is unique among living things because he thinks, learns, reasons, communicates, uses tools, constructs institutions, builds traditions, worships, and transmits culture. The group life of man is the central focus of these studies and the key question is: What does it mean to be a man in a particular situation? The breadth of inquiry encompasses society and culture, human and institutional relationships, time and space dimensions, social structures and processes.

Although the respective spheres of the various disciplines have not been carefully delineated and none of the fields has limited itself strictly to its major area of investigation, each of the social sciences is concerned primarily with a different manifestation of human life. These manifestations are numerous and complex and embrace not only the observable activities, functions and interrelationships of individuals, regions, groups, classes, associations, movements, and nations but also the values, hopes, and aspirations which constitute the forces motivating them. The specialized branches abstract different elements from the structural context and concentrate on different components of social systems. Thus, psychology devotes itself mainly to the individual as a unique organism; anthropology takes as its point of reference the individual as a member of a particular group; sociology is most interested in processes of social interaction; economics investigates how social systems are organized through systems of exchange; political science focuses on the institutions and processes of government. However, there is almost no form of behavior which is not treated, to some extent, by each of the social sciences. The anthropologist may be primarily concerned with patterns of interrelationships which differentiate one culture from another, but he cannot ignore the ways by which such basic material needs as food, clothing, and shelter are secured, or the structure of familial relationships or the system of authority. These things, from different perspectives, are the concerns of economics, sociology, and political science. The same proliferation of interests characterizes each of the fields. This situation has led one of my departmental colleagues to compare the social sciences to a rather quarrelsome family. "None has a private room, and each has a habit of wearing the others' party dresses."[1]

Terminology and research procedures are far from being standardized among disciplines, or even within disciplines. Hybridization, represented by such fields as political sociology and psycholinguistics, complicates matters still further. There is not even universal agreement on what disciplines should be included. Is law a social science? Are geographers natural scientists? Are historians humanists? These are questions to which there are no definitive answers. The scope of the various fields of inquiry will probably continue to differ from place to place and from one generation to another.[2]

Is it proper to employ the term "science" for such studies? Is it legitimate to draw parallels between conclusions established experimentally in the natural sciences and those of social science? Man's cultural environment is a human creation that is not the product of biological, physical, or chemical processes. The subject matter of natural science is basically uncontroversial but the social sciences treat sensitive matters that are frequently at the storm center of controversy. It is relatively easy to think objectively about cells, plants, molecules, electrons, fossils, and stars. The natural scientist can be absolutely neutral about photosynthesis, the dimensions of a dinosaur, the speed of light, or whether water normally runs uphill or down. But precisely because human behavior occurs in a largely symbolic world patterned by myths, traditions, attitudes, beliefs, and customs and because ideas, opinions, interests, and purposes are the "data" of social science, it is immeasurably more difficult to maintain objectivity when the subject matter involves such problems as war, nuclear proliferation, a population tide threatening to swamp the world, pollution of the environment, critical resource shortages, race relations, ancient religious animosities, taxes, unemployment, distribution of income, urban blight—to name but a few.

In a strict sense, as a "body" of knowledge, social science should have a definite content and positive boundaries. But, in practice, each social observer sets his own limits and to this extent creates his own boundaries. Consequently, in any specific case the subject to be approached does not exist entirely externally to the mind of the scholar investigating it. He, like other human beings, is an encultured person, who has in his own mind the "past" in his way of perceiving, characterizing, and evaluating present events which may affect his selection, conception, and arrangement of the material under examination. Thus, Marx's predictions, based on his observations of nineteenth-century capitalism, did not anticipate the adaptability of Western industrial enterprise, the great growth in the power of labor unions, the innovations of profit-sharing, codetermination, or employee pension fund ownership of large-scale capital in the twentieth century. No social scientist is timeless or placeless. He belongs to a particular society or age; he thinks not only at a given time in history and as an American or Zulu, Moslem or Jew, Catholic or Protestant, as the case may be, but also as a member of an age, sex, class, regional, occupational, or professional group. The "truth" is more a medley of co-existent truths in that all human history teaches us that clashes in belief and conficting interpretations are to be found both within and among societies. In Karl Mannheim's perspectivist view, there are "many" truths shared by those who have had similar experiences and who have agreed among themselves on social aims. The penumbra which encompasses our observations makes universal truth impossible. Thus, the sociology of knowledge would suggest that since freedom from all value is an unrealizable imperative and that to postulate a wholly objective social science is to demand something which is unattainable, to strive for a general theory of society is probably a mistake.

There are other intrinsic difficulties connected with the nature of our subject and the tools of analysis at our disposal. Two points on which all social scientists would agree is that human behavior is less predictable than the phenomena which the natural sciences examine, and that with present methodologies social science has not been able to produce a general integrating theory comprehending the totality of human experience. Not only does Newton's apple continue to fall at the same constant rate of acceleration, but astronomers can now map precisely the position of the stars for millennia. On the contrary, about the best social scientists can do for the year 2000 is to say: "If you decide to do thus and so, this is what will probably happen, assuming the continuation of the circumstances."

We work with an enormous number of variables; we are unable to isolate much of the phenomena in which we are interested; we can make relatively little use of the controlled experiment; most of the sequences with which we deal are unique; we cannot conduct operations research in the scientific sense because we cannot replicate historical events. Consequently, observation, history, documentary evidence, statistics, the questionnaire, and the survey must remain the greater part of our laboratory. The empirical method of science as an instrument for accumulating and authenticating knowledge has a useful, but limited application.

What, then, do the social sciences have in common with the natural sciences? Certainly, the desire to advance knowledge and to understand reality with greater precision. Equally, the necessity to develop methods and techniques of thinking which help the possessor to draw correct conclusions. Further, a certain tentativeness which applies to both in the sense that the generalizations of the so-called "hard" sciences are hypotheses which have thus far resisted disproof. It may be said of social science, as of science in general, that it utilizes procedures not so much for discovering truth as for approaching truth by progressively eliminating error. Even if it is a mistake to look for a general theory of society or to suppose that the social sciences can become as "hard" as the natural, this does not mean that we must retreat into total "a priorism." Even though we can probably never be thoroughgoing positivists, we can still try to behave up to a point as though we were. It is still possible to make many interesting and useful generalizations and to test them by methods modelled on those of natural science. Professor Runciman summarizes the situation pithily: "Although all sciences are sciences, some will remain more scientific than others."[3]

TRENDS IN CONTEMPORARY AMERICAN SOCIAL SCIENCE

The twentieth century has witnessed a tremendous expansion and professionalization of the social sciences. Today's research is often undertaken by teams of technicians making increasingly precise and focused inquiries on specific subjects. The amateur social scientist has all but disappeared as the field has become dominated by specialized academic or governmental professionals. This institutionalization has been accompanied by a growth in university chairs and departments, professional societies, and specialized journals. World War II was a major catalytic event in the history of the social sciences in the United States. Up to 1940 government activities in this field were confined largely to the collection of statistical information. But during the war social scientists carried out more than three hundred projects for the government. The range of subject matter included such diverse studies as estimation of war production requirements, analysis of war-bond sales campaigns, clothing preferences of soldiers, command problems among Negro troops, combat morale, venereal-disease control, and the strategic bombing survey.

The methodological changes made in our century have been considerable as new tools were fashioned for the study of old as well as new questions. These tools were designed to make it possible to investigate rigorously what were previously matters of impression. The theoretical structures of Darwin, Marx, and Comte crumbled, or were seriously weakened, in the face of newer modes of analysis. The Enlightenment's axiom of progress toward democracy gave way to a multilinear theory of political development. The general thrust of the new movement was to introduce greater precision and validation to the study of social phenomena. Consequently, statistical techniques and mathematical treatments tended to displace descriptive and literary discussions. Lacking such instruments as microscopes and telescopes, social scientists turned to model-building, simulation, and game-theory to test their concepts. Data collection has been revolutionized by sampling procedures based on probability theory which have made social surveys, public opinion polls, and very large-scale election and voting studies feasible. Techniques have been elaborated for analyzing small group dynamics and communications content. New functional categories have emerged as refined methods of multivariate analysis have made possible more accurate specifications of variables. The use of computers, whose efficiency permits formerly prohibitive calculations, has further revolutionized methodology. A sizable proportion of the theory that has been constructed has been noninstitutional in character, that is, it has been concerned primarily with explaining the effects of institutions on individual or aggregate behavior, rather than explaining the institution itself. Increasingly, social science has come to be dominated by what has been called the "behavioral persuasion." The sum of these developments has been encapsulated by Bernard Berelson in the following description: "The field has become technical and quantitative, segmentalized and particularized, specialized and institutionalized, modernized and groupized."[4]

The roots of the behavioral movement lie in the work of European scholars such as Max Weber, Herbert L. Tingsten, and Graham Wallas, but the most intensive development has taken place in the United States, particularly since World War II. Earlier in the century, Arthur F. Bentley and Charles E. Merriam had been influential. What has been called the "revolution in the behavioral sciences" is unquestionably the most significant movement in social science in the twentieth century. This revolution has been animated by the belief that there is a qualitative continuity of knowledge and that a universally applicable method exists for its discovery. In the words of Ernest Nagel, this means that in its method of articulating and evaluating evidence, "the social sciences will be continuous with the theories of the natural sciences."[5]

It is undeniable that this emulation of pure science, a new rigor in method, and the avoidance of policy applications have produced continuous controversy and an ongoing debate of a very fundamental nature which has persisted into the present since the second World War. Although the social sciences are not held in universal esteem in lay circles, some of the strongest (and bitterest) criticisms have come from within the disciplines themselves. One has only to attend the annual meetings of professional associations to realize this. As the devotees of greater rigor continue to reject more speculative theory as "nonknowledge," the spectrum of the "postbehavioral" critique has widened. Some adversaries have strongly denounced the pretensions

of a scientific knowledge of human behavior, have scorned the "fe-
tishists" of quantitative techniques, and have characterized the effort
to emulate the methods of natural science as the pursuit of a will-o'-
the-wisp. For these critics the whole idea of explanation as the subsumption of particular events under universal laws has no application
to social science.[6] For persons of this persuasion the attempt to con-
fine human interaction into a model of determinacy constitutes a
misleading simplicity that becomes, ultimately, a grotesque caricature
of the real world of social events. In my own field of political science,
one major difficulty has been that, in revolting against the traditional
historical/legal/institutional approaches and concentrating on the
behavior of individuals (for example, voters), most variances have
been explained in terms of nonpolitical variables. This has tended to
minimize the importance of institutional and political factors and, for
some critics, has taken "politics" out of political science.[7] More
broadly, opponents of contemporary trends charge that, in an effort
to become "powerful explainers," social science has produced a generation of technicians, who stressing method, not substance, have
extracted from an immense wealth of problems only those which can
be readily quantified. In a recent lecture, the distinguished political
scientist, Gabriel A. Almond (who was himself associated with the
behavioral movement of the fifties and sixties), went so far as to
characterize this development as "nomological frenzy" and called
upon his colleagues to reject a demeaning, mechanistic, reductionist
view of social science and to adopt a stance of "epistemic humility."[8]
Other scholars view behavioralism as an ideology using an illusory
pseudoscience to justify applications of technology to society and a
movement implicitly favoring the status quo by its emphasis on maintenance, adaptation, and consensus.[9] Dehumanization, complicity
with the "establishment," irrelevance, ivory-towerism, myopia, trivi-
ality—these are among the more polite terms that have been used.
Finally, there are those who hold that the emphasis on quantification
has limited the scope of our subject matter and has slighted its most
important parts, namely, values. These critics reject what they consider an ideological commitment to social neutrality and repudiate the
nonevaluative stance which they believe has made social scientists
impotent in society. The thrust of this argument comes from those
who believe that the world is in such a state that the time has come
for less theorizing and more application. This view challenges the so-

cial sciences for their seeming unconcern with the actual course of human events and their reluctance to grapple with such massive problems as nuclear confrontation, population explosion, resource depletion, ecological disarray, poverty for billions, and growing racial tensions facing American society and the rest of the world. This perspective emphasizes that in the world of action, we do not, and cannot, act on the basis of scientific certainty. What we can do is to illuminate expected sequences, to clarify the grounds for rational action, and to develop creative options as man searches for solutions to his dilemmas.[10] A closely related proposal advocates a breakdown of the artificial boundaries between the various social sciences so that a multidimensional effort can be employed in the solution of pressing social problems. The term "policy sciences" has been used in this connection. The call here is for confronting the basic problem of making ourselves competent to deal with ends as well as means by providing channels for rational discourse concerning the goals of policy. These demands grow out of the belief that social sciences provide an imperfect, but nevertheless important, resource for informing public-policy judgments in particular areas of behavior by formulating useful propositions about human variables and by elucidating insights, clarifications, and generalizations in terms of which social events and decisions can be more intelligently diagnosed, analyzed, encouraged, or deterred.

In sum, debate and ferment characterize the contemporary state of social science. My advice to any new teacher (or older one for that matter) is to inform himself or herself on the contentious issues of the social sciences and to stake out a position. One is bound to meet the problem of defending his stance in the classroom, possibly on the first day of teaching! I have learned that undergraduates have a way of asking profound questions. A good way to fortify oneself against the inevitable barrage, I believe, is to become knowledgeable in a broad sense about the social sciences as a whole—their origin, scope, development, present conflicts, and future prospects.

TEACHING SOCIAL SCIENCE

It seems to me that the fundamental pedagogical problem which must be faced by a social science teacher is that created by the wealth of misinformation, misconception, illusion, and dogmatism which students bring with them to class. The triple burdens of folk wisdom, represented by aphorisms and proverbs; pop culture, now derived primarily from TV; and complex "feelings" for particular situations which most students bear, are appallingly heavy. The spectrum in my own field of political science is simply stupendous, ranging from such time-honored American attitudes as "all politicians are crooks" or "socialism is evil," to the choice bit of folklore that all Americans have a constitutional right to carry guns. Since the social sciences treat human ideas and conduct, few individuals have no knowledge or interest whatsoever in them. Research on children reveals that even toddlers have views of authority, and preschool children have some sort of experience with government in the family setting. Every person has begun life in a particular culture, has learned how to behave in that culture, and will probably continue to perceive reality through the perspectives of that culture. This is a perfectly understandable state of affairs, for much of what human beings "know" and "feel" about social systems is acquired outside the formal learning process. The enormous power of TV as a social conditioner is just beginning to be understood and it is chilling to reflect how many of our students have developed their ideas of American family life, race relations, consumption patterns, law enforcement, and so on, from "Father Knows Best," "All in the Family," "The Waltons," "Sanford and Son," "Maude," "Kojak," and "Mary Hartman, Mary Hartman." On the positive side, the Senate Watergate hearings and the House Judiciary Committee impeachment inquiry constituted the largest national classroom in American government ever given. The Vietnam War, in living color, observed in millions of living rooms over what seemed an interminable period, undoubtedly contributed to the ultimate resolution of what had become the most unpopular war in American history.

The new student of chemistry or mathematics will quite readily acknowledge his ignorance in these fields. Not so in economics or politics where the teacher is likely to be confronted with a class of students who not only have fixed notions about the subject matter, but even a few who may fancy themselves as experts. One of our most distinguished professors of political science, a veteran of more than forty years of college teaching, wrote shortly before his death:

> In the folklore of government, every American is born free
> and equal, and a little know-it-all as far as government is

concerned. Little children learn to count, they learn to spell, and they learn that 2 plus 2 is 4, but nobody tells them what government is: *they already know.* [Emphasis added][11]

Two other university teachers have commented on the universal ethnocentrism which they have encountered:

> Students already have answers about the world. They will 'know" that one God is better than two (at least at the same time), that private property is better than communal property, that a nation is better than a tribe, and that the rest of the world would be happier if it were more like us. In short, we would find that students are ethnocentric. They believe that *our* way is *the* way, that what is right for us is right for everybody.[12]

If, in addition to these difficulties, the radical ethos of the late sixties which exalts impulse, feeling, and passion over thought, reason, and cerebration were to prevail among our students, I hesitate to contemplate how our teaching problems would increase.

I conceive of my very first teaching objective as giving the student the factual background, conceptual apparatus, and analytic skill, so that he can cross over the gulf from the side where a simplistic, misinformed, and common-sense view of the world governs, to the other shore where a reflective, mature, and sophisticated outlook on social reality prevails. Of course, there is a good deal to be said for what Samuelson has called *relevant* common sense, arrived at after possibilities have been excluded and probabilities have been reduced. But "the content of *pure* common sense—like that of the self-cancelling folk aphorisms of a people—tends to be nil."[13]

I could not say that there is *any one single thing* that I do to achieve this goal; *everything* I do is calculated toward this end. My whole course is dedicated to the development of the habit of rationality, respect for evidence, and the enlargement of the student's visions beyond his narrow personal experiences and immediate horizons. My hope is that each student will emerge with a wider range of factual content, a more critical attitude toward generalizations about human behavior, a healthy skepticism about the finality of our present state of knowledge, and a critically self-conscious philosophy that he can employ in making his own evaluations and decisions.

Teaching Undergraduate Courses

Preparation, Organization, and Execution

How does one proceed to organize and prepare for teaching a course? The examples which I outline in some detail below are drawn from the elementary levels of college instruction where most novice teachers are assigned. They are based primarily on my experience in teaching the introductory course in American government and politics—the single course by which most students are introduced to the discipline of political science. I have offered this course (usually to classes of more than one hundred students) over a period of thirty-two years at New York University. However, some of my suggestions grow out of upper-division courses in political parties and Congress (usually with registrations of from thirty-five to fifty), and with both of these courses I have had much experience. I hope these specifics will be helpful, although I am mindful of the extreme difficulty in recapturing the quality of a classroom experience or in evoking its atmosphere.

1. *Thinking About the Course* The first considerations to which attention should be directed are: "Where will the course be given?" "Who will be in the class?" "Under what conditions will the course be given?" In other words, will the course be offered in a community college, in a distinguished small undergraduate college, or in a large university? Will the students be primarily affluent, largely middle-class, or drawn from disadvantaged backgrounds? Or a mix? Will they be teen-agers or adults? Americans or foreigners? Is the institution located in a small city, in a teeming metropolis, or on a sylvan campus? Will the students be majors or nonmajors? Will they be pre-law, pre-medicine, pre-journalism, or general liberal arts matriculants? Will they be drawn from diverse components such as business, education, or nursing schools? Will sections be limited in size, say thirty-five, or will the enrollment be unlimited resulting in class size of several hundred? If the latter, will teaching assistants be assigned to the instructor? Will the course be offered in the day or in the evening? What library facilities will be available? These preliminary considerations are very important because they impinge directly on such central decisions as: what teaching style is appropriate (lecture, discussion, or some combination); how best to motivate the student in terms of his own background and experience; what community re-

sources can be employed for field work; how to select and organize the subject matter to be presented; what reading and illustrative materials to choose. My own experience with the introductory course has been in a large urban university, with big sections, populated by students from various undergraduate schools, with great differentials in background based on social class, age, previous preparation, nationality, and educational objective. Practically every class contains a few severely handicapped students who suffer from blindness, cerebral palsy, dwarfism, or other serious malady. Although the class always has a goodly number of majors, most of the students will take no further courses in political science.

After analyzing the setting, the teacher should then ask and answer the question: What do I want to do with and for these students? I presume that one's own views of liberal education are most relevant here. As a political science instructor, I share with most teachers in the liberal arts the common goal of fostering knowledge and effective thinking—which should be informed, accurate, critical, and independent. In my view, these two are correlative—knowledge, in any real sense, cannot be acquired without thinking and genuine thought is impossible without knowledge. I do not try to make the students into political scientists, but rather to convey the significance of politics in the social order and to make political processes understandable to those who are not technically trained. I do not attempt to give practical training in the art of politics (how best to run for office, how to manage a campaign, how to lobby, and so on), but to impart knowledge about politics in a clear, vivid, and realistic manner. I do not seek to impart values or to impose my own political preferences, but to develop the student's own talent for valuation. I make no conscious effort to produce a good citizen, but rather a human being whose intellectual power is greater at the end of the course than at the begining.

2. *"Facts" vs. "Theory"* For many years, a principal criticism of college teaching by students has been that it is too much concerned with an amassing of facts which are not readily retained and which soon become obsolescent, and that student achievement is too often judged on the basis of mere recall of informational specifics. From a different perspective, many professional educators and scholars in the social sciences agree, and have consciously tried to do something about it. As a consequence, over the past few decades a major trend

has been to discourage mere coverage, retention, and regurgitation of facts and to move in the direction of learning skills. The emphasis is more on the nature of the inquiry than on sheer information or, indeed, on the importance of the conclusions reached. The trend which puts major emphasis on methods, particularly those based on induction, has gone so far that, to many in the field, the social science disciplines have become "all medium and no message."[14] Teachers are often torn between what they deem adequate coverage of content and use of methodologies which require time for an examination of propositions, a review of evidence, reflection, and an appraisal of the proof on which knowledge claims rest.

I believe that it is possible to achieve a proper balance between the two extremes of the low cognitive level of "mere" facts and excessive preoccupation with technique. For me, Daniel Bell strikes the right note: "As between the secondary school, with its emphasis on primary skills and factual data, and the graduate or professional school, whose necessary concern is with specialization and technique, the distinctive function of the college is to deal with the grounds of knowledge: not *what* one knows but *how* one knows."[15] Of course, the heuristic questions: "How do you know that?" and "How can that be known?" are fundamental tools in instruction at the college level. Bodies of knowledge are not ever larger collections of facts, but organizations of facts into concepts, generalizations, and interpretations, and, at higher levels of abstraction, propositions, models, and theories. To be at all intelligible, facts must be grouped, classified, and arranged. However, it should be emphasized that facts are still very important in learning as essential prerequisites to an understanding of principles, concepts, and generalizations. It is necessary to construct the hierarchy of knowledge in any given field on a factual foundation. The new teacher of American government might well think about what factual information he believes the students must possess about Congress, for example, such as the size of each chamber, terms of office, methods of election, campaign finance, types of constituencies, characteristics of leaders, committee system, party organization, official rules, informal norms, and relationships with the executive branch, before undertaking to conceptualize about Congress in an analytical construct or framework based on decision-making, conflict management, communications flow, linkage, interest aggregation, structural-functionalism, or systems theory. A considerable amount of thought about the balance which the instructor wants to achieve is basic to his working out the details of his course.

3. *Preparing the Course* It is well to make an outline for your own guidance which will include the goals of the course, the subject matter which it will encompass, together with a rough approximation of how much time you will spend on various sections or modules, the textbook, package of paperbacks, or other readings which you will assign, and the term papers or special projects which you will employ in furtherance of the course objectives. From this outline, a syllabus for distribution to the students can be prepared which will also include specifics on examinations. I think it especially important in teaching undergraduates, many of whom will be freshmen, that the students know what the course attempts to accomplish and what the course requirements are, in rather precise terms. With regard to required readings, I have found it best to use a comprehensive textbook and supplement it with a book of readings.[16] It is good practice to leave some room for assignment of additional readings: for example, a major presidential proposal, an important Supreme Court decision, significant Congressional hearings, a particularly perceptive journal article, which may appear during the course of the term. I also follow the practice of leaving some leeway in the course outline for time to consider topics that the students might wish to bring up for discussion. In my field, major political events of great significance may occur during the course of the semester which are unforeseen at the time of preparation of the course (the Cuban missile crisis, the assassination of President Kennedy, President Johnson's decision not to seek reelection, the Cambodian invasion, Watergate, the New York City fiscal crisis, Jimmy Carter's unexpected primary triumphs—come to mind as examples). Another possibility to be anticipated is that the students may have special difficulties with some concepts so that more time may be required for them than originally intended. If the only choice is between comprehensiveness and depth, I choose the latter. As Alfred North Whitehead counseled: "What you teach, teach thoroughly." A frantic effort to "cover the syllabus" is not the ultimate virtue, for a too rapid survey, unmindful of the capabilities of the students, will serve no intellectual purpose.

4. *Introducing the Subject Matter* I do not begin the course by introducing any overriding "grand theme" or approach, such as the "end of liberalism" or "domination by elites." The course is not or-

ganized within a particular framework of analysis such as structural-functionalism, public policy, or systems theory. Instead, I expose the students to the ideas of several major schools, utilize the insights from a wide range of scholarship, and draw upon such theoretical interpretations as seem appropriate at different points in the course. Thus, in several contexts, the students become acquainted with the methods by which mature scholars seek to advance knowledge and understanding in the field.

Starting with the assumption that the students have only the vaguest idea of what is meant by political science, but have some notions of government and politics, we begin by discussing political activities and policy outcomes which flow from governmental decisions, rather than commencing the course at an abstract level of analysis. I begin by observing that society is a network of relationships arising out of the variety of ways that people are organized within it. From time immemorial man has employed organizations and institutions to meet the problems intrinsic to his relationships to the natural environment and to other men. He has organized to cultivate the earth, to hunt for food, to distribute produce, to trade, to move from one place to another, to worship, to procreate, to educate his young, to enjoy himself, to protect himself, to make war, to keep peace. Each of these organizational activities orders relationships by designing procedures to be followed, conferring powers or status, assigning tasks, and establishing rights. One of the most important organizations which man has created to achieve his purposes is government. The fact that of the four billion human beings in the world only a handful live outside a governmental system, testifies to the impotence of anarchism as a political movement.

From there we go on to discuss what governments do and to consider what might happen if we were suddenly deprived of government services such as the courts, education, police and fire protection, waste disposal, potable water, transportation, hospitals, welfare assistance, and so on. If you live or work in New York City, there is no dearth of vivid illustrations as several of these functions have gone awry within the memory of the students. This introductory material is handled by discussion rather than lecture. Since our focus is on the American system, a useful exercise is to ask the students to find out just what services New York City (or San Francisco, Boston, Atlanta, or Oshkosh), New York state (or Arizona, Idaho, or Virginia), and the United States provide. There are standard reference works to which the students can be directed where this information can readily be secured.

We then proceed to examine why Americans have turned increasingly to government for the solution of their problems. How are these decisions made? By whom? Who benefits? Who pays? How are citizens induced to cooperate? How does a particular segment of citizens organize itself to secure things which it desires but to which other citizens are indifferent or opposed?

From these applications, we can then turn to the ways that have been developed to study and understand them. It can be pointed out at this time that the study of political phenomena has progressed through various stages from superstition to something approaching science and that we have a rich store of material on which to draw. The student comes to appreciate that political thought has been an essential part of the study of man, with its roots embedded in the recognition since antiquity of the importance of political power in every organized society—a recognition that has led to more than two thousand years of speculation concerning the nature and scope of acceptable power and a search for principles to legitimatize it and a structure to make it effective. Because in a whole lifetime one could not possibly read what has already been written about government and politics and because relevant new facts continually appear, those who are engaged in its study must in some manner reduce to order and generalization the vast scope of the field and must search for the most revealing techniques to accomplish this purpose.

With this background, the instructor could discuss one of the major contemporary organizing constructs of political science, for example, the widely employed "political systems" concept. This concept is an abstraction which organizes a variety of participants, processes, and institutions, and which seeks to clarify the functions which decisions fulfill. It involves the whole complex of activities by which "the authoritative allocation of values in society" are made and presents the political system as a network of interrelationships by which men and women decide which goals and aspirations will be written into public policy and enforced in society. Its concern ranges from individual political awareness and interests to the complex operation of large political institutions.[17]

A final point to emphasize during the introductory section of the course is that the "known" of political science undergoes continual change as the field develops. With the help of appropriate readings the students can learn how new concepts have replaced or supplemented older ones and how systematic inquiry has expanded or reconstructed existing knowledge. Widely accepted interpretations of the pre–World War II era have been overturned when subjected to empirical test. For example, an earlier understanding of American democracy included the assumption that its efficacy depended on a popular consensus on fundamental democratic principles. Another assumption was that malapportionment of the state legislatures substantially affected political outputs. Still another supposition was that the degree of party competition is related to levels of government activity. New research on these matters has discredited these formerly universally accepted generalizations. It is now widely believed that American democracy is far more dependent upon a consensus among elites than one within the masses, that policies which might have been favored by the underrepresented are no more in evidence in fairly apportioned legislatures than in those which are malapportioned, and that the states which have vigorous competition between two parties, and which are comparable in wealth, industrialization, and urbanization, are not more liberal in welfare or education expenditures. Whether a state is dominated by the Republicans or the Democrats or whether there is a high or a low level of electoral participation make only a negligible difference. Most of the variances found were accounted for by differences in economic development among the fifty states.[18] Studies of this kind can be utilized to demonstrate how political scientists, by using new research tools and by freeing themselves from the conventional wisdom and reformist prescriptions of the past, have succeeded in demolishing a number of hoary clichés about American politics.

5. *The Role of Relevance* One of the great academic battle cries of the late sixties was "relevance." In a national study, the Carnegie Commission on Higher Education found that 91 percent of the 70,000 undergraduates surveyed wanted their course-work to be "more relevant to contemporary life and problems"; 71 percent of their teachers shared this view.[19] If by relevance is meant an aimless and endless unstructured discussion of transitory events, or a series of moral exhortations on what is good or bad about persons or groups in the public eye—I'm against it! A shortsighted quest for mere con-

temporaneity is utterly self-defeating. If the world were static, this might be possible, but precisely because it is dynamic, no education that does not deal in time, development, adaptation, progress, or decline can be valuable. Isolation in the present is as stultifying as isolation in the past. Arthur Bestor has said that the student who devotes his whole time to contemporary problems is betting that the clock will hereafter stand still, but, that by the very nature of the universe, the cards are stacked against him.[20] Loren Eiseley has made the same point: "A now that is truly now has no future."[21]

If, on the other hand, relevance is taken to mean the use of contemporary events as illustrations of fundamental issues, problems, or principles, or as examples for generalization purposes, it can be the basis for that "mix" of immediacy and perspective that is one of the best classroom tools that we have. Here are a few examples. A few years ago, my students were intensely interested in two important matters then before Congress—the eighteen-year-old vote question and the women's rights amendment. At appropriate places in the course, I used these two measures to illustrate the procedure for constitutional amendment, congressional rules, differences in House/Senate procedures, and voting characteristics of the American electorate. I believe that the students acquired much more knowledge about these matters than they would have learned if I had chosen Prohibition as the illustration—which as far as they are concerned might have taken place during the Punic Wars. The interest in these subjects was high throughout the semester and contributed to the liveliness of the discussion.

During the 1972–1974 period, a cyclonic complex of events, collectively known as "Watergate," induced the greatest crisis in American government since the Civil War. After the original break-in of Democratic headquarters in Washington, the drama proceeded through an incredible stream of revelations about the Nixon White House, including what was later characterized as the "cover-up," the so-called "Saturday night massacre," the continued claims of "executive privilege," the Ervin Senate Committee hearings, the Supreme Court decision ordering the surrender of the tapes, the indictment of several high administration officials, including the attorney general, the impeachment inquiry by the House Judiciary Committee, the resignation of the president, followed by the granting of a pardon to him by his appointed successor. During this entire period, interest of students in American government was at a peak, evidenced by burgeoning enrollments. The high drama of this unprecedented situation stimulated interest, concern, and just plain curiosity. Moreover, it provided an unparalleled opportunity to analyze and discuss almost all fundamental features of the American political system including the principle of separation of powers, the growth in the size and power of the presidency to what some have called imperial dimensions, the fragility of civil liberties under an onslaught undertaken in the name of "national security," the importance in a democracy of a free press, the independence of the judiciary, the significance of the rule of law, the powers of Congress to impeach and, last but not least, the power of an aroused citizenry. As the story unfolded, the scope and intensity of developments were reported on radio and especially TV in such a fashion as to heighten the drama and suspense and bring Watergate's multifaceted aspects to public attention in a way in which no public question had ever been presented before. For students and teachers of American government, the crisis provided a learning tool par excellence. Nor are all of Watergate's consequences yet fully known. Certainly, the moral structure of the presidency has been diminished, executive-legislative relations have entered a new cycle, and there is substantial evidence that large numbers of Americans have become disillusioned and cynical about politics and politicians—at least, incumbents. A crucial distinction must be made between the disenchantment produced by Watergate and a continuing faith in the basic political institutions of the nation. Perhaps this is the secret of Jimmy Carter's startlingly successful primary campaign for the nomination of his party, appealing as it did to the pride and not the guilt of American voters. Of all the candidates, Carter alone, in the first presidential campaign after the Watergate trauma, had the prescience to sense the people's desire for a way to restore their relationship to a political system traditionally personified by its president. This might well be one of the principal themes of classes as the nation enters its third century.

One final point on relevance. The ideal use of contemporary issues is not merely to use them as part of the passing scene in a classroom version of a rap session, but to incorporate them into a contextual framework that makes the institution or process which one is discussing more vivid and meaningful for the students. If I were asked what is the classroom method on which I rely the most, my response would be that it is the weaving together of day-to-day changes and developments with the fundamental continuities.

6. *Teaching Styles* It must be acknowledged that each of several styles of teaching has its own excellence. At least five faculty prototypes have been identified: the drillmaster, the content-centered, the instructor-centered, the intellect-centered, and the person-centered.[22] We have all, as former students ourselves, known teachers who employed particular modes of instruction with varying degrees of success. There is no single exclusive method of good teaching any more than there is a "perfect" teacher. Brilliant lecturers may be much less effective in seminars. Some teachers excel in advanced work, some perform best at the introductory level. Effective teachers are not necessarily more learned than those who are less successful, but more resourceful and creative in stimulating students. A popular teacher is not necessarily a good one, although there is probably some correlation between the identification of the student with the teacher and his motivation to learn. If instructors do not find teaching pleasurable and are consequently frustrated or even hostile to students, the learning process is inhibited. Most teachers who, in today's parlance, "turn off" the students are probably not very effective. In addition to an instructor's personal predilections, style should be closely related to the students' level of preparation and the conditions under which the class meets: size of enrollment, type of room, length of class period, library facilities and technical equipment which is available.

Most of my undergraduate teaching has taken place in large lecture halls. In the introductory course, my enrollment has ranged from 90 to 250 students; in advanced sections it has never been smaller than 35. In the typical situation of the large class, meeting twice a week for one hour and fifteen minutes, I utilize a combination of lecture and discussion. I do not share the low estimate of the lecture method which has been in vogue for several years. A well thought-out, clearly presented lecture serves several educational objectives. A major segment or unit of the course can be presented; texts or other assigned readings can be updated; the student can be provided with a structure within which he can better organize what he is learning; emphasis can be added to those points most directly related to course objectives. Dreary recapitulation of the text or an incessant recitation of facts is always disastrous. However, my classes are something less than completely formal affairs. Usually I devote the last fifteen minutes of a period to questions and comment. Structured in this way, the discussion tends to flow from the major points made during the lecture, rather than degenerating into a desultory question and answer period on factual material. If a question or comment is too far afield, I will rule it out, but if it can be related, I will make every effort to place it in the context of the main body of the presentation of that day. It has been a happy experience for me that discussion frequently goes beyond the allotted time—if the room is free.

Although there is undeniably an element of showmanship in successful lecturing, flamboyance and mere entertainment are not only in bad taste but something the students see through very quickly. One of my former colleagues used to begin his course by asking a student for a dollar bill, touching a lighted match to it and then dramatically declaiming as it burned: "That's what I think of capitalism." Pure gimmickry! Thorough preparation, good organization, clarity, vitality, honest enthusiasm for the subject, ability to excite and maintain interest and to motivate the students for further learning—these are the hallmarks of the good lecturer. In my own practice, apart from the academic aspects, there are a few things that I do which I believe conduce to these objectives. I always stand, never use lecture notes, do not use a microphone, but speak in a louder-than-conversational tone, and look directly at the students.

There is one further aspect of style on which I would like to comment. In recent years, it has become somewhat fashionable for faculty members to seek "rapport" with the students by a variety of devices such as requesting that students call them by their first names, conducting classes while sitting on the floor in a circle of students, or speaking incessantly in the rather boring street slang or obscenities of the moment—informing students that they will "tell it like it is," or "where it's at," that "President Ford is full of ——————" or that "Congress is all —————— up." This conscious aping of the style of some youths by their insecure elders is something that I do not believe a majority of the students wish or admire. After all, many of them do these things themselves purely as a result of peer pressure. In my experience, mutually satisfying relationships seem to be best promoted by role differentiation and the maintenance of a certain social distance—not to be confused with authoritarianism, stuffiness, aloofness, lack of genuine interest, unfriendliness, or hostility. Robert Frost, although not describing the teacher-student relationship, was profoundly right when he wrote: "Good fences make good neighbors."

Further, at the fees these students, their parents, or the public are paying, the very least we can do is to provide one place where they can hear the mother tongue spoken with somewhat greater elegance than that reflected in the current *Umgangsprache.*

One of my most brilliant undergraduate students, now doing advanced graduate work at Chicago, remarked a few years ago in the privacy of my office during an advisement session that at first he had been attracted by the "informal" approach of some of his "new-style" professors, but that as time went on and the novelty wore off, he was less and less impressed. His final summary was: "You know, Professor, that stuff is really ——————." I agreed with him.

7. *Examinations and Evaluations* It has been said that for many students education consists in little more than sporadic preparation for examinations. If true, this is more a reflection on teachers than it is on students. Most learning theorists view knowledge of results, feedback and reinforcement as important elements of learning. A grade or evaluation gives a student information on his performance in a specific course, an approximate measure of his relative academic achievement, and a system of rewards that can stimulate both good and poorer students to work harder. The student who is not examined, or to whom examinations are not returned or returned without comment, is deprived of the advantages of evaluative feedback, thus affecting his capacity for further learning.

Contrary to rhetorical bombast sometimes uttered at faculty meetings, grades are *not* estimations of a student's inherent intellectual ability, observations about his character or evaluations of his basic worth as a human being. Judgment of students as "persons," as demanded by some students and faculty, is, in my opinion, not only impossible and undesirable; it will tend to make relationships between students and faculty even more tenuous than they are presently in the sense that teachers may actually avoid contacts with students out of hesitation to make such personalized judgments.

In my classes, I give only essay examinations. Although there is the temptation to prepare objective tests which can be marked electronically (or by graduate students), thus saving me an enormous amount of time, the fatal defect of the objective examination, in placing far too much emphasis on mere factual recall and memorization, has impelled me to resist. My preference for the essay stems from its adaptability as an instrument for evaluating the student's understanding of principles, concepts, and interrelationships. It challenges the student's ability to organize, to make judgments, to express opinions, to demonstrate originality in a way that no objective test which I have ever seen can possibly accomplish. It has been my experience that the time spent in constructing examinations carefully is worth the effort. It is important to select questions significantly related to course objectives, to state the questions with clarity, to specify any restrictions on scope or length of answer, and to indicate the relative weight of each question asked.

When my classes have been exceptionally large, I have been provided with a graduate assistant. Among other duties, these young teachers-in-training assist with grading. My practice is to go over the examination carefully with the assistant, or even make up the examination jointly if he or she is a well-advanced student. The degree of responsibility imposed on the assistant is dependent upon his relative maturity, experience, and level of professional development. After the mid-term exams have been graded, the assistant and I share the task of counseling those students who are in academic difficulties or who, for any other reason, wish to discuss the course. I believe this practice serves a good purpose. One of the most basic deficiencies of the grading system, as I see it, is that far more attention is paid to the evaluation of student achievement at the end of the course than informing him of his progress as the term proceeds. Going over the exam, remediation suggestions, instruction in better study habits, and subject matter clarification can be very useful to some students who seek help. To engage in a plea-bargaining session with a student (If I don't get an A, I won't get into law school) is a fatal mistake—to be avoided at all costs.

8. *Term Papers and Special Projects* Another method of evaluating a student's work is by means of a term paper or special project. Advantages here are that the student has some leeway to select a topic that interests him and to handle the material in an individualistic manner.

An example of a project which I have used that the students seem to enjoy is the following. I ask each student to prepare a report on either his own congressional district or another of his choice. The student is specifically directed to find out the physical, demographic, and electoral variables which affect the district's social, economic, and political character. In other words, how many people live in the district? What are they like, in terms of age, race, religion, ethnic background, education, labor union membership, income? What are the physical characteristics of the district—urban, coastal, mountainous, plains? Does it possess significant regional characteristics? What industries are located there? What agriculture? What military installations such as army forts, air bases, navy yards? What are the identifiable pressure groups? Is the district undergoing important changes in terms of population distribution, political or economic trends? What is the election history of the district? How many qualified voters participate in elections? Are there any groups that do not? Who represents the district? What are his or her characteristics in terms of age, religion, ethnicity, occupation, previous political experience, military record? What is his seniority position in his party and in the House as a whole? What are his committee assignments? What is his area of legislative specialization? What is his relationship to the political organizations in the district? Is he a spokesman for any pressure groups in his district or state? What is his voting record on major issues? How often does he visit the district? What "errand boy" chores does he perform for his constituents? How is he perceived in the constituency? By his peers in Congress? Is he perceived differently by various pressure groups? Is the seat "safe" or "marginal?" What kind of campaign does he wage? By whom is it financed? What appear to be the future political prospects in the district?

After directing the students to the standard reference works where they can find materials (*Census Abstracts, Congressional District Data Book, Congressional Directory, Congressional Record, Congressional Quarterly,* etc.), I tell them to use whatever other means they wish in order to complete the assignment, for example, interviews with the congressman, his opponents, other local politicians, constituents, local newspaper editors or columnists, civic leaders, pressure-group representatives.

Although some of these reports turn out to be quite pedestrian, I am always amazed at the ingenuity and enterprise which this assignment evokes in many of the students. One New York student chose the district of the late Mendel Rivers of South Carolina, then chairman of the House Armed Services Committee. This student drove to Charleston over a long weekend and managed to interview Rivers, his most recent primary opponent, the leading newspaper editor, and a sampling of constituents. Another student succeeded in securing a taped interview with a senior congressman from Brooklyn who, in the most vivid and candid language, excoriated the chairman of the Senate Foreign Relations Committee. I played that tape in class not only for its "color," but to illustrate the widely differing House/Senate orientations to the war in Vietnam existing at that time. Still another student flew to his home town in Maine to interview constituents on what they knew about their congressman, how well they were acquainted with his record, what they considered the most important function of a congressman, what his reputation was, and so on. These interviews were recorded on tape and were really choice, Yankee accents and all. Playing this tape in class gave many students in the class the flavor of a small town in Maine, something completely outside the range of most of their experiences. One semester, a young man from the suburbs chose as his congressman Representative Charles B. Rangel. To get a "feel" for the district, this student visited Harlem for the first time in his life. His reactions to the sights, sounds, and smells of a part of New York which he had never visited before and his favorable impression of the congressman whom he interviewed in his district office were so powerful that he ended up volunteering to work in Rangel's reelection campaign.

I think this assignment serves many purposes. Not only does the student become acquainted with a wide variety of official sources and standard references, he is also challenged to synthesize a large body of data into an organized whole. He is dealing with a great many variables and has to order them in some meaningful way. Another inestimable value is that the student begins to acquire the "feel" of politics. Individuals, formerly only names in the newspapers or pictures on campaign literature, are seen in "living color." Several students have informed me that, as a result of work on this assignment, they have become political activists. One has been elected to a city council in New Jersey, another has been appointed youth coordinator for one of the major parties in New York state, still another "went west" where, after three years, he was nominated for the State Assembly in Wyoming. A young woman, with no practical experience in politics whatsoever, after completing her project on a Minnesota district, and pursuing numerous leads with politicians from that state, ended up on Senator Humphrey's 1972 presidential-nomination campaign staff.

Concluding Observations on College Teaching

Thomas Fuller, commenting on teaching in England in the middle of the seventeenth century, wrote as follows: "There is scarce any profession in the commonwealth more necessary which is so slightly performed."[23] Is this observation as true of college teaching in the United States in the latter part of the twentieth century? If we only knew! The visibility of our performance is still low and few people believe we have learned how to measure teaching ability. The classroom remains, in Blanche Geer's striking phrase, "a lonely eminence."[24] One thing we do know: students all over the country desire more emphasis on teaching and greater attention to teaching in considering faculty members for advancement, tenure, and salary increments.[25]

There are probably very few college teachers, whether senior, experienced veterans, or newly minted Ph.D.s who can approach the subject of teaching without trepidation or, at least, humility. This is true even though most teachers have an implicit educational philosophy and devote some thought to the problems of higher education. When we consider how awesome is our task and how exiguous our ability to test our efficacy, we can only conclude that to teach at all is to be an optimist. Our "results" may not appear for several years, and then only in the minds of our students and the society which they will fashion. We are really sowers of unseen harvests.

Fortunately, we learn as we teach. Every teacher I know will testify to this. Conscientious teachers are continually evaluating themselves in terms of their course objectives and reassessing the success of their method. Since teachers in democratic societies set the goals of their courses, they can control to some extent the means, in terms of method and content, by which they expect to achieve those goals. However, it should be recalled that such significant factors as the previous preparation of students, class size, and availability of resources to support the course-work, such as library and laboratory facilities, are frequently completely outside the control of the teacher. The current plight of the teacher in many institutions is a real one. He is required to teach an ever increasing number of students who have great unevenness of background and academic level as well as disparate expectations concerning college work. At the same time, he must attempt to cope with the knowledge explosion. In many fields, there is a veritable mountain of new material to be read, digested, organized, and prepared.

Moreover, our efforts to keep abreast of the expansion of knowledge cannot be narrowly restricted to our own discipline. Our assignment, in the social sciences certainly, is communication in the context of real-life conditions. To maximize our effectiveness, we should be prepared to spread our active awareness beyond the scholarship in our own speciality and to draw upon the rich possibilities for vivid illustration from other fields. Social science clearly does not provide the only way of looking at social phenomena. Artists, poets, dramatists, novelists, moralists, and even travelers have produced a vast literature on the life of nations, races, classes, groups, associations, and individuals. Some of our most profound illuminations about man are derived from such sources. Picasso's great painting, *Guernica,* may convey more about the Spanish Civil War than all the books written about that tragic human event.

Of course, we cannot teach everything. What we can attempt is the creation of interests, attitudes, and skills that make continuing self-education possible. This I perceive as our ultimate goal—a body of citizens who think. An operational difficulty for many teachers lies in the necessity to generalize without sufficient detail or to present so many details that the meaningful generalizations are lost. The special genius of the good teacher lies in his competence in choosing the fundamental questions to be asked. Ideally, the student should be able to relate concepts learned in one class to a mass of material considered in another and to life situations in the everyday world of reality. Our task is to assist the student in the development of intellectual powers which he can employ in various contexts. A great watershed in the learning process is reached when the student discovers that conceptual ordering can be exciting, when he strengthens the ability to relate the subject matter to his own goals and values, and when he begins, we hope, the life-long process of searching for principles and meaning in the kaleidoscopic unfolding of events. The synthesis must take place in the mind of the student.

Is teaching any better today than in the time of Socrates? What qualities make for the most effective teaching? What is greatness as applied to teaching? These are questions for which only subjective answers can be given. Despite the avalanche of theories about teaching, there remains an elusive mystique about our craft which defies the imposition of objectifiable criteria beyond the minimal requirements of intelligence, knowledge of our subject matter, and an ability to communicate. Having said that, it might be easy to conclude that great teachers are "born" and that we can do little to improve. I do not believe that. Within the limits of our capabilities and personalities, we can, by exchange of information, study of published material relating to college teaching and, most important, constant self-evaluation, improve our performance in the classroom.

To those aspiring teachers who are contemplating the academic life I can only say that for me teaching has brought profound satisfaction. I have passed through the various stages of teaching ex-GIs in the late forties, the so-called "silent generation" of the fifties, the "now generation" of the sixties, and the very serious, career-oriented students of the present. After more than three decades at a large, urban, bustling, crowded (and almost always crisis-ridden) university, I look back upon the 30,000 students whom I have taught with no regrets. Nor am I discouraged by future prospects. I look forward to a few thousand more before retirement and acknowledge my immense debt to my students from whom I have learned so much about life, teaching, American youth, and myself. Erasmus has called our vocation laborious (although not deplorable), but my own sentiments have been best expressed by B. J. Chute: "When experience joins with integrity, and discipline with delight, the process of teaching and learning can become nothing short of marvelous."[26]

NOTES

1. Alfred de Grazia, *The Elements of Political Science* (New York: Knopf, 1952), p. 7.

2. *The International Encyclopedia of the Social Sciences* (New York: Macmillan, 1968) includes anthropology, economics, geography (except physical), history, law, political science, psychiatry, psychology, sociology, and statistics (because of its close relationship to the social sciences).

3. W. G. Runciman, *Social Science and Political Theory* (Cambridge: Cambridge University Press, 1965), p. 21.

4. *The Behavioral Sciences Today* (New York: Basic Books, 1963), p. 8.

5. "Problems of Concept and Theory Formation in the Social Sciences," in *Science, Language and Human Rights* (Philadelphia: American Philosophical Association, 1952), p. 63.

6. See, for example, John G. Gunnell, "Social Science and Political Reality: The Problem of Explanation," *Social Research* 35 (Spring, 1968): 159–201.

7. V. O. Key, Jr., and Frank Munger, "Social Determinism and Electoral Decision: The Case of Indiana," in Eugene Burdick and Arthur J. Brodbeck, eds., *American Voting Behavior* (New York: Free Press, 1959), pp. 281–299.

8. "Clouds, Clocks, and the Future of Political Science," James Stokes Lecture, New York University, March 29, 1976.

9. See, for example, M. Surkin and A. Wolfe, eds., *An End to Political Science* (New York: Basic Books, 1970).

10. For a recent exposition of this view, see Robert A. Dahl, "Political Analysis—Science, Advocacy, or Clarification?", James Stokes Lecture, New York University, April 12, 1976.

11. E. E. Schattschneider, *Two Hundred Million Americans in Search of a Government* (New York: Holt, Rinehart, and Winston, 1969), p. 3.

12. Donald Johnson and Leon Clark, "Ethnocentrism and the Social Studies," in Herbert Ira London, ed., *Social Science: Theory, Structure and Application* (New York: New York University Press, 1975), p. 309.

13. Paul A. Samuelson, "What Economists Know," in Daniel Ler-

ner, ed., *The Human Meaning of the Social Sciences* (Cleveland: Meridian Books, 1959), p. 185.

14. See Herbert Ira London, *Social Science Theories: Structure and Application* (New York: New York University Press, 1975), p. vii.
15. Quoted in William Buchanan, *Understanding Political Variables* (New York: Charles Scribner's Sons, 1969), p. 1.
16. For example, in the fall of 1976, I used Raymond E. Wolfinger, et. al., *Dynamics of American Politics* (Englewood Cliffs, N.J.: Prentice-Hall, 1976), 633 pp. (including bibliography and the Constitution); and John F. Manley, *American Government and Public Policy* (New York: Macmillan, 1976), 506 pp.
17. The most influential treatments of this concept are to be found in three books by David Easton: *The Political System* (New York: Knopf, 1953); *A System Analysis of Political Life* (New York: John Wiley, 1965); and *A Framework for Political Analysis* (Englewood Cliffs, N.J.: Prentice-Hall, 1965). An excellent brief description of the "political system" concept can be found in Frank J. Sorauf, *Perspectives on Political Science* (Columbus: Charles E. Merrill, 1965), pp. 3–8.
18. See Herbert McClosky, "Consensus and Ideology in American Politics," *American Political Science Review* 58 (June 1964): 361–382; Thomas R. Dye, *Politics, Economics, and the Public* (Chicago: Rand McNally, 1966), Ch. III; Ira Sharkansky, *Spending in the American States* (Chicago: Rand McNally, 1968).
19. *New York Times,* 16 January 1971.
20. Arthur Bestor, *The Restoration of Learning* (New York: Knopf, 1955), p. 126.
21. *The New York Times Annual Education Review,* 11 January 1971, p. 49.
22. Joseph Axelrod, "Teaching Styles," in *Effective College Teaching* (Washington, D.C.: American Association for Higher Education, 1970), p. 43.
23. Thomas Fuller, *The Holy State and the Profane State* (1642).
24. *The International Encyclopedia of the Social Sciences* (1968), pp. 560–565, "Teaching."
25. A whopping 95 percent took this position, according to a report of the Carnegie Commission. See note 19, *supra.*
26. *The New York Times Book Review,* 29 November 1970, p. 30.

JOHN G. WEIGER

Teaching Foreign Language and Literature

JOHN G. WEIGER (Ph.D., Indiana University) is Professor of Romance languages at the University of Vermont. Previously he taught at the University of Colorado and Lawrence University. From 1968 to 1976 he served at the University of Vermont as assistant dean, associate dean, and dean of the College of Arts and Sciences. He is the author of *Introduction to the Youthful Deeds of the Cid, The Valencian Dramatists of Spain's Golden Age,* and *Hacia la Comedia.* His articles have appeared in various periodicals, including *Bulletin of the Comediantes, Romance Notes, Hispanófila,* and the *Philological Quarterly.*

163

Because I speak several languages (or perhaps simply because I teach a foreign one), I am frequently referred to as a linguist. (Curiously, a teacher of our own language is rarely called a linguist, but more plainly an English teacher.) When people refer to those who speak many tongues—which includes waiters and bellhops as well as professors and diplomats—they really mean polyglots. A linguist, on the other hand, may be thoroughly familiar with only one language, unlikely as this may be by virtue of his interest in the phenomenon of language in general, hence particular languages as well. A linguist, therefore, may indeed be a teacher of English *or* a teacher of foreign languages, but strictly speaking, *as a linguist* he plays a role closely related to, yet fundamentally distinct from, the teacher of languages.

Linguists prefer to speak of their field as a science, something which attracts pathetic and even sympathetic smiles from colleagues in physics, chemistry, biology or even mathematics. This is not the place to carry on that argument, but I mention it because at the heart of this claim to a linguistic science lies the search for an ultimate explanation of a *system*. There is something systematic about a given language which separates it from another language, and the same applies to the comparison of one language group with another, say, the Romance with the Semitic languages. Moreover, changes in the system of the *same* language over a period of time account for the evolution of a given language. This latter approach, commonly known as historical linguistics and referred to by specialists as diachronic linguistics, is characterized by comparing the various components of the system—phonological, morphological, syntactic, and so on—at one point in time with the corresponding elements of the system at another point in time. The most widely known application of such a study is the etymological one, but it is only a small, albeit important, aspect of the evolution of a language. The lexical elements of a language are not the total language, so that those who defend the study of Latin because of the high percentage of English *words* with Latin origins, must temper their arguments with the knowledge that, despite remote relationships in Indo-European, Latin is part of the Romance family whereas English belongs to the Germanic group, and its system as a whole has more in common with German and Dutch than with Spanish or French.[1]

The instructor of a foreign language, while he may hold a doctorate and possess a knowledge of earlier stages of the language he teaches, is normally more concerned in his classes with the instruction of the language as it is practiced today. He therefore needs to understand the system of the language at one time (the present), an approach known as synchronic linguistics. His own learning will have come about as a result of the study of how that system functions (descriptive linguistics), particularly where it *differs* from the system of the students' native language. Let me present one oversimplified example to underscore what I believe to be the most fundamental *intellectual*, as opposed to *methodological*, approach to the teaching of a foreign language.

If I tell my students that the Spanish word for "I" is *yo*, they will have no problem. If I next tell them that *yo quiero* means "I want," they will similarly encounter no difficulty. If I further tell them that the Spanish for "to study" is *estudiar*, they may be faced with a slight problem, but they will probably not have to exhaust their intelligence by accepting a difference in the two systems, namely that English normally expresses its infinitives by using two words, the first of which almost invariably is "to," whereas Spanish does the same thing by using one word. It is soon discovered that the equivalent of our prefixing the word "to" is one of only three possible suffixes in Spanish, namely *-ar*, *-er*, or *-ir*. (As a matter of fact, it is an illusion caused by our system of *writing* that makes "to study" appear as two words; the illiterate native speaker would respond to it without heeding the concept of separate words and would interpret the group of *sounds* that make up the phrase "to study" in the same way as the Spanish listener would identify *estudiar* as having the function of an infinitive by virtue of the respective affixes.) To continue with my example, if I next told my students that the Spanish word *te* means "you," they again would be confronted with a simple memorization task. (I leave aside the fact that there are several other ways of saying "you" in Spanish; the point is irrelevant to my example. Only the fact that one of these versions may be applied to a forthcoming example in this description is necessary to understand the nature of my proposition.)

If I now move on to some attempt to construct sentences, the students will readily accept that the combination *yo quiero estudiar* means "I want to study" and that *yo te quiero* requires only an explanation of one rule of word order to be understood as "I want you." (For those who are not familar with Spanish but have heard a Spanish song or two, I hasten to reassure them that this sentence may indeed mean "I love you" as well.) Finally, if I throw in the word *que* and indicate its meaning as "that," there will once again be no apparent problem.

Now, if *yo te quiero* means "I want you," and if *yo quiero estudiar* means "I want to study," the application of some logical progression of concepts would suggest that the way to say "I want you to study" ought to be *yo te quiero estudiar*. It turns out, however, that this means something else ("I want to study you") and the way to translate "I want you to study" is *yo quiero que estudies*. (Aside from the disappearance of the word which had been used as "you" in the previous instances—*te*—I could confuse the issue further by suggesting that one may indeed insert a word, but it would be *tú*, not *te*, and its positioning would not be as before, but in one of two other places: the sentence could also be expressed as *yo quiero que tú estudies* or *yo quiero que estudies tú*. The fact that the word *yo* could be omitted in any of the sentences could also be used to provide the needed evidence to reach the conclusion that the Spanish language is devoid of logic or at least that the cliché that Spanish is easy wasn't true after all!)

The above example is not intended to be a lesson in how to teach or learn Spanish. (It isn't even the ulterior motive of a hispanist to demonstrate the difficulty of Spanish!) What I have tried to show is that the first few steps are typical of the kinds of elements in one linguistic system which correspond in a familiar way to the similar elements of the learner's native tongue. All that needs to be accomplished is the memorization of a number of lexical items. Although the teacher may be of some limited help in the learning of vocabulary by means of etymological explanations, relationships to words in English or mnemonic devices, the acquisition of a working vocabulary in a foreign language (or in one's own, for that matter) clearly devolves upon the diligence of the student. As for the function of these lexical elements in the first simple steps illustrated above, their grammatical (i.e., morphological and syntactical) application is so close to the English-speaking students' experience with language that to belabor this point is not only a waste of time—enough of a sin in the teaching profession—but a risk that the teacher's insistence on the obvious fails to take advantage of the students' previously acquired linguistic facility and, worse than all else, may make the students begin *to think* about what they should simply *accept* by virtue of what they prejudged correctly!

The foregoing may sound as though I am an adherent of what I like to call the *la-plume-de-ma-tante-est-sur-la-table* school. By this I refer to the theory of language instruction which provides the student with model sentences to be memorized because the book or the teacher says it is so. Far from it. The above example in French is so closely parallel in all of its grammatical aspects to its English counterpart that to attempt to drill it home is a commission of all the sins I enumerated above, most especially that of failing to take advantage of the structure of this type of sentence which is *already* in the students' linguistic bag, so to speak, because of the seeming "normality" of it to an English-speaking student. What is new here is the vocabulary, and I have already suggested something about lexical learning. What is also new is the pronunciation, and I shall return to this as well as to vocabulary acquisition below.

What requires some explanation, perhaps, is that while it is perfectly acceptable English to say "the pen of my aunt," it is more usual, especially in normal speech (as opposed to elevated written prose) to use the alternate construction, "my aunt's pen." The explanation required is twofold: first, the perhaps startling (to the students) fact that there is no alternative in French: one simply *must* say *la plume de ma tante*; second, the student must be clear about what he is saying: to the French ear he does not appear to be speaking stilted prose, but rather he is using the everyday way of expressing possession. This is the great lesson that good translators learn: literal translation usually produces inferior results. The most exact translations are not translations at all, but rather the skillful conversion of the original to what *corresponds* to it in the other language. Let us not forget the famous Italian maxim: *traduttori traditori*. Greater comprehension on the part of the teacher is shown when he explains not that "Who is this?" becomes *Wer ist das?* in German, but that it *corresponds* to it.

The above is but another example of my earlier progression in Spanish. The first challenge facing the language teacher is to take advantage of the students' preconceived notions which *do* parallel the structure of the new language. This can be acquired by many years of experience, but it can be more systematically apprehended by studying the linguistic structures of the two languages. It is sometimes amazing to find how many teachers still know more "rules" than a textbook can describe, yet are incredibly vague about any structural knowledge of either English or the foreign language, much less of where the points of similarity and difference lie. Ask a teacher of English, or a teacher of a foreign language, whether one "may" say— it is never clarified who gives permission, or who designs the rules: God, a natural law (in which case all languages would be alike), or that old standby, Latin—in English, "it's me" or "it's I." The attempt to explain the "correctness" of the latter with ill-defined logic falls apart not only in the face of the argument that a nominative on one side of the equation requires a nominative on the other, when one asks how a third person ("it") can be a first person ("I"), but when one contrasts it with other languages. As would be expected in view of the English language's position as a Germanic language, German approximates the English, but reverses the order so that the verb agrees with the first person and not the third: *Ich bin es,* literally, "I am it."

It would appear that the structure of these two languages is more concerned with consistency of verb and subject than with the grammatical case of subject or predicate. When we look at Romance languages, the discrepancy is greater: French insists on a literal equivalent of "it's me": *c'est moi.* (Can one imagine *c'est je?*) Spanish, for its part, is the only one of my selected examples which could have a claim to logic: both verb form and subject/predicate are balanced, for the Spaniards render it as *soy yo,* literally "I am I."

Let me return, then, to my Spanish example in its final stages. As in the French example above, the points at which the native language and the "target" language are at variance, are those points which require explication, although the methodology may vary. Logic may occasionally help, as in the "I am I" example above. It is applicable in my lengthy Spanish example as well: "I want you" and "I want to study" are both instances in which I want something directly. Yet, by combining the two, I logically should want both. In fact, as the English-speaking listener knows, I want neither, for when I say, "I want you to study," I want neither you, nor do I want to study. What I want is *that you study,* which is precisely what *que tú estudies* means. Spanish is once again more logical than English. I regret to say, however, that although the use of logic, especially when the teacher attempts to preach that the foreigners' language is more logical (i.e., "makes more sense") than the students' mother tongue, may indeed explain why a particular construction "is that way," such explication does not, in most cases cause the language to be learned any more readily. It represents, in one sense, the same distinction which I drew earlier between the language teacher and the linguist. One attempts to transmit a set of skills; the other attempts to describe the structure behind them. We do not learn a foreign language by studying *about* it.

THOUGHTS ON TEACHING LANGUAGE

Language instruction, especially at the elementary level, is above all an experience in the acquisition of skills. Although the ultimate challenge lies in the application of these skills as intellectual tools when dealing with the various aspects of the total culture—literature, history, politics, economics, mythology, the arts, and so on—the elementary level is primarily, although not exclusively, a nonintellectual experience. Its analogy is learning to play a musical instrument. The teacher must possess the appropriate skills, he must have the ability to transmit these skills, and the student must have the capacity to acquire those skills by virtue of much and constant practice. Therein lies one set of challenges.

On an administrative level we face the ever present challenge of convincing deans and vice-presidents that quality language instruction, like quality piano instruction, cannot take place for fifty minutes per day among three dozen or more students. Cacophony is cheaper, and the most thick-headed administrator will not quarrel with that statement nor argue for mass instruction if it means poor instruction. The real challenge lies in the fact that senior administrators may not believe that the analogy is appropriate and will suggest everything from cutting out advanced courses to buying a few more booths for the language laboratory.

The language laboratory! The remaining symbol of the biggest hoax perpetrated on students and teachers of languages, namely the 1958 National Defense Education Act, is the language lab. During the sixties, no self-respecting foreign language department would be caught without one. Not that all faculty members really understood why; in fact, many of them viewed the tape recorder as Don Quixote perceived the windmills: giants (machines) which might take over the world if knights (teachers) did not tilt at them as they spun according to the whimsical winds. Of course, the tape recorder, like the windmill, had its purpose, and the original aim was a sincere and well-intentioned one.

Prior to 1958 and with the exception of some isolated attempts to view language instruction within the context of an understanding of language and how it functions (i.e., linguistics), the teaching of foreign languages was very often entrusted to people who either were unable to speak the language themselves or who failed to understand the discrepancy between textbook presentations and usage by speakers of the language. One traditional method was what I call the ho-hum school, because it reminds me of the learning of Latin according to the formula of *bonus, -a, -um*. This approach required students to conjugate verbs according to an arbitrary and artificial context. Thus in French, a student might be required to memorize, *and in this order,* the present tense of the verb *parler*:

je parle	*nous parlons*
tu parles	*vous parlez*
il parle	*ils parlent*

Aside from the obvious fact—though frequently ignored—that all but *parlons* and *parlez* are pronounced alike, the sin of this method consists of connecting in the student's mind a sequence which in ordinary usage will never occur in a French environment. The artificiality of connecting these six forms in a 1–6 order failed to take advantage of the young student's capacity to memorize, by not placing that capacity in a meaningful context. Moreover, if the third person plural were called for, it would require the student's memory to plow through five uncalled for forms in order to recall the desired form. Why not take advantage of a *context* and have students contrast *je parle maintenant comme il parlait hier,* a sequence which is not artificial, which forces the student's mind to contrast *je* and its corresponding form with *il* and its appropriate form, while at the same time, without ever needing to make much of the nomenclature (such as the names of tenses), forcing the student's mind to register the contrast in time through clue words such as "now" (present) and "yesterday" (past)?

The second kind of approach, often encouraged by the same members of the ho-hum school, is frequently referred to as the hunt-and-peck method or, as I prefer to call it, the blur school. It consisted of a passage in the foreign language, which the student was required to "translate" into English on the day following his homework. The most obvious fault in this approach is the complete negation of the purpose of the course. (I pass over the humor of courses entitled "Elementary French" or "Elementary German," languages which I am convinced are not spoken in France or Germany!) In one way or another, the catalogues implied the *use* of the foreign language, yet the blur method suggested that the whole thing was a decoding game.

The method was simple: with one hand holding a pencil near the foreign text, the other would hunt up (or down) the vocabulary list at the end of the book. When the appropriate word was found in the rear, the pencil would write it between the lines in the front. The result was that—assuming good hunting—when called upon, the student would pay no attention to the foreign language at all, doing his best instead to recite the English which he had scribbled the previous night. Since space between lines was limited, the struggles of the student frequently concentrated upon the efforts to decipher his own English, with no mental relationship attached to the printed text before him. In the meantime, over the course of weeks, his thumb had begun to blur the oft used vocabulary section, so that the result of all this decoding became a blurred vocabulary section, a blurred original text, an illegible penmanship in English between the lines, no thought at all about the original language, much less any thought *in* that language, and quite likely no thought at all. Hence, the blur method.

Many language teachers probably view the foreign-language requirement as being in some way the greatest challenge of all. Where it exists, its challenge may be that of dealing with large numbers of recalcitrant and intellectually unmotivated students; where it does not exist, the challenge may lie in attracting students to the discipline or it may be that of convincing one's colleagues in the other disciplines that a foreign language is an intellectually useful skill which should be required. If the reader of these pages is an advocate of foreign-language requirements, he might ponder for a moment that most of his fellow faculty members passed their foreign language requirement for the Ph.D. by means of a speed-written blur method. The most common such exam consisted of a lengthy passage or passages in the foreign language, which the doctoral candidate was to translate accurately into English, most often with a dictionary at his side. The time limit caused greater strain upon the pages of the dictionary than upon the student's intellect, with the result that as many words as could be found were set down on the "answer paper." (One can imagine the professors marking each blank spot or falsely decoded

word in the manner of Hans Sachs hammering at each error committed by Beckmesser in the latter's attempt to sing the Prize Song.)[2]
Clearly what the *mind* was attempting was an exercise in half-way
decent English prose, while the thumb was seeking the appropriate
decoded words. Certainly, the passing of such a test was regarded by
the brightest of students—the doctoral candidate—as a hurdle. Surely
he did not pretend to be familiar with the language, to be comfortable
with its literature, to be at ease in seeking scholarly research in its
journals, unless his knowledge of the language had come—or eventually came—from other experiences. Yet, these students, products
of the blur method or the ho-hum method in their undergraduate
years, and of the rapid blur method in graduate school, are now our
colleagues in the other humanities, the social sciences and the natural
sciences. And they were there when the vote was called for with respect to the retention of the requirement.

It was in the late fifties and early sixties that language teachers
gradually began to listen to descriptive linguists. Some of them listened because as intelligent scholars, they were eager to learn more.
Some of them listened because they knew how ill at ease they themselves had felt during a summer trip when trying to communicate with
native speakers of the very language they professed to be teaching!
Some of them listened because the sixties produced a cry on the part
of the students not only for "relevance," but, as I heard, a demand
from those who *wanted* to learn but were unable, either because the
methods described above produced no facility to deal *in* the language,
or because the large numbers of students who were forced into the
classrooms prevented them, the motivated students, from learning.

The linguists began by defining language. Teachers and students
alike were amazed to learn some simple facts. A language, even a so-
called dead language, develops first as a system of *vocal* symbols. Its
"rules" are determined by the social group which uses it at a given
time.[3] Hence, the French spoken in Quebec sounds different from
that spoken in Paris; the English spoken in Dallas differs from that
spoken in London; the English spoken by Churchill differs from
that spoken by Chaucer. And each one is correct, meaning that it
would be artificial, not to speak of the cultural change implied, to
force one system upon another (although it has been attempted for
various reasons). More surprising, perhaps, was the revelation that

of the thousands of languages in the world, only the smallest fraction has evolved a written form. Furthermore, since the spoken form of the language develops more rapidly than the written language, the written symbols are often hopelessly antiquated. Certainly this is evident in English or French; it is less so in German or Portuguese and even less in Spanish or Italian.[4]

The language lab was advertised by some as the solution to all the above problems. By having native speakers record their voices on tape, it was claimed that (1) only native pronunciation would be heard by the student, far superior to his native American professor; (2) the tape recorder would never lose its patience and thus would not distort phonemically important distinctions of intonation; (3) the language lab could accommodate more students over longer periods and thus provide the answer to the crowded classroom; (4) the famous Berlitz slogan, "The eye is the enemy of the ear," would at last be accepted, rather than snobbishly sneered at, by having the "real thing" come out of the earphones to combat the supposedly intellectual perceptions of the eye; (5) to run a language lab required a minimal knowledge of the workings of a tape recorder, how to splice broken tapes, and the like, all of which could divert salary money into at least three stipends for graduate students in exchange for one full-time instructor, thus also increasing the number of graduate students and freeing scholarly professors from the ho-hum routine in order to pursue the more intellectually oriented courses at the graduate level. If you were a businessman—and many academic administrators have to be—it all sounded like the long-sought panacea.

The panacea, however, often produced panic. Proceeding by the numbers, (1) it was true that the student was assured that the voice on the tape would be a native one. The fact that the region might be other than Madrid or Paris, is, I grant you, not a serious problem, so long as some measure of consistency is maintained. But if the local teacher's pronunciation was truly deficient, how could the student cope with this dilemma? Moreover, the initial tapes were simply spoken versions of the textbooks which the students held in their hands. The so-called laboratory was nothing more than a new blur method: instead of thumbing pages for written symbols, the student was now glancing at written symbols while a strange voice duly (and dully) intoned the corresponding vocal symbols. As I wandered through the language lab, I often learned that what at first glance appeared to be a student in deep concentration was in fact a person in deep slumber.

This problem was subsequently remedied to some extent by the introduction of multi-track tapes, so that the voice on the tape could initiate dialogue, which the student could continue by recording his response on another track during an appropriate pause. The advantage (2) of the tape's inability to become impatient with the student's mistakes remains, of course, but as I shall point out below, the disadvantage of allowing the student's incorrect response to go unchallenged had yet to be faced. With respect to space and numbers (3), I have already alluded to the paranoia developed among language teachers that they would soon be replaced by two-eyed monsters which made minimal salary demands (initial cost), minimal raise requests (maintenance and repair), brief sabbatical applications (units away for retooling at the factory), and never caught a cold (the possession of a master tape assured the absence of laryngitic models). It required more than a decade, however, to reassure the profession that the machines could not replace them; rather, that much of the drudgery of repetition, in fact all the nonintellectual aspects which the professor felt had turned him into a drillmaster, could be taken off his shoulders, be performed better in the lab—and certainly better than as "homework" with an unresponsive wall or helpless parent to receive the efforts of the student.

With regard to (4), the eye being the enemy of the ear, it soon became evident that Berlitz was correct, and that if the student had before him the Spanish word *como*, his eye would lead him to use his native habit of pronouncing the word as though the vowels were diphthongs, [koumou], despite the most mellifluous Spanish recording's repetition of the word as [komo]. In short, what was needed (5) for the language lab, to take proper advantage of all the points raised above, was not the presence of a graduate student who could be taught in ten minutes how to run and not ruin a tape recorder. What was required was the human presence of a person or persons thoroughly familiar with the languages and the lessons being studied, stationed at a central console and assigned the difficult task of constantly (not occasionally) listening in on the "dialogues" between tape and student in order to help the student realize what he was doing incorrectly, ranging from the improper phonetic transfer alluded to above to the fact that the student was giving a phonologically and grammatically correct answer to a question never asked of him.

This history was necessary, for in my view it explains the national trend during the late sixties and early seventies to do away with the foreign-language requirement. The abolition of the requirement was not merely the result of pressure from students who could find no relevance in learning a foreign language ("Anything worthwhile's available in translation anyway"), although this was certainly a vocal factor. Moreover, there was the opposite pressure, mentioned earlier, from language majors for smaller classes devoid of the captive audience which lowered the level of language instruction. It is ironic that this wave which opposed the foreign-language requirement hit the faculty just at the moment when reform had begun to appear and many of the abuses of the language lab—as well as the in-class abuse of memorized dialogues without an understanding of how to manipulate the phonemic or morphemic principles involved—were well on their way to correction.

One must not forget the ultimate political factor, as I hinted earlier. The members of the faculty had not forgotten their unhappy experiences with the ho-hum and the blur methods, not to mention their memories of the Morpheic (not morphemic) language lab. Moreover, even the good scholars who wanted, in fact demanded, the knowledge of foreign languages, had to throw up their hands when students told them that they were unable to read certain materials because they had "only taken two years of the language." Yet they had been given the stamp of approval: they had *passed* the language requirement. Clearly, the language profession—with many exceptions—had failed to meet the challenge presented by hordes of captive enrollments.

As we reach the end of the seventies, we need to rethink the nature of the challenge facing us and what some of our responses might be. (I leave aside the important question of the greater scarcity of dollars and students which the next decade will bring, because the basic challenge and our responses to it are only made that much more dramatic, and perhaps traumatic, because of it.)

First let me say that as I have observed it in the past dozen or so years, instruction in the foreign languages *has* improved. Not only on my own campus but on several that I have visited, the fact that students speak the foreign language so fluently in ordinary—as opposed to textbook or classroom—situations that it now appears as a commonplace, is an amazing stride forward. I suspect that the reason lies not in one but a combination of developments. The loss of the language requirement on some campuses decreased the size of foreign language faculties and, with some exceptions, left the better ones on the campus. The retirement of life-long adherents of the old methodologies helped to free departmental discussions of curriculum from the iron hand of the past. (Perhaps the Italian quotation cited earlier should be changed to *traduzione, tradimento, tradizione!*) The concurrent decrease in the size of classes also raised the level of instruction: students no longer could count on being called upon once or twice, but had to be on their toes every minute. The fact that both students and teachers were travelling more raised the level of preparation for both groups before the semester even began. Finally, with some exceptions, students were enrolling in these courses more often because they wanted to learn. Perhaps this is the most important factor of all, particularly in a language course which does not promise much stimulation until the basic elements have been mastered.

There are three perspectives from which I see the challenges and the responses. First, for the profession itself, the matter of survival dictates that students must be attracted to our discipline. One clearly does not do this by means of posters which illustrate the alluring (and expensive) tourist attractions. Nor, I must insist, does one accomplish this by an all-encompassing rule which requires of all students a certain amount of credit hours in a foreign language. (Proof of proficiency rather than "passing" the course would be an improvement in intent, but I fear that this would merely become another weapon in the language teacher's hand, a weapon he would at times rather waive than wave, if the student's career were at stake.) Although it may prove to be politically fruitless by giving rise to the question, "And what will you do for us?" I believe an effort must be made to have *other* disciplines either require a foreign language for their majors, or ideally, make so evident the importance of a foreign language to another discipline, that students will discover on their own the "relevance" to their primary interests.

If all the social sciences, for example, were to require a language as it pertains to the student's principal interest, the relevance becomes defensible, and the quality of the *social science department's offerings* is enhanced. I need give only one example: a political science major whose prime concern is the governmental structure of the Soviet-dominated portion of the world evidently would benefit from a knowledge of Russian or some other Slavic language.

From here I would progress to the more ideal situation I mentioned above. If a professor of economics, in his daily performance in the classroom, consistently reveals a knowledge of up-to-date Latin American views on and developments in the economic theories and situations of our southern hemisphere, theories which are not found in the *New York Times* and situations which were not yet known when even the latest textbooks were sent to press, it will soon become evident that the professor has another source of information. If it can be made obvious that the professor is reading not just Associated Press dispatches, but editorials and current journals in publications from Latin America (available in the library), the student will realize that for a more clarified comprehension of the material, he needs a proficiency in Spanish or Portuguese or both. If the student is serious about his major, he will draw his own conclusions about what has turned out to be relevant to it.

My second perspective concerning the challenge of foreign-language teaching is our own isolation in the field of language and literature. The language may be the tool a culture uses to communicate, and I share with most of my colleagues the conviction that literature—which includes carefully and well written biography, philosophy, history and other works which belong in the world of letters—is the highest esthetic form of language. However, nothing could be more narrow-minded, less liberal, if you will, than to insist or even suggest that the foreign culture is acquired, assimilated or even just studied through us, the teachers of language and literature, alone. I shall return to the teaching of a foreign literature below. For now, I merely wish to state a truism which my colleagues sometimes tend to forget: neither the language nor the literature *is* the culture; even the literature constitutes only one aspect of the culture, and must share its place alongside not only other arts, such as music, sculpture or architecture, but among such parts of the culture as its history, its politics, its philosophy, its economics, and the like.

I don't think the above has surprised the reader. What is surprising is how many professors who belong to the Modern Language Association do not see their role as going beyond language and literature on the one hand, and the number of professors of other disciplines who see us basically as walking dictionaries or minds incapable of making intelligent observations beyond our literary exegesis, on the other hand. In short, what I am suggesting is that the teaching of a foreign language begins with at least an introduction to how that language relates to the total culture and it should reach—I dare not say "end with"—the joint approach of as many talents as are available on a particular campus or consortium of campuses and as can be mustered during a student's four-year stay in college.

To start with, the study of a foreign language can begin in English. Heresy, or a return to the ho-hum era? Hardly. An explanation of what language really is (it is *not* communication any more than is the telephone) is a proper beginning for a course which proposes to deal with language. Such an explanation also is a sobering experience for those who think that one language about which they know a good deal is English. (This should be of comfort to those whose chief demand for Latin is based on the notion that its ultimate value is a better understanding of the English language.) Ask your students about some of the elementary facts about the structure of their native language and be prepared for a barrage of nonsense. Ask about the intonational patterns of English; about how many vowels there are in English (no, not five: "a, e, i, o, u, and sometimes (!) y and w") and you will discover that they have confused five or seven *written* symbols with over a dozen *vocal* symbols; ask about the meaning of "would" in a sentence such as "Whenever I saw my uncle, I would ask him for money," and ask the difference between that usage and the same word in "If I had an uncle, I would ask him for money." In short, not only will such a prelude provide some understanding about the languages of the native and foreign cultures, but it will make subsequent grammatical explanations intelligible.

The need to make the workings of a language intelligible to intelligent people is what differentiates the challenge of language teaching in college from that in the elementary school. This self-evident fact escaped the well-intentioned reformers in the sixties when they not only made us all construct language labs (at a handsome profit for those involved in their construction), but forced us to stick longer with a given textbook because of the large investment we had made in the accompanying tapes (an unhappy state for new authors who had ideas which could improve on the state of the art, but who faced the tremendous competition of well selling books whose tapes almost literally tied them to the market). In an attempt to reform the endless rules and complicated explications of their predecessors, the linguistically aware leaders of the sixties took to heart the Berlitz slogan. They properly proclaimed that an explanation may not help the learning of much of the material (e.g., the explanation that the "formal" version of "you" in Spanish, spelled out as *usted* but commonly abbreviated as *Vd.* or *Ud.,* developed from *vuestra merced* ["your grace"], may be interesting, may explain how a word which means "you" is found as a third person, but does not in the least aid in the everyday use of the verb forms or their functions). Hence the sixties were the apogee of the oral-aural method, the homonymous pair requiring a new baptism as the audio-lingual method.

It was an important stride forward for it recognized that the learning of a foreign language is indeed the acquisition of skills, and not the intellectual inquiry into the nature of language which is the domain of the linguist. Unfortunately, many of the summer institutes set up with the support of the NDEA and run by linguists, stressed so heavily the discipline of linguistics that many well-meaning teachers returned to their classes and taught neither the language nor its grammar. Instead, they introduced their newly acquired linguistic vocabulary and forced their beginning students to learn about phonemes and morphemes, segmental and suprasegmental, and so on. The whole thing ceased to be a class in a language and became a course about linguistic principles. In short it became irrelevant, quite suprasegmental.

The favorite device created by the new approach was the memorization of connected dialogues. The story is told—it may be apocryphal, but its lesson is to the point—that a young lady initiated dialogue #18 on a train in France, and to her surprise, the answer was the same as the answer in her textbook back home. (What would one expect: how many answers are there to *ça va?*) What amazed her, the story continues, is that when she tried the next line of dialogue #18, she again received a familiar reply. She continued this until the stranger responded with an expression that the author of the textbook had not prepared her for. The joke soon loses whatever humor it has, however, when the real point is understood: not only the dialogues of lesson #18, but those of most of her book were memorized in a sequence without any comprehension of what she was saying or what the replies meant. But she surely pronounced her phonemes well.

This brings me back to the intelligence of the college student.

Whether it is an apathetic age or a generation which demands relevance, nothing is more antithetical to the students' nature than what
appears to be mindless memorization. This does not mean that memorization is meaningless—in fact, purely as an exercise it has its
value, analogous to the apparently purposeless running around a
track. One must, after all, *memorize* (not "understand") that "house"
is *casa* in Spanish, or *maison* in French, *Haus* in German, and so
forth. But I am glad to see that the latest textbooks generally avoid
the former standard practice of listing in each chapter the new vocabulary items in alphabetical order! Surely nothing could have been
better devised to produce confusion than the pairing of words that
look alike. How else explain the perennial error of my former students who learned *cansar* and *casar* in alphabetical order only to confuse later *está casado* ("he is married") with *está cansado* ("he is
bored" or "he is tired")? In short, the eye *is* the enemy of the ear for
the literate person. The challenge is quite distinct from that confronting a teacher of five-year-olds or a group of illiterates from what is
now called the "inner city."

For this reason, my own view concerning the challenge of teaching
a foreign language begins with a clear presentation, lasting perhaps
as much as two weeks, of the nature of language in general, the basic
ingredients of the system of English, and a brief introduction to where
the English system will not correspond with the new system. To go
back to my earliest example in Spanish, students will begin to encounter difficulties primarily where the two systems differ. For mature minds, these differences must be explained, sometimes after the
first encounter, although it certainly does not usually require long-
winded rules with nine exceptions, the learning of which often turns
out to be more difficult than the foreign language itself.

Once the rudiments of the structure of the two language systems
are understood at least in principle, then it is time to speak normal
(not "elementary") Spanish, French, German or what have you. The
distinction I make between "normal" and "elementary" in a first-year
context has already been touched on in two places above. It is not
normal to learn verbs by conjugating them out of context in the dor-
mitory all night; nor is it normal to learn vocabulary by memorizing
words in alphabetical order. It is normal, on the other hand, to begin
a conversation, accompanied by appropriate objects and gestures,
such as, "Good morning. I am Professor Jones. I shall open the win-

dow. Oh, I feel cold. You, young man, please close the window."
This may take ten minutes on the first day before the young man,
aided by a series of gestures, actually gets up and closes the window.
But before half the period is over, the class will have learned at least
the word for "window," a form of the verbs "open" and "close" and
perhaps the words "cold" and "young man." In the remainder of this
first day of class, the professor can start counting windows, which will
not bring about automatic memorization of some numbers, but it will
provide a first important morphemic clue to the system: how to form
(at least some) plurals, a clue which can be confirmed by holding
first one pencil, then several, first one book then several. The practice
of the verbs "open" and "close" can similarly be performed on the
door(s), books, and drawers. If after fifty minutes of class time, a
perspiring group of students follow a dripping professor out of the
room with the knowledge of four lexical items (the words for "door,"
"window," "open," and "close"), one morphological item (the plural
form for nouns), a clue to the workings of the verb (the implicit distinction between "I close" and "please close"), not to mention a great
deal of practice in proper pronunciation, the class is off to a good
start. It is at this point that a properly supervised language lab, coor-
dinated with the lessons of the day and required not only for attendance but for spot checks on the students' performance, becomes the
valuable instructional device it is.

Finally, aside from residence in the foreign country, the ultimate
way to produce speakers of the language is to demand of and provide
for them the same sorts of things a music teacher will demand and
provide: models to imitate (live or recorded), places in which to
practice and as much time as possible in which to do this. Here is
where the language teacher has the advantage if he will but work with
his colleagues as I suggested above and if he and his department
chairman (and, if necessary, his dean) will use the dormitories wisely.
One cannot expect a music major to do his history course on the
oboe; one may, however, expect the German major to do *his* history
course in German. By this I have two things in mind.

The first I have already alluded to, and in itself constitutes nothing
novel, namely that professors in the language departments can use
their knowledge and experience outside their home departments.
One's Ph.D. may have been the ticket to enter the pigeon hole we call
a department. I trust, however, that Ph.D. does not really stand for

Pigeonhole Department. At the very least, a professor of French drama, say, ought to be able to provide a perspective for the theater department, or the course on world literature, that adds richness in a way the professor whose doctorate did not take him to the deeper study of French culture most likely could not do. This can be done in English, of course, and does not in itself constitute what I have in mind. This is why it is not novel, for the area studies concept, or the comparative literature curriculum, among others, has done this for decades. But it is a nucleus to build on.

Cannot some, in fact many, of the courses in a college have sections taught in one or even two foreign languages? Cannot a course in Latin American history—an area of some importance—be taught in English, in Spanish, and in Portuguese? And would it not be an exciting finale to have a weekend seminar of all three groups (in English) to compare viewpoints, sources, poor translations of recent documents, and so forth? I am convinced that those who have spent a semester studying the original documents will display to their fellow students the relevance of a foreign language in a most dramatic fashion.[5]

But my suggestion mentioned dormitories as well. To have a "French House" or a "Spanish House" is nothing new. Certainly where these are successful, they should be continued and strongly supported. What I have in mind here is something much less dramatic. Can the faculty not cooperate with those in charge of dormitories so that language majors room either with majors in the same language or with fluent speakers of that language? Can these roommates then not be required to speak consecutively—depending on their level of proficiency—on some other course, e.g., philosophy, *in the foreign language*? If we have taught them to use the language, surely two seniors who have majored in French should be able to discuss coherently some of the philosophical ideas of, say, Plato? This could subsequently form the basis of a presentation by the students in the advanced conversation class. In turn, this would raise the intellectual level of what all too often degenerates into an exercise of ordering meals or some other artificial conversation. Moreover, since presumably the professor of the conversation class is familiar with French thought, French literature, and even the neoplatonic movement, the class could prove to be a valuable asset to those students enrolled in courses on Plato and on French literature as well.

TEACHING A FOREIGN LITERATURE

I said earlier that I viewed the challenges to our profession from *three* perspectives. Although I strongly urge foreign language teachers to broaden their field of experience to encompass either the subject matter or the methods of the social sciences in a joint effort to bring our field of expertise to bear on theirs while they provide us with their approaches to the study of human culture (in the long run we are all really humanists), our training is nonetheless centered around the language and the literature of the culture with which we deal. I hope that we, too, have our "minors" or "related fields," particularly in one of the traditional humanistic areas, such as the arts, although a continuing serious interest in a social science or in some other aspects of the relationship between man and his environment within the context of the particular culture can be an equally rewarding and reinforcing experience.

Nonetheless, most of us did earn our doctorates in literature. I assume this presupposes a love for books, particularly those books which challenge the mind, present the creations of great minds, explore the human species, pose stimulating hypotheses or even simply tell stories which enrich the imagination.

No one has described this better than Charles Lamb: "I love to lose myself in other men's minds. . . . Books think for me."[6] A more dramatic assessment is Ezra Pound's definition: "Literature is language charged with meaning."[7] Some scholars may quarrel with this statement, but the thought assuredly strikes a responsive chord among those of us who by choice have devoted our lives to literature.[8] Although literature can be defined more broadly (and etymologically, more accurately) as encompassing the field of letters, thereby enabling us to include within our ranks philosophers, historians, musicologists (in fact all those who do not limit their learning to mere data collection), my task here is to restrict myself to the challenges inherent in the teaching of the more narrowly defined genre we call literature and, further reduced, the teaching of foreign literature.

Earlier I observed that language cannot be defined as communication. As long ago as the seventeenth century, Milton unequivocally declared that "language is but the instrument conveying to us things useful to be known."[9] We must also attempt a definition of literature. I regret to say that I cannot accept the definition posed by Northrop

Frye: "Literature is a specialized form of language, as language is of communication."[10] Not only is language not communication; it is not a form of communication, for the latter is a process and language is a vehicle for that process of communication. Similarly, literature is not a form of language, but is the *result* or product of a specialized formation of language.

I have used the phrase "the teaching of foreign literature," yet I wonder whether it is possible to *teach* a literature. Perhaps we can play our role in teaching people *how* to read literature, particularly at the earliest stages where the literature is often used as a vehicle for the acquisition of the language (which implies that the converse ought to be occurring as well). The same might be said of the most advanced stages, such as in courses on stylistics, exegesis and techniques of criticism. The real challenge, however, begins at the beginning.

Just as I have criticized some approaches to language teaching, so must I point out that one of the surest ways of turning off the student in either language or literature is by starting him out with artificially constructed readings in "elementary" language. We are dealing with mature people who are dealing with intellectually rigorous reading matter in other fields. If we insult them in our own courses with little stories, many of them allegedly humorous, that deal with Pedro's *burro,* Johann's *Katze* or Marie's *tante,* we not only engage in the sowhat school of pedagogy, but we encourage the growth of beliefs which will persist when our students are our colleagues, such as the oft cited question, "So Cervantes wrote *Don Quixote*; what else is there to Spanish literature?" (It is curious to note how many so-called educated people believe that the Don Juan legend had its origins in Italy [*Don Giovanni,* composed by an Austrian] or in France [Molière]; mention Tirso de Molina and one is greeted with a blank stare.) Whose fault? Not the students' who were brought up on stories about *burros, sombreros,* and *toros.* Our fault, for not beginning with simply constructed Spanish in good editorials of Spanish newspapers, followed by gradual promotion to the literary pages of newspapers and magazines, and eventually to some of the less complex—but not watered down—passages of Unamuno, Sarmiento (whose writings about the United States deserve a place alongside those of de Tocqueville), Ortega y Gasset, among others. I am not suggesting that no one is doing this; I am lamenting that it did not begin sooner and that even now, the connection between, say, Sartre's philosophy, his language, his impact upon French culture, his ties to world culture, is not solidly made but allowed to be compartmentalized.[11]

The challenge, therefore, lies not in persuading students to appreciate the beauties of style and content in great literature. Cervantes, Shakespeare, Goethe, Dante, Corneille, Tolstoy and others have already done that better than we can. We not only face a challenge; we owe a challenge to the student. I see no reason, for example, why a first-year student of Spanish, a few months after he has gone beyond closing windows and opening doors, cannot be challenged with a reading of the windmill adventure in *Don Quixote*. Never mind if he reads it in English at home; the vocabulary required will soon make him aware that if he is to be at home with the work, it had better be with the original. I can think of no argument which could nullify the linguistic and literary advantages of an hour-long discussion of this adventure in a context other than that of the idealistic fool versus his imaginary giants. Why not discuss the fact that windmills first appeared in Spain only thirty years before the publication of *Don Quixote*; that a man who had spent his life in a library would easily, particularly in the heat of La Mancha, mistake these huge entities waving in the distance for the only thing he had been trained to expect; that Sancho, whose life as a farmer would more likely have led him to come in contact with windmills before, would quite routinely accept them for what they are; that the puzzling question remains why Sancho continues to follow a master who seems to be mad? Surely this sort of discussion is possible with a minimal vocabulary in the presence of a teacher whose function is to foster discussion.

I maintain, therefore, that to avoid the charges that "Spanish is easy," that foreign-language teachers are drillmasters, that sophisticated machines can replace language instructors, all of which amounts to the charge that language instruction is less intellectually challenging than most other courses taken by college students, we must accept the challenge as one of challenging them. The underlying premise of a liberal education, after all, is the stretching of the mind as far as is possible for each individual. The intellectual tools for constantly pushing the apparent limits of the mind ever farther include the linguistic tools described above. But tools have a purpose, and intellectual tools are for the exercise (and enjoyment) of the intellect. We, then, must make intellectual use of even the rudiments of language as early as possible. I am not suggesting that after six days of lectures about the systematic nature of language, an introduction to the two linguistic systems (native and "target"), and a day or two of "open the window" exercises, we should at once plunge into a discussion of Dostoevsky's world view. But even here, where the learning of a new alphabet is involved, I submit that by the beginning of the second semester, an at-home reading of, say, the Grand Inquisitor scene from *The Brothers Karamazov,* in English, could still form the basis of a stimulating discussion the following day in Russian, with the professor somewhat slyly dropping hints that the original Russian presents an ambiguity or a clarity that the English rendition failed to reveal. This should not "put down" the student, but rather spur him on to greater mastery of the tool with which to excite his intellect.

With regard to the more advanced levels of courses in the literature, the personality of the instructor, his own interests beyond literature, the background of the students, and the prevailing issues of the day are all variables that cannot be put in a uniform mold. However, it seems clear that a familiarity with Wagner cannot fail to enhance an understanding of Thomas Mann's *Tristan,* in the same way that a knowledge of Beethoven is fundamental for a reading of Romain Rolland's *Jean Christophe.* I need not, I think, heap example upon example to make my point: not only does the professor's store of knowledge increase his ability to explicate; perhaps more important is that the relation of a book to some other field or fields encourages the student to seek further relationships, thus giving meaning to the word "relevance" as well as to our catalogue cliché of expanding horizons.

Students *qua* students, however, are very quick to see what is relevant to their grades. I cannot stress enough the importance of relating our examinations to the intentions which we profess. By this I mean that if a course on Dostoevsky is spent discussing psychological analyses of human character, life in an absolutist country, the search for utopian societies, and so on, but the examinations deal with the author's chronology, the date of the books' first editions, and an essay question or two about the plot, then the word will spread rapidly that although the professor enjoys holding forth on certain interesting propositions, what really counts is a series of dull facts and the knowledge of these will determine the professor's only enduring way of expressing approval: the final grade.

An example I have used in a Cervantes class will serve to show what I have in mind. Although certain facts are important for even undergraduates to memorize (e.g., *Don Quixote* is not a medieval work nor a Romantic novel, hence the date is of some significance), my expressed intentions for the class include that of eventually not needing me. In other words, if I have shown my students how to read Cervantes, how he employs the language, what his philosophy consists of, what his favorite allusions are, then a reading of *Don Quixote*, the *Exemplary Tales* and some of his plays should have set the students on their way to dealing with other works which presumably they have not read. I therefore include in my final examination a passage from, say, *Persiles and Sigismunda*, a novel rarely read by undergraduates. I allow the students a period of an hour to read the passage and a half hour to write a critical interpretation of it based on the techniques we have used throughout the course as well as a consistent familiarity with Cervantes's ways of approaching his subject matter. Naturally, if the selection is atypical, I would expect the students to perceive this, to explain in which ways it differs from the other works studied, and perhaps even to doubt its authorship. There is only one way to prepare for such an examination and it cannot be begun the night before. A steady participation in the course together with a growing ability to deal with literature—at least this literature —is the proper preparation for the final examination, an exam which in reality is symbolic of future dealings with further reading.

One final word: although at all levels of foreign-literature teaching there should be as little use of English as possible—ideally, none at all—an occasional reversion to English should not be viewed as a sin. If the professor observes that neither the text nor his lecture can clarify the obvious confusion on the part of his students, a brief attempt to find the source of the mystification (usually an idiomatic use of an otherwise differently understood word or set of words—e.g., *desde* in Spanish means "since," and *luego* means "then" or "later," yet *desde luego* does not mean "since then," but "of course," a confusion which could destroy the meaning of an entire page), can be carried on in English. Of course, the class must immediately continue in the foreign language or else there looms the danger of daily explanations

188 / John G. Weiger

188 / John G. Weiger

in English and the concomitant degeneration of the course. The principle of an occasional explanation in English should be kept in the teacher's bag of tricks, however; with experience, the instructor will learn to anticipate these moments and may prepare in advance a clear explanation in the foreign language. If it appears that I have spent too much time on the matter of a word which can cause the more important matters to be thrown into confusion, then let me remind my colleagues who teach Shakespeare that the common undergraduate error of confusing "wherefore" with "where" in the famous balcony scene in *Romeo and Juliet* explains why the opening line itself is the stumbling block to a discussion which centers around *why* they had to be born into feuding families (i.e., names).

To sum up: the challenge to the professor of foreign languages at the college level is to remember that he is faced with people who *think*, who will ask *why* even as they claim not to be concerned with grammar, and who will require an understanding of how language functions and how the foreign language differs from the student's native tongue. This implies that the professor is challenged by the curious mind and conversely, that the student wishes to be challenged by the professor. The latter should have recourse to related aspects of the foreign culture, so that the students may use the newly acquired tool in a more demanding (and perhaps, interesting) context. Naturally, those who find the very study of language fascinating, should be encouraged to explore the fields of linguistics, psycholinguistics, speech pathology, philosophy and etymology. Finally, the demands of great literature upon the mind as well as on the emotions, should be the vehicle for a direct experience of one of the artistic aspects of another culture. As the inscription on the facade of the University of Colorado's library reads: "He who knows only his own generation remains always a child." I believe that this extends to one's own culture as well as to one's own time.[12]

NOTES

1. I do not wish to take issue with my colleagues who teach Latin
    with respect to the importance of this classical tongue, which is
    by no means "dead." Not only does it live on in its evolved
    forms of the Romance languages, as well as in the lexical roots
    of other tongues, including English, but it is as alive as Goethe,
    Dante, Cicero or Chaucer. My "mixed bag" of examples is in-
    tentional: it is the *cultural* aspects of these giants, one of whom
    happens to have made his contribution in Latin, that make the
    study of the Latin language most important. To argue that such
    a study imposes clear thinking upon the student or that one will
    understand English that much better, misses the mark, in my
    opinion. A well-taught course in logic (or even physics) may
    accomplish the former just as readily, if not more so. As for
    greater familiarity with English vocabulary, I submit that a well
    developed love of literature with its consequent lifelong desire
    to read a great deal, is the best way I know to absorb the mean-
    ings and nuances of English words. To repeat, the study of Latin
    is most important because of the various facets of Roman civili-
    zation that are opened up for us.
2. See Wagner's *Die Meistersinger*, act II.
3. The teacher's explanation that certain elements "agree" with one
    another (a ludicrous attribution of the faculty of will to inani-
    mate parts of speech) is really an attempt to describe the agree-
    ment of a social group and therein lies the "it's me" or "it's I"
    distinction, just as the elements of pronunciation, intonation,
    kinesics, or any other peculiarity of a linguistic system are the
    product of the particular group which employs that system.
4. It is inaccurate, however, to describe languages like Spanish or
    Italian as "phonetic" (which presumably conveys the notion that
    they are pronounced as they are written). The phonetic distinc-
    tion of the "d" in the Spanish words *amado* and *amando* pro-
    hibits such a description, as does the pronunciation of *che* in
    Italian.
5. At a recent meeting of the Modern Language Association, this
    idea was confirmed by a professor from a leading liberal arts
    college in the midwest. The professor, who is an established

literary scholar, pointed out that she taught *Don Quixote* in Spanish in her Spanish classes and in English in another class and despite the guidance of the same instructor, the end result was a totally different reaction to the same work on the part of the two groups.

6. Charles Lamb, "Detached Thoughts on Books and Reading," in *The Last Essays of Elia* (Garden City, N.Y.: Doubleday Dolphin, n.d.), p. 252.

7. Ezra Pound, *ABC of Reading* (New York: New Directions, 1960), p. 28. Still more dramatic is his statement, "Great literature is simply language charged with meaning to the utmost possible degree." (Cited by Pound from his own *How to Read.*)

8. I have expressed my views on what literature (and professors of literature) may contribute to us in "Chaucer, the English Department, and a Liberal Arts Education," *Bulletin of the Association of Departments of English* 45 (1975): 21–24, originally delivered at the 1974 convention of the National Council of Teachers of English in New Orleans.

9. John Milton, "Of Education," in *Complete Poems and Major Prose*, ed. Merritt Y. Hughes (New York: Odyssey, 1957), p. 631.

10. Northrop Frye, *Anatomy of Criticism* (Princeton: Princeton University Press, 1971), p. 74.

11. Without any intention on my part to make a judgment on the particular book, I am pleased to note the opening lines of a recent review of a textbook as descriptive of a trend: "*Vivir hoy* continues the trend of editing for intermediate students collections of non-literary writings, mainly newspaper and magazine articles. . . . The topics in *Vivir hoy* are current enough to be of interest, yet not so current as to become dated soon. . . ." See William Woodhouse's review of Gloria and Manuel Durán's *Vivir hoy*, in *Hispania* 58(1975):995.

12. I trust that the reader has not lost sight of my emphasis on the word "culture." My closing remark is not an argument for a centrally decreed language requirement, unless that language is carried to its humanizing potential as merely *one* part of the total culture, as I have explained earlier in the text. A typical language requirement does not in itself provide sufficient experience with the culture, which is why I stress the philosophical,

artistic, economic, political, historical and other aspects which, *together* with a facility with the language may bring about that liberalizing acquaintance with a culture other than one's own. If I were to prescribe a single requirement for the liberal arts aside from intellectual tools and skills, it would be that of stepping outside one's own culture, and the language, of course, is the tool with which to begin. The crucial point remains the necessity to carry through beyond "passing" a language requirement.

Teaching Music

L. MICHAEL GRIFFEL (Ph.D., Columbia University) is associate professor of music at Hunter College and the Graduate Center of the City University of New York. He holds degrees in historical musicology, music theory, and piano, and appears in concert frequently. In 1975 he was named the first "Teacher of the Month" by one of Hunter College's student newspapers. He has contributed to various periodicals, including *The Musical Quarterly, The Journal of Aesthetics and Art Criticism, Music Library Association Notes*, and *Current Musicology*, which he edited from 1970 to 1972.

Music is somewhat different from the other disciplines discussed in this book. It is an art and a science, a humanistic study and a practical profession. It is taught in the college, the graduate school, the conservatory, the private studio, the teacher's college; in a classroom, on a stage, in an electronic studio, in a listening lab. Its study can lead to a B.A., a B.S., a B.M., an M.A., an M.S., an M.M., a Ph.D., a D.M.A., and other degrees; its students become singers, instrumentalists, composers, conductors, arrangers, historians, theorists, critics, writers, educators, private teachers, therapists, and enlightened music fans. Therefore, when a person reveals the fact that he is a musician or that he teaches music, he knows that no one can be quite sure what he actually does.

I am always at a loss in filling out a bureaucratic questionnaire when I come to the line "Profession." If I put down "Musician," I imagine that people might envisage me entertaining at the piano in some cocktail lounge. If I enter "College Teacher," I worry that my very special musical talents and interests, such as giving piano recitals, will be completely overlooked. If I go on record as "Musicologist," I assume that no one will have the foggiest notion of what I do, although a fairly recent American motion picture, *What's Up, Doc?*, seems to have "educated" the public somewhat. Now many people think that a musicologist is a bumbling scholar who looks like Ryan O'Neal!

Musicology is indeed the study of music but is an academic, systematic, and historical study about music, as opposed to training in the creative and applied skills of a musician. It is "the scholarly or scientific study of music, as in historical research, musical theory, the physical nature of sound, etc.," according to a recent definition.[1] Therefore, it is truly musicology that is taught on the undergraduate level at most of today's liberal arts colleges in this country, even though the names most often used for designating a student's major are music, music history, and music theory. To be sure, composition, performance, and music education have also become major fields of study in the colleges during recent years. They involve special profession-oriented skills, however, and must be considered separately, beyond the focus of the liberal-arts education. This essay, then, will be devoted primarily to a discussion of teaching music history, literature, and theory in the four-year college, to music majors and nonmajors, and to students with or without a scholarly inclination.

Most people are surprised to learn that music was one of the fundamental subjects taught among the intelligentsia of the medieval era. Among the seven liberal arts of the Middle Ages, music, then regarded as a mathematical science, belonged to the quadrivium, along with arithmetic, geometry, and astronomy. In the trivium of language arts were grammar, rhetoric, and logic. The study of music incorporated consideration of the regular movements of heavenly bodies, the harmony between man's health and the functioning of his internal organs (and between his body and soul), and actual sounding, practical vocal and instrumental tonal arrangements. Clearly, only the last-mentioned aspect, which was termed *musica instrumentalis* in the Middle Ages, remains today as the study of music.

As early as the sixth century the theorist Anicius Manlius Severinus Boethius distinguished between two types of musicians: those who sang, played, or composed, whom he called the *cantores* (we call them the practitioners), and those who could judge, understand, and explain the numerical proportions among the sounds being heard, whom he called the *musici* (we call them the theorists). The true musician, wrote Boethius, is he who "assumes the skill of judging," sees "that the whole is founded in reason and speculation," and "possesses the faculty of judging" anything musical "according to speculation or reason."[2] It seems to me, then, that to this day the primary function of the liberal-arts college teacher of music remains to train students to listen critically, to formulate judgments based on reason, and to become musically literate and articulate.

Times have changed since the writings of Boethius, and music in our schools and colleges is no longer deemed a fundamental subject in one's education. On the contrary, it is often termed a luxury or an extravagance; and when departments are to be pruned or eliminated for financial reasons, music can be expected to appear near the top of the list of nonessentials.

Such an attitude is most alarming in an era in which one of man's greatest problems is and will continue to be how to spend his leisure time and retirement years profitably. Being safe from war, disease, and poverty is to be hoped for, of course, but what good is a long, healthy, or rich life if there are no intellectually enjoyable, enlightening, and stimulating ways of filling it? As one of the humanities, music teaches us how to listen. The humanities can provide no more crucial services than to help students learn how to listen, how to look, how to read, and how to write. With these four weapons in hand, the individual can face life fully armed. But until more politicians and administrators change their attitudes about music, instructors of music will have to continue teaching it under the shadow of its "nonessential" status.

In the college there are four traditional areas of undergraduate training in music as a humanities subject: (1) the introductory course, (2) music literature, (3) music history, and (4) music theory. Let us now turn to a discussion of each of these in turn.

The basic-training college experience in music is an appreciation and rudimentary course most often with a title like "Introduction to Music." Designed for students with a very limited or nonexistent background in music, this course is most commonly thought of as the bread-and-butter course of a music department. The main reason is that this is the music course which can usually be credited toward the fulfillment of a distribution requirement in the humanities. At Hunter College of the City University of New York alone, there were seventeen sections of the "Intro" course offered in the Spring 1976 semester, with roughly from thirty to one hundred students in each section. These statistics are more impressive when one realizes that in the same semester there were only nine sections of various music literature courses and only seven of history, with these classes normally being limited to about thirty students each. It is therefore not surprising that the various college-textbook publishers are competing for this market with about eight new "Intro" textbooks each year.

In colleges an introduction to music is different from most other humanistic introductions, such as an introduction to English literature, because most students come to college with only a kindergarten-level background in music and because music is a "foreign" language, with its own vocabulary, grammar, and rhetoric, and its own highly complicated notational systems.

Yet music cannot be translated from or into any other language. The terminology one learns in a music course merely enables one to verbalize about what one hears; it does not enable one to listen accurately—except on the most superficial level—nor can it make one "think in music." Such automatic responses are possible only after many years of personal experience with music, especially by performing it. Therefore, the instructor in the introduction class finds before him a group of adults with not even an elementary grasp of the subject, unable to "speak," "read," "write," or "think" in its language, but wanting to have a college-level understanding of it after a meager forty-five hours of instruction. Yet, hopeless as the task may seem, these students are able to comprehend an enormous amount of music and benefit greatly from this course, *if* the teacher and the students make a point of reminding themselves frequently that the course is just an introduction to music, a very first step.

Students in the introduction course become frustrated when they cannot readily hear musical phenomena such as modulations, intervals, or meters. The teacher's duty here is to explain to the class that listening is not altogether different from playing an instrument or singing. A person begins to perform well only after years of daily practice, and listening really well cannot be expected to occur much sooner. The teacher must stress that a composition is dependent upon the skills of the composer, the performer, and the listener in roughly equal amounts, and that none of these three skills can be gained overnight. If students can be made to realize that an introduction to music is of necessity a remedial course and that the colleges are doing the jobs which the primary and secondary schools failed to do, then a proper frame of reference for this course can be established and students can be made to feel more comfortable throughout this experience.

The teacher of the introduction course must make it clear from the first class that the main goal of the course is to acquire perceptive listening habits. The emphasis is not on gathering facts about music history, nor on chronology, nor on reading or writing or performing music but on listening attentively, verbalizing the listening experience, and learning to base critical evaluations of music on an understanding of that music rather than on immediate physical reactions to it. Since everyone is a potential listener, the reactions of each student should be of interest to all the others, so that they can compare their respective levels of listening expertise at each stage of the course. It is well known that pianists and singers attend so-called "master classes" in order to listen to, criticize, and learn from one another. Listeners, too, need this kind of learning opportunity, and so the teacher should set aside some time each meeting for students to comment on music heard in or between classes.

A listener has a right to his own opinion about a piece of music, and it is important for the teacher to respect this right at all times. Naturally, one is expected to support an opinion with reasons, and this is precisely what gives most students a lot of trouble at the start of the course. I have often been upset at hearing a student condemn Bach as "dull" or Mozart as "juvenile," but I have always encouraged students to say exactly what they feel, so that I can find out how best to educate them and alter their opinions through the appropriate information and music.

There is an easy way to show even the best students in the class how very little they know about music at the outset. It takes the shape of an initial assignment, in which I ask them to listen to *any* piece of music (art music, popular music, jazz, etc.) and then ask themselves the following question: how could I describe this music (without reference to author or title) to someone else in so vivid a way that the other person would be able to recognize it from among a large selection of compositions? I explain how much easier this assignment would be if a film were involved: one could comment easily and profusely on various characters, plot developments, settings, climaxes, flashbacks, length, colors, sounds, and so on. As the students quickly learn, the dimensions of a musical composition are more difficult for them to fathom. A second purpose is ultimately served by this exercise: when, on the final exam or during the last week of the term, the same question is asked, the students are easily able to delineate the texture, timbre, genre, form, main melodic and harmonic features, meter, tempo, and other attributes of any random piece of music, and they are tremendously pleased by their awareness of their growth as listeners in the course.

Some music teachers consider their role in this course to be evangelical in nature; they wish to convert people from popular music, notably rock, to art or "classical" music. While there may be nothing wrong with this end, the means taken toward achieving it are often questionable. "Make the students like good music by making the course very easy," these teachers suggest. "Give simple tests, little or no homework, and very high grades. The student will leave the course with a very positive, happy feeling and a concomitant love of music." My own views are radically different. I feel that this course should be extremely challenging, with many and difficult tests, plenty of homework, and a fair grading procedure, in which a grade reflects nothing other than achievement in the course. The student will love art music if the teacher can expose the right amounts of the right music to the student at the right time. Anyway, not everyone wants to, can, or even should love art music. A teacher should teach, not preach.

There is a better tack to take. Tell the class that hardly anyone likes all kinds of art music but that almost everyone derives immense enjoyment from at least one type. Tell them that one of the purposes of the course is to expose them to enough different kinds of music so that each student may latch onto something. An introduction course must *introduce* the class to many pieces, composers, epochs, places, and styles of music. Almost every meeting should offer something new to the student, whether it be a Mozart opera, a Stravinsky ballet, or a Joplin rag. Sooner or later the listener feels attracted to some kind of music, and this experience often leads to a lasting love. Explain to the student that, once he finds something to his liking, for instance, organ music or Beethoven or Renaissance vocal music, he could fill all of his spare time for the rest of his life with the study and enjoyment of just that one type of music (if he wanted to).

I make a point of allowing students to decide for themselves that good music is its own reward. I do not even require attendance at a live musical event (although I encourage it), because I am instinctively averse to forcing people to have a good time. As I tell each class, "I will not insist that you eat a steak dinner, drink champagne, or attend a concert. If you really want to get the most out of a course like this, you'll see an opera or go to a concert as frequently as you can." All I can tell my readers is that this soft sell has met with great success through the years. Surely, there are a few students who do not attend a performance and, therefore, may never in their lives see an opera or a symphony orchestra; however, there are many more who, because nothing is forced upon them, and because no resentment rises in them, attend with an open mind and an open heart—and go on to become avid fans.

What ought to be covered in the introductory course? Certainly a rudimentary discussion of the fundamentals of music is beneficial at the outset of the course, if one is going to be able to articulate verbally about the music to be heard in the remainder of the term. These lectures on sound, melody, harmony, rhythm, form, and the like can become tedious, especially to students who had hoped to be listening to and discussing Beethoven's Fifth Symphony by the end of the second class. However, this basic training is indispensable, just as learning to play a C-major scale is tedious but indispensable to a piano student aspiring to play a Mozart concerto. The teacher must work the hardest during these first six to nine hours; he must be at his best in order to make some rather dry subject matter seem fascinating. He must bring to class myriad musical examples of each point discussed, such as consonant chords, duple meter, monophonic texture, or woodwind instruments. And he must contrast examples of new music with those of old; ones of art music with others of pop, rock, and jazz; some of Western music with some of African, Asian, or other ethnic musics. Students should be encouraged to clap rhythms, sing melodies, and express what they like and dislike about each excerpt heard.

Interspersed with these exercises should be aesthetic and historical considerations, such as: (1) what is music; (2) what are the functions and duties of the composer, the performer, and the listener; and (3) how does the history of music divide into stylistically distinguishable areas. To answer these questions the students should consult the opening chapter or two of several textbooks designed for such a course, which the teacher should place on reserve.

Teachers of Introduction to Music have varying opinions on the need for a textbook in this course. While almost everyone feels that a paperback dictionary of music is requisite, many professors deem a textbook of limited use because these teachers prefer their own syllabus and favorite musical compositions to the regimented sequence of chapters and the prefabricated musical analyses of some author's chosen pieces which are contained in any textbook. These teachers often claim that no good instructor of this course has any need for using a textbook. That may be well and good; however, they ought to consider the problem from the student's point of view. A textbook is good to have for those days when a student is absent, late, or not feeling well. It is also useful for times when the teacher is not thorough or clear (every teacher is guilty of these sins once in a while) and when he is replaced by a substitute. Furthermore, when a student is reviewing for an examination, a book serves to tie all sorts of loose ends together and puts everything into place. And when time has frayed the pages in the student's notebook, the textbook will still sit on a bookshelf, ready to serve whenever needed. From the student's point of view, then, a textbook is worth its price (about ten dollars), and I therefore feel that one ought to be used in this course.

One other purpose that a textbook can serve is to provide a chapter on the notation of music, with clear diagrams of musical symbols and enough explanations to enable an interested student to read simple tunes and rhythms. The teacher should also spend a day or two in class explaining the basic symbols, such as staves, clefs, note-values, pitches, and time signatures; however, he should stress the fact that learning to read music is accomplished in other courses dedicated to that end and that in this course students are not required to read music and will not be quizzed on it. The interested student whose appetite is whetted in class will turn to the textbook again and again for lasting assistance in understanding musical notation.

Having established a foundation for the rest of the course, the instructor is ready to introduce various types of music to the class. The difficulty of selecting this body of music is overwhelming, as the teacher owes it to the students to provide a broad scope, and yet he ought not teach topics with which he is not familiar or comfortable (e.g., many academicians find it impossible to teach their students much about rock or the music of Indonesia). Furthermore, he should realize that these students are not likely to become professional musicians but need preparation for active participation as concert-goers and listeners, and so they ought to be taught how to listen to that music which is most frequently performed in concert halls, namely, the art music written between about 1700 and 1940.

With the above in mind, the core of the introduction course ought to be the music of the late Baroque, Classical, Romantic, and early twentieth-century eras. Examples of medieval, Renaissance, contemporary, popular, and ethnic musics can be inserted at appropriate times. Chronology, while making the historical flow clear, can make for a duller course, and it might be more stimulating to compare operas, symphonies, cantatas, melodic styles, and so on, from various ages. However, the choice between the chronological and topical approaches should be made in terms of what is more comfortable for the particular teacher.

This brings us to a consideration of who should teach this course. All too often departments place these students in the hands of a novice instructor or graduate student; the feeling may be that since this is the most rudimentary of courses, it can be taught by the beginning teacher. What a mistake! The course is rudimentary, but it is also the most difficult one given by the department and, as mentioned earlier, a most important one. Accordingly, a department chairman should schedule the very best professors to give one section each of this course, thus ensuring that as many sections as possible will be taught by an experienced teacher. These professors may be historians, theorists, composers, or performers—it does not matter which. Of course, each one will emphasize his own special interests, but that is certainly desirable. Nonetheless, the teacher should be a virtuoso of sorts, who incites the students to a frenzy of interest in the topic. The virtuosity can take the shape of speaking dynamically and eloquently, singing, playing, throwing in humor, drilling students as in a language course, setting up debates on aesthetic points, and, of course, handling the phonograph and tape deck effortlessly.

It is most important that this course be taught without reference to lecture notes. The teacher must have virtually memorized the entire content of the course, be able to extemporize on any musical topic which comes up in class, allow students to ask questions at all times (certainly at the start of each meeting, at least), willingly go off on tangents, and move the course along according to the tempo of the students on hand rather than to a fixed rate of progress. After all, it is better for the class to understand x ideas very well than x + 3 less well. This course has no quantitative goals, only qualitative ones. In these terms the reader can certainly sense the folly in having no one but graduate students offer this course. These young scholars do need opportunities to gain teaching experience, but, if they are to get it in this particular course, they should be supervised by an experienced teacher of Introduction to Music.

The virtuoso instructor of this course should also be other things, namely, patient, sympathetic, and kind. The fastest way to lose these students permanently is to make them nervous and fretful. Music should be enjoyed, and students worrying about being called on for answers in class or about surprise quizzes cannot concentrate on the music itself. The classroom should be a type of listening laboratory, in which the instructor demonstrates musical phenomena and students volunteer to respond to questions.

Concerning homework assignments, some readings in the textbook are required, but the main object is to listen to a lot of music. After all, students have enough other courses in which reading and writing occupy their time. This course offers one the opportunity to develop a different skill, the art of listening. Writing interestingly about the music heard is, as mentioned before, not really possible until the end of the course; it is far more useful to have classroom discussions, during which the teacher can guide the students, who in turn can complement each other's perceptions.

Frequent testing is necessary, so that students can find out where their problems lie before it is too late to remedy them. This is especially important for freshmen, who comprise a large percentage of the class and who are somewhat apprehensive about college anyway and are also inexperienced in taking tests on a college level. Exams should include objective-type questions, definitions or essays, and, most important, listening problems. When a student does poorly with the listening questions, the teacher should meet with this student individually and work on overcoming the problem. There are very few people who are really tone deaf; most can be brought to a passing level of listening acumen.

So much for the introduction course. Turning to the courses in the literature and history of music, one runs up against different types of problems. The main one usually is how to teach the subject matter so that both music majors and nonmajors can understand and be kept interested in the course. This is really a severe problem. There is a tremendous difference between talking about (or around!) music and explaining a piece of music. Anyone can understand the biography of a composer, his letters, his goals, the nature of the world during his lifetime, the reception of a piece at its first performance, and so on, but only the superior music students are able to analyze a composition and derive from that analysis ideas about the structure, efficacy, or style of the work in question.

In order to undertake such an analysis, one needs prerequisite courses in music theory, counterpoint, harmony, orchestration, and sundry other areas, depending upon the music in question. For instance, one cannot comprehend many of Stravinsky's late works without being steeped in serial and dodecaphonic theory. Nor can one analyze some of Machaut's motets without understanding the theory of isorhythm. The music major can acquire only so many skills per semester, just as the high school student proceeds from algebra to trigonometry before taking on calculus, and he is well nigh ready for graduation before he is able to discover meaning in a musical work. For the nonmusic major, moreover, such understanding is normally next to impossible.

Where musical comprehension is unattainable, the next best thing for the student who loves music is to acquire at least a greater familiarity with it; for, in the life of the listener familiarity breeds anything but contempt. In fact, impresarios have to cope with this vicious cycle all the time. The public wants to hear what it knows best again and again and, of course, continues to know only what it perpetually hears. To make students more familiar with music, music departments offer literature courses, in which a single body of music, such as the works of Monteverdi, the Romantic art-song, or jazz, is investigated throughout the semester. Such courses presuppose only that the student has previously taken Introduction to Music. They are usually geared to the nonmajor and avoid detailed technical analyses of the music. The students in these classes tend to listen to music mainly on what Aaron Copland has called "the sensuous plane," on which one is "listening to music for the sheer pleasure of the musical sound itself," and on "the expressive plane," on which one is looking for "a meaning to music," or "the expressive feeling that it gives off."[3] Copland distinguishes between these two planes and "the sheerly musical plane," where "music does exist in terms of the notes themselves and of their manipulation."[4] One of the aims of these courses, then, is to guide both the majors and the nonmajors as far along "the sheerly musical plane" as is possible for each.

The literature courses bear a close relationship to the introductory course. In the latter, students listen to a little bit of many types of music; here they listen to a great deal of one type of music. The experience of the earlier course enables the instructor to conduct these courses on a much higher level, on which the interrelationships of musical events within a piece and the comparisons and contrasts among related pieces can be discussed. Also, at this point there can be a de-emphasis on tests and constant checking of the student's comprehension, resulting in a very much more relaxed atmosphere, in which teacher and students jointly submerge themselves in the subject matter. Since these courses are electives, there is rarely the problem of having to force people to work or learn.

A textbook for the literature courses is helpful, but usually there is no single good and adequate study of the subject matter. It becomes the instructor's duty to comb through the existing literature and compile a reading list of the most useful articles and chapters, all of which must be made available in the college library. Recordings and scores of each work studied in class or assigned must also be procured for the library; and the teacher should also advise the class as to which performances on record and which editions of the score are best, so that students who can afford to purchase them know how to spend their money most wisely.

As quickly as possible, the instructor should find out how experienced the class is in music history, theory, and performance; which instruments they play; which compositions they would like to investigate; and what they are hoping to learn from the course. This information is easily obtainable by means of a questionnaire which can be completed the first week of class. In terms of the answers to the above questions, the teacher can prepare a syllabus which is most useful to the specific group of students at hand. To take an example, if one were offering a course on Brahms, and if 80 percent of the students in the class had studied the piano but only 30 percent had ever taken a theory course, the teacher would be wise to spend many hours on Brahms's piano works, some on his Lieder and on his chamber music with piano, and just a token amount of time on his choral works or chamber music for strings. Moreover, the teacher would do well to emphasize the historical factors surrounding a work, the problems faced by the performers of it, and an overview as to its structure and expressive content, rather than to dumbfound his ill-equipped audience with subtleties and technicalities of musical analysis. To a student unfamiliar with, for example, the laws of harmony, a teacher's enthusiasm over Brahms's substitution of a Neapolitan sixth chord in one variation of a theme for the flat subdominant in the previous variation will be met by weak smiles on confused faces. Suffice it for the teacher to play these two chords in succession and allow the class simply to hear the difference first out of context and then in context, as the two entire passages are replayed.

The main problem of the student in the literature class is that, in order to discuss music, one needs to learn to read a symbolic language and to acquire a whole new vocabulary of terms descriptive of strictly musical events. The most inexperienced student can immediately see two different shades of blue in a painting, but only a trained listener is aware of the two different "shades" of harmonic color in the aforementioned Brahms illustration. To make matters worse, whereas the painting is all there at once before the eyes of the beholder, by the time the Neapolitan sixth chord arrives in the musical composition, the flat subdominant will be dozens or hundreds of tones removed.

And so, to return to the sample Brahms class, the teacher should strive to make the course relevant for those enrolled. If those able to sing or play are willing to perform Brahms works for the class, they should be encouraged to do so. If composition students are enrolled, they should be asked to write some music in the style of Brahms. The performers and composers should comment on the specific difficulties encountered in this style. If there are sociology majors in the class, they should be allowed to present a report on the interactions between Brahms and the cities of Hamburg and Vienna. If religion majors are present, they might investigate the spiritual message of the Brahms Requiem. Class discussions, assignments, and term papers, then, should be suited to the specialties and wishes of the students.

In the music literature class the lecture method of teaching seems advisable for several reasons. First, although there are reams of books about music, they tend to be either too technical for the undergraduate or too elementary (taken to the lowest common denominator of student comprehension). The greatest challenge in the field of musicology is to describe musical events in words, and only the rarest of authors have been able to do that well. Thus, the teacher must add to or subtract from the assigned readings and make the level and amount of information meted out match the capacity of his audience.

Second, the music teacher often has a bit of the performer in him. He has a certain charisma or, at least, a memorable personality. He can infuse his lectures with his love and enthusiasm for music (enter the purple prose) and with theatrical and rhetorical gestures which enliven the classroom. The printed page that describes music seems stillborn in comparison.

In the third place, any given book or article on a musical subject will stress only one or a few aspects, and its interpretation will be bound up with the time and place of its publication. As a performing art, music is ever in need of renewal and changing interpretation, and in his lectures the teacher is able to provide this service, as well as to collate all the bits and pieces of information scattered among the secondary sources. The teacher must be the arbiter for his class in instances of disagreement among authors. To take an example, one of this country's most capable musicologists, Joseph Kerman, once wrote of Act II of Richard Strauss's *Der Rosenkavalier* that "the scene of the presentation of the rose has all the solidity of a fifty-cent valentine,"[5] while Donald Grout, a musicological legend in his own time, wrote that "the presentation of the silver rose thus moves in an atmosphere of ideal, magical, passionless beauty, unsurpassed anywhere in the whole realm of opera."[6] Should the teacher not help his students come to terms with such an issue?

This very point, however, raises another question. Can the teacher settle the issue, or can he merely voice his own opinion? I think that the best teachers are those who remind their students repeatedly that every opinion backed by scholarship and sincerity has merit, that in a subject like music there is room for differing opinions, that none of these opinions is really provable or disprovable, and that, certainly, the teacher's own opinion is not always fact, nor is it the final say on the subject.

A fourth reason for using the lecture method in music-literature courses is that the alternative manner of running the class as a discussion group necessarily enables the inexperienced students to bore the advanced, the indolent to foil the industrious, and the garrulous to infuriate the reticent. While allowing for questions and comments at any time during the session, the teacher ought to do most of the talking; his students, who could listen to music and read on their own, have signed up for his class to hear what he has to say. A few questions at the start of the class, however, about the most recent assignment, may serve as an incentive for the students to keep their work up to date. As usual, only volunteers should be heard, so that the others can pay attention to the discussion instead of fearing that they will be called on.

Before leaving the literature course, let me stress that here more than in any other music course, the instructor must, by the second week of class, announce the objectives of the course, the work load, and what students will be expected to know for the final exam. Only in this way can certain students—and there are always some of these —know that they had better withdraw because the course will be too easy or too difficult.

The courses in music history are of two kinds: those that stress history and those that stress music. The former are so much like any other history courses that they need no elaboration here. The courses that stress music (and these are the ones which will be referred to here as music-history courses), if they are to rise above the most dilettantish level of some of the literature courses, must delve into analytical problems dealing with musical structures, procedures, and techniques. If the literature course is for the amateur, the history course is for the connoisseur. Consequently, only music majors or other highly trained music students should be encouraged to take music-history classes.

Music history is the study of primary and secondary musical sources; chronology and periodization; geographical distribution of musical activity; sociological data, such as the functions of music, the status of musicians, institutions, and patronage; biographical data of composers and performers; theoretical, critical, and aesthetic systems, concepts, and attitudes; performance practices, including instrument technology; and musical styles. In examining styles one has to contend with the elements of music, including medium, texture, sonority, tonality, harmony, rhythm, tempo, meter, theme, and melody, with musical genres, forms, and structural procedures, and with such special problems as word-tone and musico-dramatic relationships.[7]

Students of music history are expected to be able to use a music library skillfully. Their teacher must expose them to the joys and hazards of using music dictionaries, encyclopedias, periodicals and periodical indexes, full scores, piano-vocal scores, complete-works editions, phonograph records, reel-to-reel tapes, cassette tapes, and the like. If an English major looks up Shakespeare's *Hamlet* in a library card catalogue, he will easily find the play and the edition he is seeking. On the other hand, if a music major looks up Mozart's *Don Giovanni,* he will find cards not only for various editions of the score but for piano-vocal reductions, miniature orchestral scores, phonograph discs, and taped performances. The teacher, then, must either make a working knowledge of the music library a prerequisite for the course, incorporate the explanation of bibliographic and research techniques into the course, or give private assistance to those in need of it.

Teaching music history at the undergraduate level is challenging, because it is quite impossible to reach a proper balance between breadth of coverage through generalizations and summaries, on the one hand, and in-depth study of a given piece, on the other. One can talk about Mahler's life and works—his post-Romanticism, his obses-

sion with death, his conducting, his total output—for hours and yet
not understand any single piece of his at all. Or one can spend a week
talking about only the first movement of his Symphony No. 2 and
commit the work to memory without realizing its purpose, its place
in Mahler's life, in the Romantic era, or in history in general.
Neither extreme is helpful to the students, and yet a happy medium
is hardly possible in the time allotted to a course, especially when one
considers that some classroom time will have to be spent on listening
to at least a part of such a lengthy work.

After a few years of experimentation and juggling, I have come to
the conclusion that books and articles must be depended on for most
of the historical overview and that class time ought to be spent primarily on investigating the music itself. As in the literature course,
the professor must fill in gaps, choose the best wordings of ideas and
the most helpful quotations, take a side on controversial issues, and
augment the secondary sources with first-hand knowledge; however,
here he must dispose of generalities as succinctly and unambiguously
as possible and proceed to the music at hand. If I had a week (three
hours) to devote to Mahler, I would spend the first hour on his life
and works in general and would play one or two of his Lieder, the
second hour on the opening movement of one of his symphonies, e.g.,
the Second, or *Das Lied von der Erde,* and the third on bits and
pieces of some or all of the other movements of the same work. In
this way I would have looked at Mahler through three different lenses.

Planning a syllabus is another insoluble problem in a one-semester
history course, such as Music of the Baroque Era. How can 150 years
of music be covered in 45 hours? Where does one find the time to
discuss opera, oratorio, cantata, sonata, concerto, motet, mass, an-
them, fugue, suite? How can one do justice to France, Italy, England,
Germany, Spain, and other nations, or to Monteverdi, Frescobaldi,
Schütz, Purcell, Lully, Alessandro and Domenico Scarlatti, Corelli,
Torelli, Vivaldi, J. S. Bach, and Handel—by no means a complete
list of the great Baroque masters? These questions are not rhetorical;
they are real, and the answers to them are disheartening.

One has to choose between a very superficial treatment of a great
many topics and a deeper one of a few. I, for one, much prefer the
latter option. A judicious selection of some of the most important
subject matter pertaining to the course and a few of the pertinent immortal works should provide the class with an ample understanding

of the area under study. Again, the teacher can make some of his choices in terms of the composition of the student body; however, in these courses there are certain requirements which are unalterable. For example, if a Baroque class includes some organists, then, perhaps, the study of a Handel organ concerto could be substituted for a Torelli violin concerto. However, the course could not overlook Monteverdi's *L'Orfeo* or *Poppea* or Bach's Mass in B Minor. To close some of the gaps, the teacher can arrange to have the term paper, as well as shorter essays, relate to some of the music and composers that he is unable to treat in class. But even this is not really necessary, for everyone should keep in mind the fact that music-history students are merely beginning their studies at the undergraduate level. They will have ample opportunities to further their scholarly quests in graduate school and beyond.

Concerning the term paper, the history teachers of a music department must cooperate to train students for their future careers as scholars. It is foolish to assign the same type of paper in each and every history course, when there are several different kinds of skills that ought to be developed. At Hunter College several colleagues and I devised the following schedule of term-paper assignments for our courses.[8] In the special introduction course for music majors only, the paper is conceived as a series of précis to insure that students can read, understand what they read, and reproduce in their own words the essentials of an essay. In the medieval and Renaissance course the paper is to investigate the relationship of musical life at some point during those eras to other areas of contemporaneous cultural life, such as painting, architecture, literature, or sociology. The Baroque paper is the study of a genre, such as cantata or trio sonata: to discover what it is, to describe it, to tabulate findings on it. For the course on the Classical period, the assignment is thought of as an exercise in the organization and structuring of a paper, with special emphasis upon the crafts of quotation, footnoting, and bibliography. The Romantic paper is an analytical exercise, in which the student is to account for the characteristics of a musical style by reporting the results of analysis by means of prose, musical examples, charts, tables, and diagrams. In the twentieth-century course the students undertake reviews of books, recordings, and concerts.

These courses require substantial reading and listening assignments. The teacher should prepare book and recording lists near the beginning of the semester in order that the students can accurately gauge the amount of work for the course right away. Listening examinations might test not only the recognition of styles in general but also that of specific assigned compositions.

Lest the reader think that the history class is always a humorless, dry arena of profound scholarly work, it ought to be stated that the teacher can and should lighten the atmosphere regularly. There is plenty of humor in the history of music and a good deal in the music itself. Every teacher has collected a series of anecdotes, clever stories, witticisms, and jokes, and the insertion of these at appropriate moments can offer much enjoyment to the students. Enjoyment seems to spur interest in the subject matter and also tends to lead to better results. Storytelling naturally has its dangers and must be used sparingly. Also, the teacher's stories should be about the music and musicians under study, not about his wife, children, car, home, or travels, as is all too often the case.

The first music histories, in the modern sense, were authored toward the end of the eighteenth century. However, writings on both practical and speculative music theory extend back to Greek antiquity, to the fourth century B.C. There is hardly any Greek music extant, but there are lucid texts treating the theory of music. This is why Walter Wiora could honestly claim that "musicology has been called the youngest of the sciences of art, but it is in truth the oldest."[9] The numerical proportions which Pythagoras found in the sixth century B.C. are as true and basic to music today as they were then; and in studying theory, students can truly enjoy their historical links to the past.

Expertise in music theory requires some knowledge of such fields as acoustics, perception, mathematics, and computer science, but on the undergraduate level, theory tends to concentrate on the basic tools of the trade, namely, counterpoint, harmony, orchestration, and analysis. This is as it should be, since very few musicians want and are able to become professional music theorists providing modern-day treatises and speculation. There are plenty of theory majors, but these are customarily people planning to become teachers, performers, and composers. Thus, the courses in theory must assist one to write, play, or sing better and, of course, to understand what previous composers were trying to accomplish.

Music involves a purposeful use of sound intended to create an impression in the listener. Composition requires organization. Art is not random but controlled, intended, constrained. Music is a language. These platitudinous assertions help explain why a theory course must proceed in a deliberate, logical, additive manner. It must adhere to the strictest type of syllabus, not allowing for the personal whims or interests of the members of the class *or* of the teacher. The rules and regulations of species counterpoint, tonal harmony, and the like must be laid down, explained, memorized, and obeyed, so that students can understand the nature of music at various times in the past. Few individuals really like rules, but just as few like to be without them. Even if rules are made to be broken, they are the starting points in every discipline.

As in any language course, a textbook is indispensable in a theory class. More than in the history and literature courses, the teacher here must not settle for the cheapest, prettiest, lightest, or newest book, but only for the best. The instructor's role is to explicate the necessarily intricate subject matter, demonstrate the approaches to solving problems, select the most useful questions for homework assignments, and correct those papers with the finest of tooth combs. For students who are having difficulties with the assignments, it is imperative that the teacher give them individual assistance during his office hours. He should not wait to be asked, since some students are shy, ashamed, or foolish, but should require the weak students to meet with him until and unless the problems are solved. It is cruel and wasteful merely to hand back F papers repeatedly and watch students sink slowly into despair. Of course, some people are hopelessly inept, and these should be encouraged to withdraw from the course when all efforts to help fail.

How can the theory instructor make his course exciting and most beneficial for the students? He should explain a certain problem very slowly and carefully. The problem should be worked out visually at the blackboard and also aurally at the piano. Throughout the demonstration he can question members of the class to ensure that each step is understood. A first exercise having been completed, he might begin a related one and stop along the way for opinions and advice from class members (upon whom he should call in this case) as to how to proceed. A third problem should then be undertaken. This time a student ought to be asked to go to the board to solve it. Other class members may offer suggestions as needed.

The theory teacher must be very critical but, it seems to me, can be so without frustrating his students through fear and pressure. Unending patience is called for, as kindly suggestions and constructive corrections do more good than embarrassing remonstrances. As in performance lessons, the student is in constant need of help and encouragement, and only the cockiest type might benefit from a verbal spanking once in a while, since it is really dangerous to overestimate one's own abilities in these areas.

There are two often overlooked aspects of every music-theory course, even the most elementary one, which the teacher must include in his classes. One is composition, and the other is analysis. A person does not learn how to solve mathematical problems so that he can accumulate high scores on mathematics tests. Similarly, realizing a figured-bass line with paper and pencil may not be of much assistance in the student's future. On the other hand, composing one's own four-part chorale or a portion of a three-part sonatina movement, according to the rules and methods learned in class, is the surest way to appreciate and understand the achievements of a Bach or a Clementi. Doing a fifth-species counterpoint exercise in three voices is good, but composing a sixteenth-century-style motet is even better. Certainly, one must do first things first, and the exercise precedes its application. Nonetheless, a little bit of composition is possible on a continual basis, even if it is restricted for a while to creating good melodic lines —by no means an easy feat.

In addition to synthesis, or composition, there is analysis. Teachers must choose from the wealth of music literature effective examples of good music illustrating possible solutions to the problems under study. Scores must be provided for each student, and analytical questions based on this music should be assigned for homework at least once a week.

Analysis is a key toward the proper execution or performance of a piece of music; it is the basis for one's interpretation of a work. Musical tones relate to each other according to various hierarchical systems. Through proper analysis the student learns which tones to play (or sing) softer, which louder, which faster, which more slowly, which to highlight through some type of accentuation, which to embellish, which to pedal, which to double. Analysis should not be saved for the analysis course. It belongs, in small, proper dosages, to every theory and history course.

Along with academic theory courses, all music students must receive lessons in sight-singing and ear-training (solfège) and in keyboard. Solfège is the backbone of the beginning student's education in music. By singing intervals, scales, modes, and melodies and by clapping rhythms, the student learns the "feel" of these musical events; he learns what they sound like, experiences them, begins to "think" in them. He trains his ears to pick out these same sounds in the context of musical compositons. Sad and sorry is the individual who can solve a problem with paper and pencil but cannot hear in his mind what he has written. Two or three years of practice in solfège can make the student's future in music more meaningful and enjoyable. Keyboard training is of similar importance, so that the student can learn to hear harmonies, as well as interactions among melody, harmony, and rhythm. (Furthermore, all musicians, be they performers, composers, scholars, or teachers, need to know how to play the piano.)

The solfège or keyboard teacher, even more than the theory professor, must be careful not to frighten or shame his students in front of each other. Students are most sensitive about their singing or playing abilities and hate nothing more than suffering criticism in front of their peers. Indelicate treatment of students here can create a mental block, hang-up, or other disabling state for the student which is sometimes impossible to correct. The teacher must remind students that the quality of their singing voice or the beauty of their piano tone is not important in these courses. Their goals are only an accurate execution and an ability to hear and match sounds correctly. The teacher must give students time to think and opportunities to correct errors. Students should be encouraged to assist and teach each other between classes, since, when working alone, one cannot be sure of one's accuracy.

Before I close this essay, I would like to make a few remarks about teaching performance—to be more precise, giving private lessons in the college classroom. Students and teachers should have common goals, namely, to improve the student's command of the voice or instrument gradually from lesson to lesson and to realize the student's potential as far as is possible. The goal should not be what it all too often seems—to become a world-famous performer. Many students suffer from this desire for stardom, and there have been teachers, too, who have hoped to get fame vicariously through their students. But success at this level is reserved for only a chosen few, whose talent shows its face usually before they reach college age, and, with rare exceptions, involves those who attend conservatories or study privately with master teachers. Of course, one has to keep an eye out for those few gifted students who have slipped through unnoticed theretofore, but the average college teacher will most likely go through life without ever seeing any of his students become famous performers.

With this sad fact in mind, it is a primary duty of every teacher (whether in college or not) to give the students an honest, realistic evaluation of their talents and abilities in performance. False hopes ultimately do far more damage to the student's morale than an immediate disillusionment. (Private teachers are the worst culprits here, since they fear that such disappointment will lead to the student quitting and, in turn, to the loss of income for the teacher.) Keeping in mind that singing or playing just as well as one can is indeed a rewarding experience, the teacher should work on technical problems, whether or not he thinks the particular student will ever be able to solve them, and discuss the problems of interpreting the music.

Teaching music is indeed a challenge. Almost all the students who opt for music like it and many are in love with it. The teacher's difficult job is to enlighten students without detracting from their love of music. Love is easiest when it involves little sacrifice; it becomes a problem when the target of that love makes demands. Music is a most demanding subject, on one's pocketbook, one's time, and one's stamina. The music teacher must show his students how to cope with these sacrifices, how to pace their progress, and how to relate the various branches of music to each other, for there is no room for schisms among musicians.

It pays to remember that music exists for people, not the other way around. Stories of cutthroat competition among musical performers and among students are all too common in the history of music. Teachers have to discourage students from such behavior. Music is a wonderful, logical discipline, which teaches people to think clearly, perceive sharply, and feel deeply. The teacher of music should try to serve as a model of articulateness, sensitivity, and compassion. He should seek to exhibit the graceful and harmonious personality which Plato, in Book III of the *Republic,* viewed as the result of a musical education.

NOTES

1. *The Random House Dictionary of the English Language* (New York: Random House, 1967), p. 943, "Musicology."
2. From *De institutione musica,* as translated in Oliver Strunk, ed., *Source Readings in Music History* (New York: W. W. Norton & Company, 1950), p. 86.
3. Aaron Copland, *What to Listen for in Music,* rev. ed. (New York: McGraw-Hill, 1957), pp. 9–16.
4. Ibid., pp. 16–19.
5. Joseph Kerman, *Opera as Drama* (New York: Vintage Books, 1959), p. 260.
6. Donald Grout, *A Short History of Opera,* 2nd ed. (New York: Columbia University Press, 1965), p. 517.
7. For this profile of the study of music history, I am indebted to Professor William B. Kimmel of Hunter College of the City University of New York.
8. My gratitude here is extended to Professors William B. Kimmel and John Reeves White.
9. Walter Wiora, *The Four Ages of Music,* trans. M. D. Herter Norton (New York: W. W. Norton & Company, 1967), p. 76.

Appendix: The Uses and Abuses of Grades and Examinations*

STEVEN M. CAHN (Ph.D., Columbia University) is professor of philosophy and chairman of the department at the University of Vermont. Previously he taught at Dartmouth College, Vassar College, the University of Rochester, and New York University. He is the author of *The Eclipse of Excellence: A Critique of American Higher Education; A New Introduction to Philosophy;* and *Fate, Logic, and Time.* Among the books he has edited are *The Philosophical Foundations of Education; Philosophy of Religion;* and *Classics of Western Philosophy.* His articles have appeared in such publications as *The Encyclopedia of Philosophy, The Journal of Philosophy,* the *American Philosophical Quarterly, The New York Times,* and *The Chronicle of Higher Education.*

---

* Although this essay originally was written for this volume, it appeared first as part of the author's work *The Eclipse of Excellence: A Critique of American Higher Education* (Washington, D.C.: Public Affairs Press, 1973). Reprinted here by permission of Public Affairs Press.

It is astonishing to realize how little a college teacher may know about the academic lives of his students, and conversely, how little his students may know about the academic life of their teacher. I recall one professor who taught a large lecture course for several years without ever realizing he was addressing a captive audience, since unbeknownst to him, the course was required for graduation. On the other hand, I have spoken to students unaware that just as a student can be required to take a course he would prefer not to take, so a teacher can be required to teach a course he would prefer not to teach. How many teachers, even in a very small class, know whether their students are sophomores or seniors, a matter of some importance to the students? But again, how many students know whether their teacher is an assistant or full professor, a matter of some importance to the teacher? It may never occur to a teacher that the sleepy students in his 8 A.M. class are there only because all other sections of the course were already closed when they registered. But, likewise, it may never occur to the students in the 8 A.M. class that their teacher is standing wearily before them at such an hour only because he lacks the seniority to claim any other time.

Such mutual ignorance extends over many aspects of academic life and is nowhere more apparent than in matters regarding examinations and grades. A basic source of the misunderstandings which surround evaluations of student work lies in the fact that normally such evaluation has vital consequences for the one being evaluated, whereas it has no such consequences for the one who does the evaluating. The grades a student receives not only determine whether he graduates with honors or fails out of school; they may also guide him in choosing his field of specialization, affect his plans for graduate study, and ultimately influence his choice of career. On the other hand, the grades a teacher gives do not affect his professional stature, his commitment to a field of study, or his future success as a scholar. A student may for a long time harbor a deep resentment against a teacher who grades him harshly, but were he to confront that teacher years later, the teacher might not even remember the student and would almost surely not remember the grade. Indeed, the teacher would most probably be astounded to learn the student cared so deeply about the grade. I once heard a woman who had taught for over thirty years remark in a faculty meeting that she could not understand why students were so interested in grades. Apparently in moving from one side of the desk to the other she had developed amnesia.

Some students believe that teachers are fond of examinations and grades, that they employ these devices in order to retain power over the students. But although undoubtedly a few teachers do possess such motives, most do not. A scholar enjoys reading and writing books, not making up questions to test the knowledge others may possess. And a great many more fascinating things can be found to do than read one hundred or so answers to the same question and try to decide how many points each answer is worth. Whether Johnny understands the problem of induction is not crucial to Professor Smith's intellectual life, for Professor Smith finds the problem highly stimulating, even if Johnny neglects to study it.

The system of examinations and grades thus places important decisions affecting students' lives in the hands of those who are comparatively unaffected by these decisions and perhaps quite uninterested in making them. Such a situation is fraught with unpleasant possibilities, these often compounded by the difficulty of constructing and applying suitable examination and grading procedures. But to refer to "suitable examination and grading procedures" implies that such procedures are intended to fulfill certain worthwhile purposes, and so we would do well to consider just what those purposes are. Why bother with examinations or grades at all?

Examinations ideally serve at least four significant purposes. First, an examination provides the opportunity for a student to discover the scope and depth of his knowledge. Much like an athlete who tests himself under game conditions or like a violinist who tests himself under concert conditions, a student tests himself under examination conditions and thereby determines whether he is in complete control of certain material or whether he possesses merely a tenuous grasp of it. It is one thing to speak glibly about a subject; it is something else to answer specific questions about that subject, relying solely upon one's own knowledge and committing answers to paper so they can be scrutinized by experts in the field. A proper examination procedure makes clear to the student what he knows and what he does not know and thus can serve as a valuable guide to further study. By paying close attention to the results of his examination, a student can become aware of his strengths and weaknesses. He can learn whether his methods of study are effective, and he can recognize the areas of

220 / Steven M. Cahn

a subject in which he needs to concentrate his future efforts. In short, an examination enables a student to find out how well he is doing and assists him in deciding how he can do better.

Students, however, are not the only ones who are tested by an examination, for the second purpose examinations should serve is to provide an opportunity for a teacher to discover how effective his teaching has been. By carefully analyzing his students' examination papers, a teacher can learn in what ways he has succeeded and in what ways he has failed. Of course, many teachers would prefer to believe the reason three-quarters of their students missed a particular question is that the students are not bright or have not studied hard enough. But in this matter, college teachers have something to learn from those who teach in elementary school. When three-quarters of an ordinary third-grade class find multiplication confusing, the teacher does not assume the students are not bright or have not studied hard enough. He assumes his teaching methods are in need of improvement. A college teacher ought to arrive at the same conclusion when three-quarters of his class are confused by a fundamental point he thought he had explained clearly. In one sense, then, teachers as well as students can pass or fail examinations, for by paying close attention to the results of his students' efforts, a teacher can become aware of the strengths and weaknesses of his instruction. He can learn whether his methods are effective, and he can recognize the areas of a subject in which he needs to concentrate his future efforts. In short, an examination enables a teacher to find out how well he is doing and assists him in deciding how he can do better.

We have thus far considered examinations only as tests of learning, but they can be more than a means of evaluating previous learning experiences: they can be themselves worthwhile learning experiences. During an examination most students are working with an extraordinarily high degree of concentration. If the examination questions place familiar material in a slightly unfamiliar light and thereby lead students to develop for themselves significant connections between various aspects of the subject matter, then the students will be working intensely on challenging, important problems and so gain intellectual perspective. Ironically, in this day of large lecture classes, examinations sometimes provide greater opportunity for active learning than any other part of the course. It is not unusual to hear student complaints about uninspired, unrewarding examinations. Such complaints are entirely legitimate, for a boring, banal examination indicates pedagogic laziness and is a waste of a potentially valuable learning experience. Long after completing a course, students who have forgotten virtually everything else may still remember some of the examination questions. They should be worth remembering.

An examination, however, consists of more than the two or three hours spent sitting in the examination room. Most students prepare for examinations, and such preparation itself possesses significant educational value. The nature of an examination requires that one not know what questions will be asked or which aspects of the subject matter spotlighted. The only adequate preparation for an examination is a thorough study of all the subject matter and a careful consideration of as many as possible of its various interconnections. In trying to anticipate the examination questions, a student is led to analyze and synthesize the course material, thereby strengthening and solidifying his grasp of the subject matter.

In this connection it is important to note that the writing of a term paper, though potentially a beneficial educational experience, is not a suitable substitute for preparing for an examination. In writing a term paper, even one which is given a strict time limit and misleadingly dubbed "a take-home examination," a student need only master those parts of the course material bearing directly on his topic. Rarely does a term paper require mastery of most or even very much of the course material. Furthermore, it is not difficult to copy ideas from a book, alter them slightly so as to avoid the charge of plagiarism, and use them in a term paper without ever thoroughly understanding them. Such a tactic is almost impossible in an examination, for few students have a strong enough memory to answer questions intelligently without understanding their answers. Thus, preparing for an examination is in some ways, though not all, more demanding and more rewarding than writing a term paper.

This fact was strikingly brought to my attention several years ago by a student who came to see me after I had returned her examination paper. She had received a C and was very disappointed, for, as she explained, she had always been an A student. I asked her whether she had studied as hard for this examination as for previous ones, and to my surprise she informed me that never before in her academic career had she taken an examination. As it turned out, she had gone to a "progressive" secondary school where examinations were considered outmoded, and she had then attended a college that prided itself on having replaced all examinations with term papers. I was fascinated by this woman's academic background and inquired whether she thought she had been helped or hindered by it. She replied that until she had taken this examination she had always assumed it was to her advantage to have avoided the pressure of examinations, but that now she believed her grasp of previous course material rather flimsy. She had learned how to write term papers but never had thoroughly mastered an entire body of material so that she could draw upon it at will and utilize it effectively wherever it was called for. In short, she had never received the benefits of preparing for an examination.

Of course, examinations serve yet another purpose, for they are in part the basis on which course grades are determined. However, since we have already seen that examinations provide an opportunity to discover the scope and depth of a student's knowledge, we have little reason to doubt that if grades are to be given, they should be based, at least to some extent, on the results of examinations. The crucial question is: why should grades be given?

Ideally, a grade represents an expert's opinion of the quality of a student's work within a specified area of inquiry. Viewed in this perspective, a grade serves a variety of significant educational purposes. First, it is to a student's advantage to be aware of his level of achievement, for that information can be a valuable aid to him in assessing his past efforts, evaluating his present abilities, and formulating his future plans. Knowing whether one's approach to a subject has been fruitful is a helpful guide toward further study; recognizing one's strengths and weaknesses is vital to intellectual growth as well as to decisions regarding how one's abilities might most effectively be utilized in and out of school. A college student is directly concerned with questions such as "Which courses should I take?", "Which fields should I specialize in?", "Which graduate schools, if any, should I apply to?", and "Which career should I choose?" Intelligent answers to all these questions depend, among other factors, upon the individual's academic abilities and accomplishments, and he can measure these reliably, though not infallibly, by his grades. Granted a teacher's judgment may occasionally be mistaken, at least his judgment is based upon relevant expertise and experience and is not subject to the sort of delusions which so often distort self-evaluation. A student may not always be pleased by the knowledge grades afford, but the important point is that such knowledge is almost always useful to him.

Students, though, are not the only ones to whom such knowledge is useful, for in order for a teacher to provide the detailed educational advice often so helpful to a student, he needs to have an exact record of the student's academic performance. How can a teacher intelligently advise a student in choosing his program of study and in planning for the years after graduation if an accurate measure of the student's level of achievement is unavailable? If, for example, a chemistry teacher does not know how well a student has done in his various science and mathematics courses, how can the teacher intelligently advise the student which level of chemistry to study, which areas in the student's background need strengthening, and whether it is reasonable for the student to continue work in graduate school? And if the student should decide to become a political science major, how can a teacher in that discipline intelligently advise the student what course of study to follow without knowing his level of achievement in history, economics, sociology, philosophy, and nowadays even in mathematics? In short, students' academic records are a great aid to those teachers who try to use their knowledge and experience to advise students wisely. But if a student's record is sketchy, vague, and inadequate, the advice he receives will most likely also be sketchy, vague and inadequate.

We have already noted that grades can be a valuable guide to a student in planning for the years following his graduation, but we should note as well that grades are a valuable guide to those who must make critical decisions directly affecting a student's future plans. Graduate work usually presupposes a firm command of undergraduate work, and thus most graduate schools necessarily employ selective admission policies. Those who face the difficult task of deciding whether a particular student is to be admitted to graduate school can make that decision intelligently only if they are aware of the student's level of achievement in his various college courses, and grades are a reliable, though not infallible, measure of such achievement.

On occasion, however, it is proposed that instead of receiving an applicant's grades a graduate admissions committee receive instead recommendations written by each of the teachers with whom the applicant has studied. But this proposal is impractical and, even if feasible, would nevertheless be inadvisable.

The proposal is impractical for at least two reasons. First, the members of an admissions committee do not have the time to read twenty-five or thirty letters about each applicant. In the case of some of the larger graduate schools, an admissions committee with twenty-five letters for each applicant would be facing more than twenty-five thousand letters and could not possibly be expected to spend the time necessary to do justice to that amount of material. Second, the large size of so many college classes makes it virtually impossible for a teacher to know each of his students personally. Thus he would be reduced to writing such conventional comments as "DeWitt is an excellent student who has mastered all of the course material" or "Davis is a fair student who has mastered some, though not much of the course material." But what do these comments mean except that De-Witt did A work in the course and Davis did C work?

However, even if it were feasible for every one of a student's teachers to write a personalized comment about him and for an admissions committee to read all of these comments, still they would not be an adequate replacement for grades. Recommendations sometimes contain valuable information, but taken by themselves they are often difficult to evaluate. A remark one teacher considers high praise may be used indiscriminately by another, and a comment employed by one teacher to express mild commendation may be used by another teacher to express mild criticism.[1] Furthermore, many recommendations are hopelessly vague and tell more about the teacher's literary style than about the academic accomplishment of the student. Thus although letters of recommendation may be helpful when used in conjunction with grades, alone they are no substitute for the relatively standardized measure of achievement grades effectively provide.

Such a standardized measure of achievement also affords a reasonable basis upon which to decide whether a student ought to be permitted to continue in school, whether he ought to be granted a college degree, and whether he ought to be awarded academic honors. These decisions, however, have all been the subject of controversy, and so we would do well to consider each of them separately.

A student who consistently does unsatisfactory work is squandering the resources of his college, wasting the time and energy of his teachers, and failing to contribute to, perhaps even interfering with, the education of his classmates. Such a student does not belong in the school he is attending, and, for the benefit of all concerned, should be asked to leave. But which students are doing unsatisfactory work? In answering this question it is clearly most sensible to rely upon the expert judgment of the faculty, and their judgment, as noted previously, is reliably reflected by a student's grades.

The faculty's expertise ought also to be relied upon in deciding whether the quality of a student's work justifies his being granted a college degree. Because most students are charged tuition fees, it is tempting to conceive of a college as an educational store in which the student customers pay their money and are then entitled to a degree. But a college degree is not purchased; it is earned. It represents to the community the college's certification of a student's academic achievement, certification respected because it is backed by the expertise of the faculty. If every student who paid his tuition automatically received a degree, or if degrees were awarded by the vote of the student body, then they would become educationally meaningless and functionally worthless. In order for a college degree to retain its value and for a college education to retain its significance, the granting of degrees must be based solely upon substantial academic achievement as evaluated by recognized experts. The experts are the faculty, and their evaluations are indicated by the grades they give.

Grades also provide an effective means of determining which students are deserving of academic honors. Such honors are both an added incentive for students to pursue their work diligently and a symbol of a college's commitment to academic excellence. But in order for honors to possess such significance, they must not be granted indiscriminately or on the basis of a student's popularity. Rather, they must be awarded only to those who have attained a high level of scholarly achievement. And grades provide a standardized measure of such achievement.

Grades serve one final purpose: to motivate students to study. In the classroom, as in most areas of life, those who expect their work to be evaluated tend to do that work more assiduously. Without grades, many students might possess sufficient interest to casually peruse the course material, but few would be strongly enough concerned to devote themselves to the mastery of that material. Of course, there are a handful of students who would thoroughly study all of their course material even if they did not receive any grades. These are the saints of the academic world. But a teacher should no more assume all his students saints, than he should assume all his neighbors saints. In both cases he would do well to hope for the best but prepare for the worst. What should be remembered is that grades have helped many students who otherwise would have neglected their work, and have led some to discover for themselves the intrinsic joys of scholarship.

We must recognize, however, that notwithstanding the many worthwhile purposes examinations and grades are intended to fulfill, much criticism has been directed against these educational tools. It has been claimed that examinations fail to provide a sound basis for evaluating a student's achievement but, instead, have the effect of inhibiting his independence and stifling his creativity. It has also been claimed that grades are inherently inaccurate devices which, in attempting to measure people, succeed only in traumatizing and dehumanizing them. These charges are certainly serious, and each of them ought to be examined in detail.

Consider first the claim that examinations do not provide a sound basis for evaluating a student's achievement. Those who defend this claim argue that examinations require a student to demonstrate his knowledge under adverse conditions; he must answer a restricted set of questions within a limited amount of time, and the implicit pressure prevents many from doing their best work. Thus the results of examinations are said to be invalid.

But this line of argument overlooks the vital consideration that although examinations put pressure on students, such pressure exists whenever an individual attempts to prove to experts his competence in their field. For instance, an athlete feels pressure when he tries out for a professional team; likewise a violinist when he auditions for an orchestral position. Pressure is inherent in such situations, for experts have high standards difficult to meet, and one must be able to meet those standards at an appointed time. The ballplayer who appears skillful in practice but plays poorly in league games lacks effective control of the requisite skills. Similarly, the student who sounds knowledgeable in conversation but performs poorly under examination conditions lacks effective control of the requisite knowledge. Thus the pressure of examinations does not invalidate the results of examinations; quite to the contrary, if there were no such pressure, the examination process would be amiss.

A second criticism of examinations is that they inhibit a student's independence, that they discourage him from pursuing topics of interest to him and instead force him to study topics of interest to his teacher. Thus, it is said, examinations impede rather than promote the learning process.

This criticism, however, rests upon the mistaken assumption that learning a particular subject matter involves nothing more than learning those aspects of the subject matter one happens to find interesting. For example, to attain a thorough knowledge of American history, it is not sufficient to learn the history of the American Indian, no matter how interested one may be in the Indians, for American history, like any significant area of inquiry, has many important aspects, all of which must be mastered in order to attain a thorough knowledge of the field. But who is to decide which aspects of a subject matter are most important? The teacher is the recognized expert, and so he is in a position to make intelligent curricular decisions. Furthermore, the teacher's responsibility is to use his expertise to further a student's education, to guide him in studying important aspects of the subject matter he might otherwise neglect. Such guidance, in one sense, interferes with a student's independence, but in another, more significant, sense, liberates him from his own narrow preoccupations and leads him to less restricted, more independent thinking. And that, after all, is one of the essential purposes of a liberal education.

Another criticism of examinations is that they stifle a student's creativity, that they emphasize the mindless reiteration of facts and techniques instead of encouraging original, imaginative thinking about significant issues. Thus, again it is said, examinations impede rather than promote the learning process.

But this criticism is mistaken for at least two reasons. First, not all examinations emphasize learning by rote, only poor examinations. Good examinations, as pointed out previously, place familiar material in a slightly unfamiliar light, so that in preparing for and taking examinations, students are led to develop for themselves significant connections between various aspects of the subject matter. Of course, an examination does not normally require the same degree of original, imaginative thinking required by a demanding term paper topic. But it must be remembered a term paper does not require mastery of most or even very much of the course material; only examinations do. In other words, the two tasks serve different purposes, and there is no point in criticizing one for not fulfilling the purposes of the other.

The second reason why the criticism in question is mistaken is that it overlooks that in order to master any significant field of inquiry, one must acquire secure control of certain fundamental information and skills. As Whitehead wrote, "There is no getting away from the fact that things have been found out, and that to be effective in the modern world you must have a core of definite acquirement of the best practice. To write poetry you must study metre: and to build bridges you must be learned in the strength of material. Even the Hebrew prophets had learned to write, probably in those days requiring no mean effort. The untutored art of genius is—in the words of the Prayer Book—a vain thing, fondly invented."[2] It is simply unrealistic to suppose that original, imaginative thinking of a sustained and productive sort flows from the minds of those ignorant of the fundamental information and skills related to their field of inquiry. Of course, it has been said that the mark of a knowledgeable person is not what he knows, but whether he is adept at looking up what he needs to know. But if this were so, then the most knowledgeable people in the world would be librarians. The fact is that a person who lacks fundamental information and skills is not in a position to understand and intelligently evaluate material confronting him, so he is unable to connect ideas in the ways necessary for sustained, productive thinking. And even if, as is highly doubtful, such an individual had the time to research everything he needed to know, he would not know what to research, for he would not be aware of all he needed to know. But how can it be determined whether an individual possesses the fundamental information and skills related to his field of inquiry? Examinations enable both teacher and student to make such determinations effectively, and thus, rather than stifling creativity, help to provide the framework within which original, imaginative thinking can be most productive.

Turning now from criticisms of examinations to criticisms of grades, consider first the claim that grades are inherently inaccurate. Those who defend this position argue that the same paper would be graded differently by different instructors, and therefore a student's grade is not a reliable measure of his achievement but merely indicates the particular bias of his instructor.

However, a student's work is generally not judged with significant difference by different instructors. In fact, teachers in the same discipline usually agree as to which students are doing outstanding work, which are doing good work, which are doing fair work, which are doing poor work, and which are doing unsatisfactory work (or no work at all).[3] Of course, two competent instructors may offer divergent evaluations of the same piece of work. But the fact that experts sometimes disagree is not, of course, reason to assume there is no such thing as expertise. For example, two competent doctors may offer divergent diagnoses of the same condition, but their disagreement does not imply that doctors' diagnoses are in general biased and unreliable. Similarly, two competent art critics may offer divergent evaluations of the same work of art, but such a disagreement does not imply that a critic's evaluations are usually biased and unreliable. Inevitably, experts, like all human beings, will sometimes disagree about complex judgments, but we would be foolish to allow such disagreements to obscure the obvious fact that in any established field of inquiry some individuals are knowledgeable and others are not. And clearly the opinions of those who are knowledgeable are the most reliable measure of an individual's achievement in that field. Thus, although teachers sometimes disagree, they are knowledgeable individuals whose grades represent a reliable measure of a student's level of achievement.

A second criticism of grades is that they traumatize students. Those who support this criticism argue that grades foster competition, arousing a bitterness and hostility which transform an otherwise tranquil academic atmosphere into a pressure-filled, nerve-wracking situation unsuited for genuine learning. In such a situation, it is said, students are more worried about obtaining good grades than about obtaining a good education.

But this criticism emphasizes only the possibly harmful effects of competition while overlooking its beneficial effects. Often only by competing with others do we bring out the best in ourselves. As Gilbert Highet once noted, "It is sad, sometimes, to see a potentially brilliant pupil slouching through his work, sulky and willful, wasting his time and thought on trifles, because he has no real equals in his own class; and it is heartening to see how quickly, when a rival is transferred from another section or enters from another school, the first boy will find a fierce joy in learning and a real purpose in life."[4] In short, competition fosters excellence, and without that challenge most of us would be satisfied with accomplishing far less than we are capable of.

However, even if competition did not have beneficial effects, it would still be an inherent part of academic life, for it is an inherent part of virtually every aspect of life. Many people have the same goals, but only a comparatively few can achieve them. For example, not everyone who so desires can be a surgeon, a lawyer, an engineer, or a professional football player, and, indeed, marked success in any field of endeavor is necessarily quite rare. Thus competition arises. And since academic success is desired not only for its own sake but also because it relates to success in many other competitive fields, competition will always exist in academic life.

The question then is not whether competition should be eliminated from the academic sphere, but how it can be channelled so as to maximize beneficial effects and minimize potentially harmful effects. The key to this difficult task lies in encouraging each student to strive as vigorously as possible to fulfill his own potential, in praising his efforts when he tries his hardest and in appealing to his sense of pride when his energies flag. Treating him so does not lead him to emphasize good grades rather than a good education, for he cannot achieve a good education without striving for mastery of subject matter. And if grades are awarded as they should be, on the basis of accurate measures of a student's level of achievement, then they will indicate his mastery of subject matter. Thus a student concerned with grades is concerned with a prime component of a good education.

A third criticism of grades is that in attempting to measure people, they succeed only in dehumanizing and categorizing them, depriving them of their uniqueness, and reducing them to a letter of the alphabet. Thus, it is said, grades defeat one of the essential purposes of an education: to aid each individual in developing his individuality.

A grade, however, is not and is not intended to be a measure of a person. It is, rather, a measure of a person's level of achievement in a particular course of study. To give a student a C in an introductory physics course is not to say that the student is a C person with a C personality or C moral character, only that he is a person with a C level of achievement in introductory physics.

Grades no more reduce students to letters than batting averages reduce baseball players to numbers. That Ted Williams had a lifetime batting average of .344 and Joe Garagiola an average of .257 does not mean Williams is a better person than Garagiola, but only that Williams was a better hitter. And why does it dehumanize either man to recognize that one was a better hitter than the other?

Indeed, to recognize an individual's strengths and weaknesses, to know his areas of expertise, his areas of competence, and his areas of ignorance is not to deny but to emphasize his individuality. If Delaney and Delancey are known to their teachers only as two faces in the classroom, then their comparative anonymity is apt to lead to their individual differences being overlooked. But if Delaney has a reputation as an excellent history student with a weakness in mathematics, while Delancey is known as a generally poor student, but one who has a gift for creative writing, then these two students are no longer anonymous cogs in a machine, and their education can be tailored to suit their needs. Thus grades do not dehumanize an individual; on the contrary, they contribute to a recognition of his uniqueness and to the possible development of his individual interests and abilities.

Yet there is one further challenge to the entire system of examinations and grades, for as was pointed out earlier, this system places important decisions affecting students' lives in the hands of those comparatively unaffected by these decisions and perhaps quite uninterested in making them. Such a situation is indeed hazardous, and the potential problems are, of course, compounded by the difficulty of constructing and applying suitable examination and grading procedures. Of course, suitable procedures are the ones most likely to fulfill the worthwhile purposes examinations and grades are intended to serve, and we have already seen what those are. But what specifically are the procedures most likely to fulfill those purposes? And how can it be ensured that teachers will be cognizant of the proper procedures and apply them conscientiously? These are important questions, and they deserve careful consideration.

Constructing a good examination is a creative endeavor, and, as in the case of all creative endeavors, there are no surefire formulas for success; the most one can reasonably hope for are broad guidelines to provide a sound basis for at least partial success. The first such guideline is that an examination should be representative of the course material. Consider, for instance, a course in the history of modern philosophy that devotes two or three weeks to the study of each of five philosophers: Descartes, Leibniz, Berkeley, Hume, and Kant. If the final examination is to serve its proper function as a test of the scope and depth of a student's knowledge of the course material, then the examination should be structured so that a student is called upon to demonstrate considerable knowledge about all five of the authors studied. The examination would be unsatisfactory if it tested only a student's general philosophical ability, not his knowledge of the five authors studied, or if it tested a student's knowledge of only one or two authors studied and permitted him to neglect the others. For whatever such unsatisfactory examinations might be intended to test, they would fail to test adequately the scope and depth of a student's knowledge of the history of modern philosophy.

Of course, an examination representative of the course material need not deny students a choice as to which examination questions they wish to answer. Such a choice is an attractive feature of an examination, since it allows students an opportunity to demonstrate their special interests and abilities. But the crucial point is that such choices should be so arranged that a student's answers will adequately reflect his knowledge of the entire course material. And if certain course material is so essential that all students should be familiar with it, then no choice should be given. For contrary to common practice, students need not always be offered a choice of examination questions. What they should be offered is an examination representative of the course material.

A second guideline for constructing good examinations is posing questions that require detailed answers. Perhaps the most serious fault of college examinations is that they allow a student to talk around the subject matter without ever having to demonstrate more than a superficial knowledge of the course material. Again in contrast to common practice, much can be said in favor of questions that have answers, answers to be found in or at least closely related to the course readings. An examination lacking such questions is not merely a poor test of a student's knowledge but leads him to suppose that thorough knowledge of the course material amounts to no more than knowing a few stray bits of information strung together by some vague generalizations about some even vaguer concepts. Such an examination is worse than no examination at all; it is an educational travesty that leads a student to suppose he has mastered material about which he knows virtually nothing.

But the fact that examination questions ought to require detailed answers is no reason why students should be overwhelmed with true-false or multiple-choice questions. Though these can sometimes be of educational value, unless they are well-constructed and appropriate to the aims of the course, they turn the examination into a guessing-game that stresses knowledge of minutiae rather than the understanding of fundamental concepts and principles. For instance, only a foolish examination in the history of modern philosophy would be filled with questions such as "The title of Section IX of Hume's *An Inquiry Concerning Human Understanding* is (a) Of Liberty and Necessity, (b) Of the Reason of Animals, (c) Of Miracles, (d) All of the above, (e) None of the above." On the other hand it would be equally foolish for such an examination to be filled with questions such as "Does it seem to you that anything in the work of Kant helps us to understand ourselves?" What is needed is neither a trivial nor vague question but a sharply defined, significant, challenging question, one such as: "Both Descartes and Berkeley raise doubts about the existence of the material world. Compare and contrast (1) the arguments they use to raise these doubts, and (2) their conclusions concerning the possible resolution of these doubts." An examination with questions such as this not only provides a rigorous test of a student's knowledge but also clearly indicates to the student that mastery of the subject matter is a demanding enterprise, requiring far more intellectual effort than the memorization of trivia or the improvisation of hazy, high-flown vacuities.

If an examination adheres to the two important guidelines just discussed, then there is reason to suppose it will fulfill the worthwhile purposes it should serve. However, several other pitfalls must be avoided in order for an examination to be as effective as possible. First, the examination should not be so long that most students are more worried about finishing than about providing the best possible answers. Of course, if a student takes too long to answer a question, it is clear he does not have secure enough control of the required material. But basically an examination should not be a race against time; it should be constructed so a student working at a normal pace has sufficient time to read the questions carefully, compose his thoughts, write his answers legibly, and reread his work to make corrections. No matter how well constructed examination questions may be, if there is not sufficient time to answer them thoughtfully, the examination will turn into a shambles and be of little use to anyone.

A second pitfall to be avoided is the omission of clear directions at the top of the examination paper. Imagine sitting down to begin work and reading the following directions: "Answer three questions from Part I and two questions from Part II, but do not answer questions 2, 3, and 6 unless you also answer question 9. Question 1 is required, unless you answer questions 3 and 5." By the time a student has fully understood these directions and decided which questions he ought to answer, he will already be short of time.

When a student sits down to take an examination, he is understandably tense and liable to misread the directions, answer the wrong questions, and bungle the examination. If he does so, the fault is probably not his, for the teacher has the responsibility to make the directions so clear that the student will find them virtually impossible to misunderstand. A teacher has sufficient time to work out clear directions, and he owes it to his students to provide such directions. The examination should be a test of a student's knowledge of the course material, not a test of his ability to solve verbal puzzles.

A third pitfall is the failure to inform students of the relative importance of each answer in the grading of the examination. Suppose a student begins work on an examination in which he is required to answer three questions, but is not told the teacher considers the answer to the third question more important than the combined answers to the first two. The student will probably spend an equal amount of time on each, not realizing he should concentrate his time and effort on the third. But his mistake indicates no lack of knowledge on his part. It is simply a result of the teacher's keeping his own intentions a secret. And this secret serves no other function than to distort the results of the examination. It is only fair that a student be informed as to how many points each question is worth, so that he can plan his work accordingly.

One final pitfall must be avoided in order for an examination to fulfill its proper purposes, and this pitfall relates not to the construction of the examination, but to its grading. A teacher is responsible for grading examinations as carefully and fairly as possible. To do otherwise is to waste much of the effort put into constructing and taking the examination, for an examination graded carelessly or unfairly does not provide an accurate measure of a student's knowledge. Of course, the most essential element in the proper grading of examination papers is the teacher's serious effort to carry out his responsbility conscientiously, but many teachers have found a few simple suggestions about grading techniques helpful. First, a teacher should grade papers without knowing whose paper he is grading. An answer from a student who does generally good work is apt to seem more impressive than the same answer from a student who does generally poor work. Next, it is best not to grade a paper by reading it from start to finish but to read and grade all students' answers to one question at a time. This procedure ensures that a teacher will pay attention to each answer a student gives and not skim the paper after reading only the first one or two answers carefully. Furthermore, correcting papers in this way makes much less likely the possibility a teacher will alter his standards as he moves from one paper to another, for it is far easier to stabilize standards for answers to the same question than for entire examination papers. Finally, before grading a question, a teacher should list for himself the major points he expects students to mention in their answers. He can then check each essay against this list, providing yet another safeguard against altering standards as he moves from one paper to another. And such a list also provides a teacher with the means to justify his grades, since he is in a position to indicate to students what a good answer should be. Such information makes clear that grades have not been meted out arbitrarily and also aids each student in achieving both a better understanding of the material tested and an increased awareness of his own strengths and weaknesses. Of course, in order for such information to be most useful, examinations should be graded, returned to students, and discussed in class as soon as possible.

Examinations that adhere to these guidelines and avoid these pitfalls are almost sure to be reasonably successful. It should be kept in mind, however, that good examinations reinforce one another, since each one a student takes guides him in future study. Thus if he takes a number of good examinations in a single course, as that course proceeds he learns how to derive the greatest possible benefit from his study time. Multiple examinations in a single course also serve to discourage students from the popular but disastrous policy of wasting almost the entire term and then cramming for one final examination. The more frequent the examinations, the less need for cramming. Thus it is not, as some have said, that examinations encourage cramming. Infrequent examinations encourage cramming. Frequent examinations encourage studying. And good examinations encourage useful studying.

Having now discussed suitable examination procedures, we should next consider suitable grading procedures. Much discussion has taken place about alternative grading systems, but the basic principle for constructing an effective grading system remains quite simple: it should contain the maximum number of grade levels teachers can use consistently. A grading system should be as specific as possible because grades serve as a guide for the educational decisions of both students and faculty: up to a reasonable point the more detailed the guide is, the more helpful it is. If a student's academic record is sketchy and vague, then most likely he will have a sketchy, vague idea of his own abilities and accomplishments and will be hindered in his attempts to assess his past efforts, evaluate his present capabilities, and formulate his future plans. And not only will he himself be hindered, but those who try to advise him or evaluate his accomplishments will be at a serious disadvantage. It is just not sufficient to know that Kubersky passed a course. Was he an A student, a strong B student, a weak C student, or a D student? Without an answer to this question, neither Kubersky nor anyone else knows much about his level of achievement.

But there is a limit to how specific a grading system should be. Ultimately we reach a point where no reasonable basis exists for deciding whether a student's work is at one level or another. There is little sense, for example, in trying to decide whether an English composition should receive a grade of 86.32 or 86.31, for no teacher can consistently differentiate between work on these two levels.

The question is then, using the principle that a grading system should contain the maximum number of grade levels teachers can use consistently, how many such grade levels should there be? My own experience has led me to believe that in college the most effective grading system is the traditional one, consisting of ten symbols: A, A-, B+, B, B-, C+, C, C-, D, F. This ten-level system is specific enough to provide the needed information about a student's level of achievement while enabling teachers to differentiate consistently between work on any two of the ten levels. Of course, borderline cases will sometimes arise, but the distinction between work on any two levels is clear, despite the possibility of borderline cases, just as the distinction between bald men and hirsute men is clear, despite the possibility of borderline cases.

Perhaps the most controversial aspect of the traditional ten-level system is its grade of F, for many have claimed that if a student knows he will have a failure permanently on his record, he may become so discouraged he will give up on his education altogether. In order to preclude such a possibility it has been proposed that the grade of F be replaced by a grade of NC (No Credit), which would indicate to the registrar both that the student should receive no credit for the course and that his transcript should show no record of his having taken the course.

Such a grade, however, would obviously be pure deception, for the student *did* take the course and he failed to master any significant part of it. If he should take the same course again and pass it, his transcript should indicate as much. Otherwise, those who are trying to evaluate his work will be mislead, since, for example, it is likely a student who had to take introductory chemistry two, three, or four times before passing lacks the scientific or study skills of someone who passed the course on his first try. It is not a tragedy to fail a course, but it is a failure, and we must learn from failures, not give them another name and pretend they did not occur. Indeed, one mark of a mature individual is facing up to and taking responsibility for failures. As a colleague of mine once remarked during a faculty meeting in which the NC grade was being discussed: "When I die and stand before the Heavenly Judge in order to have my life evaluated, it may be that I will receive a grade of F. But let it not be said that my life was a 'No Credit'."

A suitable grading system, however, does not ensure suitable grading, for unless the system is used properly, grades will not achieve the worthwhile purposes they are intended to serve. And, unfortunately, improper uses of the system are all too common.

One such misuse is to award grades on bases other than a student's level of achievement in the course work. Irrelevant bases for grades include a student's sex, race, religion, nationality, physical appearance, dress, personality, attitudes, innate capacities, and previous academic record. None of these factors should even be considered in awarding grades. To repeat what was said earlier, a grade ought not to be a measure of a person; it ought to be a measure of a person's level of achievement in a particular course of study, and the only reasonable basis for measuring this is the quality of work which he does in that course.

The most effective way for a teacher to assure his students that no extraneous factors will enter into the awarding of grades is to state clearly at the outset of the term exactly how final grades will be determined. How much will the final examination count? How much will short quizzes count? How about the term paper and other shorter papers? Will laboratory work count? Will a student's participation in class discussion be a factor? By answering these questions at the very beginning of the course, a teacher sets a student's mind at ease and, in addition, enables him to concentrate his time and effort on the most important aspects of the course. Of course, some teachers assume that if they do not discuss their grading policy, the students will not worry about grades. But quite to the contrary, a teacher's failure to discuss his grading policy increases uncertainty and worry and furthermore provides no guidance as to how the students should work to do their best and get the most out of the course. And, after all, such guidance is precisely what the teacher is expected to provide.

A second obvious misuse of the grading system, exceedingly rare nowadays, results from the reluctance of some teachers to award high grades. Such teachers pride themselves on how rarely they give an A or B, and how frequently they give C's, D's, or F's. But low grading is a foolish source of pride, for such grading suggests the teacher is unable to recognize good work when he sees it. That a student's work does not deserve immortal fame is no reason it does not deserve an A. Just as a third-grade student who receives an A in writing need not be the literary equal of a college student who receives an A in English composition, so a college student who receives an A in English composition, need not be the literary equal of Jonathan Swift or Bertrand Russell. Giving a student an A in a course does not mean he has learned everything there is to know about course material or that he is as knowledgeable as his teacher; giving a student an A simply means that, considering what could reasonably be expected, the student has done excellent work. If a third-grade teacher rarely gives an A or a B, his principal does not assume this teacher always has poor students in his class. He assumes, rather, that this teacher has a distorted sense of academic values. A similar conclusion should be reached about a college teacher who rarely gives an A or a B. Such a teacher is misapplying the grading symbols and preventing grades from fulfilling their important educational functions.

A third misuse of the grading system, one especially prevalent today, results from the reluctance of many teachers to award low grades. These instructors pride themselves on never giving students a hard time or underestimating the value of a student's efforts. But high grading, like low grading, is a foolish source of pride; it suggests that the teacher is unable to recognize poor work when he sees it. Not to differentiate between two students, one doing poor or unsatisfactory work and one doing fair work, is a subtle form of discrimination against the better student. Giving a student a D or an F in a course does not mean that the student is a foolish or evil person; the low grade simply means that, considering what could reasonably be expected, the student has done poor or unsatisfactory work. If a third-grade teacher rarely gives low grades, his principal does not assume this teacher has the school's most brilliant students. The principal assumes, rather, that this teacher is giving his seal of approval to incompetent work. A similar conclusion should be reached about a college teacher who rarely gives low grades. Such a teacher, like the teacher who rarely gives high grades, is misapplying the grading symbols and preventing grades from fulfilling their functions.

A fourth and final misuse of the grading system is the practice commonly referred to as "grading on a curve." The essence of this widely adopted practice is deciding what percentage of students in a class will receive a particular grade, without considering the level of work actually done by any of the students. For example, a teacher may decide before a course ever begins that 10 percent of the students will receive an A, 20 percent a B, 40 percent a C, 20 percent a D, and 10 percent an F. Distributing grades in this way produces an aesthetically pleasing curve on a graph, but the procedure is invalid, for how well a student has learned a particular subject matter does not depend upon how well his fellow students have learned the same subject matter. Perhaps in many large classes approximately 10 percent of the students actually do A work and a similar percentage F work, but this fact is no reason at all why in any specific class exactly 10 percent of the students must receive an A and another 10 percent must receive an F. Suppose 25 percent of the students in a class do excellent work and 5 percent unsatisfactory work; then the 25 percent should receive an A and the 5 percent an F. Or suppose 5 percent of the students in a class do excellent work and 25 percent do unsatisfactory work; then the 5 percent should receive an A and the 25 percent should receive an F. For the grade a student receives is not to be a measure of his rank in class; it is to be a measure of his level of achievement in a particular course of study. And though judging a student's level of achievement does depend upon considering what can reasonably be expected of him, such a judgment does not and should not depend upon the level of achievement of other students who happen to be taking the same course simultaneously. Since the Procrustean practice of grading on a curve rests upon such irrelevant considerations, the practice ought to be abandoned.

Having now provided an answer to the question, "what specifically are suitable examination and grading procedures?", only one question remains for consideration: how can it be ensured that teachers will be cognizant of suitable examination and grading procedures and apply them conscientiously? The answer to the first part of this question is for those who administer graduate school programs to provide courses in methods of teaching for students intending to enter the teaching profession. These courses should be required of all students who are to be recommended for teaching positions and should include a detailed discussion of suitable examination and grading procedures. The person chosen to teach such a course ought to be himself a productive scholar and an outstanding teacher, for he is in the best possible position to make clear to graduate students that good scholarship and good teaching are not incompatible, that publishing develops a teacher's ability to think critically by leading him to submit his ideas to the judgment of his peers, while teaching encourages a scholar to express his views clearly enough to communicate them effectively to those not as knowledgeable as he.

But even if a teacher is cognizant of appropriate procedures, how can it be ensured he will apply them conscientiously? There is, of course, no practical way to ensure that anyone whether doctor, journalist, or taxi driver, will do his job conscientiously. A chairman has the responsibility to make certain no member of his department is guilty of gross negligence. But, ultimately, a teacher must decide for himself whether to be conscientious. If he is deeply committed to maintaining high academic standards, he will be willing to spend the time and effort required to make the most effective possible use of examinations and grades. But if he is unconcerned about promoting excellence and is satisfied with exalting mediocrity, he will be unwilling to give of himself in order to provide his students with effective examinations and accurate grades. What no teacher must be allowed to forget, however, is that if he chooses to ignore proper examination and grading procedures, both his students and his society will be the losers.

NOTES

1. Grade designations, however, are few in number and have a relatively standardized meaning. Therefore, teachers who use them idiosyncratically are not the victims of linguistic ambiguity but of pedagogic inadequacy.
2. Alfred North Whitehead, *The Aims of Education and Other Essays* (1929; reprint ed., New York: Free Press, 1967), p. 34.
3. These five levels of work are commonly symbolized by the letters: A, B, C, D, F. Teachers who misuse these symbols are an educational menace; their sins are discussed later in the essay.
4. Gilbert Highet, *The Art of Teaching* (1950; reprint ed., New York: Random House, 1954), p. 132.

Index